PEACE AT BATTLE MOUNTAIN

PEACE AT BATTLE MOUNTAIN

ALYSTAIR WEST

Quansus

ISBN: (Soft Cover): 979-8-3303-9185-1
ISBN (Electronic): 979-8-3303-9184-4

Proof reading by Granville Sydnor Hill
Cover and interior design by Frank Gutbrod

Library of Congress Number: 2024918817

Printed in the United States of America

First Edition

"Oh my God,
What might I have made of thy fair world,
Had I but loved the highest creature here?
It was my duty to have loved the highest;
It surely was my profit had I known;
It would've been my pleasure had I seen.
We must love the highest when we see it,
Not Lancelot nor another."
Alfred Lord Tennyson, Idylls of the King

"Living a just and holy life requires one to be capable of an objective and impartial evaluation of things: to love things in the right order so that you do not love what is not to be loved or fail to love what is to be loved or have a greater love for what should be loved less, or an equal love for things that should be loved less or more, or a lesser or greater love for things that should be loved equally."
Augustine, On Christian Doctrine

"Love is the foundation of everything desirable or good."
Charles Sanders Peirce

"To love a person is to desire the best for that person and to make any reasonable and moral sacrifice for that person to achieve happiness and fulfillment."
Ahn Winchester

This book is dedicated to my wife, Kathy,
our children, grandchildren, extended family, our many
friends, and the congregations
we have been privileged to serve over the years.

CONTENTS

Characters and Terms

MAJOR CHARACTERS

Battle Mountain Energy is a San Antonio-based oil and gas pipeline company usually referred to as Battle Mountain.

Patrick Armbruster is the former managing partner of Winchester & Wells.

Juan de la Cruz Bardero (Juan Bardero), whose former name is **John Mirador**, is a former Special Forces officer known as the Watcher who currently lives near San Miguel de Allende.

Buddy Bennett is the president of Battle Mountain Energy, a former subsidiary of E-Titan.

Cheetah, Ltd. and its successors are **Special Purpose Entities** (see below) formed by E-Titan to remove certain assets and liabilities from its balance sheet. They are generally referred to collectively as the Cheetahs.

Dobie Dawson Jr. ("Junior" or "DD") is the reclusive chairman of Dawson Corporation, a privately held oil and gas company founded by his father, and chairman of the board of E-Titan Energy, formed by Dawson Corporation as a publicly traded energy trading company in which Dawson Corporation has a substantial interest.

E-Titan Energy, or **"E-Titan,"** is a diversified energy trading company headquartered in Houston, Texas.

Claire DuFort is the child of Lance and Gwynn DuFort.

Lance DuFort is a former investment banker and acquaintance of Arthur Stone, now the president of E-Titan.

Gwynn DuFort, previously **Gwynn Murray,** is the wife of Lance DuFort and the former wife of Arthur Stone. Gwynn is a well-known Houston attorney and social figure.

Sheila DuFort is Lance DuFort's former wife.

Brad Gilliland is the chief financial officer of E-Titan

Heather Gilliland is Brad Gilliland's wife.

Thomas (Tom) L'Orangelo Mallory is a senior associate at Winchester & Wells and protégé of Arthur Stone.

Alicia Mallory is the wife of Thomas L. Mallory. She works for the law firm founded by Gwynn Stone.

Marjorie "M&M" Melton is an executive at Dawson Corporation and a general partner of the Cheetahs. She was also Dobie Dawson's former lover and Brad Gilliland's mistress.

Maria Mendoza is an accountant in Houston. She knows Ahn Winchester and Arthur Stone.

Eddie Morales is a trial lawyer in San Antonio, Texas. His firm, Morales & Nichols, is the lead trial firm working with Winchester & Wells and Arthur Stone regarding litigation between E-Titan and Battle Mountain Energy.

Roger Romny is the managing partner of Winchester & Wells.

Arthur Stone is the chairman of the executive committee of Winchester & Wells and its most famous trial partner. He is the former husband of Gwynn DuFort.

William "Bill" Stone is the father of Arthur Stone and a retired Presbyterian minister living near Kerrville, Texas.

Ben Stone is a retired FBI agent, the brother of Bill Stone, and Arthur Stone's uncle.

Betty Stone is the wife of William "Bill" Stone and is the mother of Arthur and John Stone.

The Rev. Dr. John B. "John" Stone is the brother of Arthur Stone and is currently the senior pastor of First Presbyterian Church of Houston.

Murray Stone is the 14-year-old son of Arthur Stone and Gwynn DuFort.

Stephen Winchester Stone (Stephen) is the younger son of Arthur and Gwynn. He was named after Ahn Winchester's deceased husband, Stephen Winchester.

Margaret Stone is the daughter of Arthur and Gwynn.

Javier Velasco, also known as **El Halcón**, is the leader of a wealthy Mexican family and a former high-ranking official in the Mexican government.

Javiera Velasco is Javier Velasco's granddaughter.

Ahn Winchester is the widow of Stephen Winchester, a partner at Winchester & Wells, until his untimely death in a car bombing. She was born in Vietnam, where she met her husband during the Vietnam War.

Adrianna Wong is the chief financial officer of E-Titan, having been appointed when Brad Gilliland suddenly died.

SPECIALIZED TERMS

Financial Accounting Standard (FAS) 140 is a policy that deals with situations in which a corporation like E-Titan (the originator or sponsor) transfers assets and related debt to a particular purpose entity (SPE), in this case, the Cheetah, Ltd. and its progeny. The relevant issue in the novel is whether such a transfer should be treated as a sale or secured financing. If the vehicle is merely a disguised financing (loan), FAS 140 prevents the originator from recording the asset transfer as a sale. It also requires the originator to recognize the debt obligation transferred to the SPE on its balance sheet.

Mark-to-Market Accounting (MTM) is an accounting method that measures the fair value of accounts that can fluctuate over time, such as assets and liabilities. MTM attempts to provide a realistic appraisal of an institution's or company's current financial situation based on current market conditions. However, it can be manipulated and is challenging to use when the assets or liabilities are not easily valued. In the case of publicly traded securities and similar financial assets, markets function to allow an easily calculated value. However, when used by E-Titan, the method was used on assets that were inherently unable to be employed in this way to show profits where there were, in fact, losses.

Post-Traumatic Stress Disorder (PTSD) is an anxiety disorder associated with severe traumatic events and characterized by such symptoms as survivor guilt, reliving the trauma in dreams, numbness and lack of involvement with reality, or recurrent thoughts and images.

Securities and Exchange Commission (SEC) is a federal regulatory agency responsible for protecting investors and maintaining fair and orderly functioning of capital markets. The SEC requires disclosure by public companies, protects the investing public from fraudulent and manipulative practices, and monitors corporate takeovers. It approves registration statements where public companies issue securities to the investing public.

Special Purpose Entities (SPEs) are business entities formed to develop, own, and operate a specific project while isolating financial risk and minimizing bankruptcy risk (making it "bankruptcy-remote") for its parent company or owners. In the case of E-Titan, these vehicles were used to reduce losses and obscure the actual debt position of the creator of the entity. The SEC has ruled that, in order not to be consolidated with the parent company, the outside equity should be comparable to that expected for a substantive business involved in similar leasing transactions with similar risks and rewards. One factor leading to misuse is the unrealistic position that, for accounting purposes, a three percent outside equity position is sufficient. In the case of Cheetah, Ltd. and its progeny, even this low equity requirement was avoided.

*P*REFACE

PEACE AT BATTLE MOUNTAIN IS the second novel in a series beginning with the book *Marshland,* written under the pen name Alystair West. In *Marshland,* a young attorney, Arthur Stone, stumbles into a mystery in the 1980s in Texas. That novel unfolds on personal, legal, political, moral, and spiritual levels. In the beginning, a mysterious watcher observes a plane exploding in an even more curious storm. The tragedy leaves the pilot and two passengers dead. The event also threatens an important transaction for Arthur Stone's law firm. Worst of all, his life and those of others he cares about are in danger.

The mystery in *Marshland* involves a diverse cast of characters, including members of a prestigious law firm, family members, a special forces officer, drug dealers, high-level financiers, local and other business people, and intelligence community members. The story takes place from the coast of Africa, where a hurricane is forming, to central Mexico, Houston, and San Miguel de Allende. As the plot thickens, it becomes clear that earthly and unearthly powers are at play, their intentions unknown.

The mid and late 1980s in Houston, Texas, were a time of financial crisis when excessive lending and risk-taking devastated an entire industry. Changes in tax laws, a deep recession, economic deregulation, and other factors led to a massive crisis. The overconfident lending and financial wheeler-dealing that characterized the banking crisis in Texas have been repeated many times in American history before and since. One interesting question is, "What is in human nature that encourages these kinds of problems?" Central to *Marshland's* plot is the love affair between Arthur Stone and Gwynn Murray, an associate at Winchester & Wells with whom Arthur works. Their relationship enables Arthur, a young attorney trying to become a partner in a large firm, to survive and unravel the mystery.

Peace at Battle Mountain, the sequel to *Marshland*, unfolds about fourteen years later. Recovering from the Great Recession of the 1980s, Houston is a bustling city where business is booming. Just as in the 1980s, when accounting principles were manipulated, the early 2000s saw accounting rules stretched in unintended and ultimately unfortunate ways. These unique elements set the stage for the narrative.

Peace at Battle Mountain reveals a new chapter in the lives of Arthur and Gwynn. Unfortunately, their love story has taken a dark turn. This novel, like its predecessor, is a blend of murder, economic problems, and moral and spiritual forces at work within the lives of its characters.

Peace at Battle Mountain, while delving into a tragedy of deceit, murder, and economic foolishness, also poses a profound spiritual question: *Why do humans find it so challenging to maintain healthy relationships in all areas of life?* This thought-provoking theme, woven into the narrative, adds a layer of depth to the story. I trust that readers will find this exploration as intriguing as I did while writing it.

Alystair West

Pentecost 2024

San Antonio, Texas

1

Blue Norther

WINTER STORM
STATE OF TEXAS
FEBRUARY 2001

HARDLY ANYONE THINKS OF THE winds of the Arctic as having anything to do with the weather in Texas. Nothing could be further from the truth. The movement of arctic air into Texas can bring rapid and dangerous changes in temperature. In Texas, the phenomenon is called Blue Northers. The term Blue Norther describes a rapidly moving cold front that causes temperatures to drop quickly and often brings with it ice, sleet, and snow, followed by clear, ice-blue skies. The phrase is unique to Texas, for a Blue Norther drives out of the Panhandle under a dark, black, and blue sky like a stampeding herd of cattle in a 19th-century cattle drive. There have been many famous Blue Northers in Texas history.

In November 2000, swirling cold air masses surrounded the north and south poles. This is normal. During the winter, atmospheric pressure shifts back and forth between the Arctic and the mid-latitudes of the North Pacific and North Atlantic. So long as nothing disturbs the rough and unstable equilibrium, the freezing air stays in place. In this case, however, a northern polar vortex appeared. A northern polar vortex occurs when warmer air comes from the south and presses against the vortex. The vortex becomes distorted, and the impacted air is pushed north. A bulge is formed in the swirling air mass, pushing freezing air violently to the southwest.

This particular winter, that is precisely what happened. Late in the year, warm air began to press northward. By January, a bulge began to appear—the largest bulge of Arctic cold air anyone could remember. The mass of air pushed southward, across Canada, the Northwest, and down into Texas, plunging the state into the coldest period of its history. This "Blue Norther" was colder than the coldest on record, leaving some regions in northwest Texas several degrees below zero. Even Houston, San Antonio, and South Texas were not spared the impact of the breath-taking cold.

Like the legendary saying, the system entered Texas over the Panhandle, then furiously plunged through North Texas, Central Texas, and finally, into freezing South Texas. Behind that initial front was a much larger front, "An Ice Monster Front," as one weatherperson described it. It was as if a freezing monster from a comic book sprayed the entire state of Texas with a giant freezing oscillator of cold.

Soon, Austin, San Antonio, and Houston, the major cities of Central and South Texas, were covered in ice, snow, and sleet. In Houston, it snowed. In San Antonio, some snow drifts were measured in feet, not the inches that would generally occur even in the coldest winters in South Texas.

The fruit crops in the Rio Grande Valley were ruined. Fragile fruit trees could not survive the winter cold. Harris and

Bexar Counties—and all the counties in between— experienced temperatures in the teens. The temperatures reached five degrees in College Station, north of Houston. The freeze lasted for more than a week and strained the power generation capacity of the entire state.

Human beings did not escape the impact of the cold. Several people, especially among the poor without heat or living in uninsulated homes, died. Even those with means were not spared, as heart issues, apoplexy, bronchial problems, and other illnesses were caused or spiked by the cold. Hospitals were filled to capacity with the sick and even dying. It was a human tragedy nearly unheard of in the generally warm climate of Texas.

Ultimately, the Great Freeze impacted millions of Americans, driving up the price of energy, causing power blackouts, bursting pipelines, closing roads, and causing accidents, including a 500-car pile-up in Dallas. The final cost was estimated at twenty billion dollars.

Of course, one person's bad news is another person's good news. In Houston, the energy traders at E-Titan Energy worked feverishly to profit from other people's misery. In fact, they attempted to worsen it to increase their profits. Trading oil, gas, and electric futures on the spot market drove up the price of energy, making millions of dollars for the traders of E-Titan Energy—and other traders as well. As the saying goes, they were trading like "hogs at the trough."

2

Study of Death

IN THE WESTERN PART OF the Houston metropolitan area, in a subdivision known as Sandlewood, in a small study in a warm house overlooking a small lake, Brad Gilliland stared at financial statements late in the evening, right in the middle of the Great Freeze. Brad was old school. He did not like to read spreadsheets on a computer screen. He preferred to read them on paper. This was especially true when the statements were complicated—and these statements were as complex as one could imagine.

O, what a tangled web we weave when first we practice to deceive, he thought to himself.

There was a timid knock on the mahogany-stained door to the study located on the first floor overlooking the lake. His first reaction was annoyance, and he ignored the interruption. After a second knock, he reluctantly told the knocker, "Come in."

Heather Gilliland stepped meekly into the room wearing her negligée and dressing gown. Laying a cup and saucer of fine china on the large desk, she stopped to speak.

"It is cold tonight. I brought you hot chocolate and put just a little schnaps in it, but not enough to interfere with your work."

"Thank you."

Once, there had been a warm intimacy between them. If he tried (which he seldom did in recent years), Brad Gilliland could remember the first time he met Heather at Texas A&M. She had seemed the loveliest creature in the world. He asked her out on the spot, and to his surprise, she accepted. In those early years, they had "chemistry," but that was a long, long time ago. They married during his senior year. For a short time, they were deliriously happy.

Then came his career, the long, calculated climb up the ladder of success, and finally, the achievement of his life dream. He became the chief financial officer of E-Titan Energy. Not that E-Titan had been his ultimate goal. He had always wanted to become the chief financial officer of a Fortune 100 company. When the call came to rejoin an old pal from his banking days in New York and become the CFO of E-Titan, he jumped at the chance. Besides, the money was much more than he ever made in banking—or ever would make, for that matter.

Success and money did not translate into happiness or increased love, as he expected. Instead, years of overwork and exhaustion created a barrier between them. Brad Gilliland despaired that the barrier between them could be torn down and intimacy restored.

"Are you coming to bed?"

"No. I have to finish looking at these financial statements before tomorrow. I am scheduled to have my deposition taken in the Battle Mountain case."

They seldom slept together in the same room, much less the same bed. Until recently, Heather had put up with an increasingly distant and moody husband. The late-night meetings, the trips to New York to visit with bankers, and the constant necessity to respond to emergencies in the far-flung economic empire of E-Titan Energy had become a part of the cold and dreary reality of her daily existence. She also remembered their love, a distant and vague memory.

Then came the disclosure of her husband's and others' shenanigans at an "Executive Planning Retreat" in Mexico. Not only did she learn of her husband's behavior, but so did her friends when an expose was published in the *Texas Quarterly* magazine—complete with pictures of the revelry. Since then, their cool distance had been increasingly replaced by something else—something dark, cold, and dangerous.

Gilliland looked up, bringing an end to the conversation.

"I am sorry, Heather, but this is an emergency. I have to be ready for the deposition tomorrow. A lot rides on this deposition. You cannot imagine how much. I promise to make it up to you later, honestly."

Heather had heard it all before. Even if it were true in this case (which it was), she could care less.

"Everything is an emergency, or at least you call everything an emergency. We need to talk. Things simply cannot continue this way any longer."

Gilliland had no time for conversation, however necessary. Tomorrow was going to be a big day. Long and difficult.

"I am sorry, but I must be alone and look at these numbers before tomorrow. I promise we will talk soon."

Heather shrugged helplessly and left, carefully closing the door behind her. Gilliland was alone, as he wanted. He went back to the numbers before him.

Some months earlier, E-Titan counter-sued a former subsidiary, Battle Mountain Energy, and its president for failure to disclose certain matters as part of its divestiture a few years earlier. The company had not wanted to file the suit. The lawsuit was only filed after E-Titan shareholders began alleging that the subsidiary was sold at an artificially low price, defrauding investors in E-Titan. In response, Lance DuFort, the president of E-Titan, was interviewed by a financial news outlet and alleged that "E-Titan had been defrauded and misled" during the negotiations.

Aware of the danger of litigation, Battle Mountain filed its suit for defamation of title in Bexar County, Texas, where it had its headquarters. In response, E-Titan Energy filed its counterclaim. Battle Mountain defended itself from the charge that it had misled E-Titan, alleging that E-Titan knew the asset's value but had sold it for less than it was worth to raise cash to offset a loss it had incurred trading natural gas futures. The litigation was proving a danger to E-Titan. The stock market, which had considered E-Titan a darling since its public offering, was beginning to ask questions.

There will be a lot more questions after tomorrow. If only Lance had listened to me.

Gilliland had opposed granting an interview with the financial press and advised against the countersuit. At the end of one explosive meeting, he had warned the chief executive officer.

"Lance, you need to think about what you are doing here. These guys are smart. They have fine lawyers and have arranged to try this case in San Antonio, where they have the home court advantage. Buddy Bennett (the president of Battle Mountain) is no fool. We have more to lose than gain by his litigation."

Lance DuFort, the CEO, had wearily nodded but could do nothing.

"I don't want to do this, but we must do it to protect ourselves from our shareholders and the feds. Sooner or later, I will settle the case with Buddy in a way that protects E-Titan. I just have to make a show for now."

Gilliland was undeterred. "Lance, making a show for stock analysts, shareholders, and the SEC is short-sighted. If the facts, as we know them to be, are ever revealed, E-Titan and you will not look good. This is not a case we can count on winning. Far from it."

Nothing more was to be said on the subject, but the results had been as bad as Gilliland feared. The litigation gradually exposed a lot of dirty financial and corporate laundry that Gilliland and DuFort would rather have remained hidden. Worse, E-Titan's fundamental business strategy was slowly being made public. This was dangerous not just to E-Titan but to the industry as a whole. Competitors were just as upset at E-Titan as were the shareholders and the principals of Battle Mountain.

I wish Lance had listened to me; God, how I wish he had listened.

Gilliland thought to himself as he returned to his tedious and weary analysis of numbers in columns on a page. The numbers, unfortunately, were impossible to explain away, assuming someone with experience looked at them. As Gilliland prepared to testify, he realized he had limited options.

- He could lie. The problem was he would be caught.
- He could cooperate with the other side. The trouble was that he would be fired.
- He could try to deceive the opposing counsel. Unfortunately, Eddie Morales, San Antonio local counsel for Battle Mountain, was a very experienced and capable trial lawyer, while Arthur Stone, chairman of the lead outside law firm

for the other side, Winchester & Wells, was known to be the finest (and luckiest) lawyer in Houston. He was also thought to hate Lance DuFort's guts.

Those who worked with Arthur Stone were also very smart. There was no way out of tomorrow—and no significant possibility of a successful day. Brad Gilliland had a lot to lose, no matter what happened. There was one last potential way out. He reached into his drawer and took out his 9mm Beretta. He stared at the gun.

MURDER FOR HIRE
SANDALWOOD SUBDIVISION, HOUSTON, TEXAS
FEBRUARY 14, 2001

BRAD GILLILAND LOOKED AT THE gun, thinking about the likely outcome if he told the truth or lied. Neither outcome held much hope of success. He remembered the promises conveyed by opposing counsel to his attorney—assurances that, if he told the truth, they would try to be helpful if they could. They refused to do more.

Is suicide the way out?

Lance was always a combination of upbeat ("Hey, there is nothing wrong here") and threatening ("You better not do anything stupid, Buster"). Lance would try to protect him because he had no choice. Gilliland knew too much. On the other hand, Lance would have to live with the results of his testimony, which, if truthful, would not be helpful to E-Titan. At worst, it would be devastating. If Lance could find a way, he would leave Gilliland holding the bag, or worse. Worse yet, Lance was as devious as they come—and generally merciless.

Why didn't Lance just listen in the beginning? I tried to warn him.

Gilliland went back to the numbers. His problem, quite simply, was that the original transaction with Buddy had not involved any fraud on Buddy's part. E-Titan had known the actual value of Battle Mountain on the day it was sold. Then, the so-called "Tarantula trade" was an obvious disaster. (Whoever thought up these names never considered litigation and juries.) The losses were enormous. To cover up the losses and raise cash, E-Titan engaged in other trades that were even more significant than Tarantula. In addition, it hastily sold Battle Mountain to raise cash, book profits, and impress the market. For a time, it worked. The losses were covered. Profits were recorded. Then, things began to go south.

By the time of Tarantula, Buddy Bennett wanted out. Buddy never liked Lance or E-Titan's trading strategies. He wanted to leave. Lance was tired of Buddy's oversight and influence. Therefore, Lance agreed to sell Battle Mountain and set the selling price to get rid of Buddy and book earnings before the first of the year—earnings that were needed to cover the bad trades (Tarantula and others) made by a subsidiary of E-Titan, E-Titan Energy Trading, which everyone referred to as "ET" because its earnings were extraterrestrial, at least on paper.

What am I going to do?

Gilliland looked at the gun again and at the spreadsheet. Shrugging his shoulders, he returned to the sheets on his desk.

There has to be a way to explain this without a disaster. I just need to find it.

As Gilliland looked down, a bullet came through the window overlooking the lake and entered the back of his head, blowing off the front of his face. As his shoulders and what remained of his head and neck fell onto the desk, the hot chocolate spilled, and the cup spun off the desk onto the floor. Blood spattered across the room. Ice-cold air blew into the room through the shattered glass. Then, there was a cold and deadly silence.

Across the lake, an athletic, medium-sized figure dressed in black walked from the little dock from which the shot was fired, opened the trunk of a late-model Ford rental car, placed a rifle into its case, and drove away.

Three hours later, the dark figure boarded a plane to Atlanta, from which he took an airplane to Edinburgh, Scotland. From there, he took a flight to Rome. In Rome, he rented a car and disappeared into Eastern Europe.

THE MORNING AFTER
MEMORIAL VILLAGES, HOUSTON, TEXAS
FEBRUARY 15, 2001

HEATHER GILLILAND WAS A HEAVY sleeper but an early riser. Since their younger son went off to Texas A&M for his first year of college (and the article in Texas Quarterly), she had begun taking sleeping pills. The shot that killed her husband had been fired from an automatic rifle fitted with a silencer. Other than breaking glass, there was no noise.

Because of the cold wave, she slept with an electric heater in her bedroom. It made a humming noise throughout the night. The door was tightly closed. When she woke to make coffee, she immediately noticed ice-cold air in the hallway. She walked to the bedroom where her husband usually slept. It was empty. Brad Gilliland was not usually an early nor easy riser. She walked down the stairs, calling his name. She noticed a bullet hole in the door to his study. Opening the door, she found her husband lying dead in a pool of blood.

She slowly backed out of the door, her hand to her mouth to stop herself from screaming. She fell into a chair in the hallway outside the office and stared for what seemed an eternity until she finally got up, dialed 911, and reported the death. Halfway into the report, she broke down, screaming incoherently. When the police arrived, Heather Gilliland sat alone in the entryway, staring into space.

Ricardo "Rico" Diaz had investigated many crimes, but never one quite like this. The Gillilands lived on a small lake in an exclusive neighborhood in the Memorial area. It was only a few minutes from the E-Titan offices in the Galleria area of Harris County. His study was deliberately placed at the rear of the home when the Gillilands built it shortly after he joined E-Titan. He enjoyed the view of the lake when working from home. Almost 180 degrees across the home-lined lake was a small pier and dock for canoes and other small watercraft that residents were allowed on the lake.

Generally, it would have been nearly impossible to fire a shot at someone from the dock without being observed by someone, but the prior evening, the temperatures in Houston dropped to around 25 degrees, and there had been a snowy mix of snow and sleet. The entire Houston metropolitan area was in a complete shutdown. Weather reporters had done their best to emphasize the danger of being outside in such conditions. (Even though the weather in Houston would have been typical in other areas of the country in February.) No one was outside—and most of the residents would not have been able to see anything if they had been looking, which they were not. Between the wind and snowy mix, no one could hear a shot fired from a rifle with a silencer.

Diaz had a forensic team at work. They had recovered the bullet embedded in the hallway wall. It appeared to be a .300 BLK, generally used with a Swiss-made B&T USA .300SPR Pro, a sniper rifle known for minimizing noise. One of the guys on the investigating team, a former sniper, recognized the bullet. He immediately said, "My Auntie Jane did not fire this bullet."

The B&T USA .300 has been in production since the 1960's. There were many such weapons in service worldwide, most used by special forces, secret agencies, or criminals. In the United States, such weapons are registered. Diaz was pretty sure they would not find the person who fired the fatal round by looking at the ATF records. This looked like a professional job—one shot, one bullet fired in poor weather. Whoever fired the shot that killed Gilliland was not an amateur. He was professional. Very professional.

After viewing the body and the study, Diaz carefully walked around the house, pondering the crime. There were no footprints on the lawn around the house. The shot must have been taken from across the lake. The weapon had to be a rifle with a scope to be accurate enough to make the kill.

He then went across the lake to look at the little dock and found tire tracks nearly obscured by the snow. He asked that imprints be made of the tracks and then drove back to the house.

This was a professional job. Someone ordered this guy killed.

❄

Diaz hated interviewing sudden widows. It was always emotional. He hated tears. He walked into the living room, where the detectives and forensic people had asked her to wait. He was surprised. Heather Gilliland was quiet and composed. Too composed. She seemed to be in shock. It was as if she was both surprised and not surprised by her husband's death.

This woman is not reacting normally, he thought to himself. Then he began.

"Mrs. Gilliland, while things are fresh in your memory, I would like to ask you a few questions if that is OK."

"That is fine."

"When was the last time you saw your husband alive?"

"A little after 10:30. I watched the news until about then, made him some hot chocolate, and took it to him in his study." She gestured towards the study in the back of the home.

"When you visited with him, did he seem disturbed?"

"Not really. He was anxious about a deposition he was scheduled to give downtown today. He wanted to be left alone to review the facts and figures he would testify about. I know he did not like this lawsuit."

"I see."

"Did you know your husband had a gun?"

"Yes. He kept it in his desk."

"We found a gun, a 9-millimeter Beretta, on his desk. Is that the gun?"

"I don't know anything about guns, but I think so. I saw it on his desk when I found his body."

"If he wasn't worried, why would he have a gun on his desk? Do you have any idea?

"No."

"Do you think your husband could have considered taking his own life?"

"I don't think Brad was the type, but he was under a lot of pressure at work. Was that the gun that killed him?"

"No, actually, it was not. We believe he was killed by a bullet from a high-powered rifle fired from across the lake."

Heather Gilliland sat and stared into space with a blank face for a few moments. To Diaz, it seemed she was either trying to think of what to say or letting something sink in, something she never dreamed of happening.

This lady is no fool. She is pretty and well-kept. But she is not dumb. She is trying to figure out what happened. I need to be careful. A pretty face has outsmarted many a cop.

"Did you hear anything unusual during the night?

"No. I take sleeping pills and am a heavy sleeper."

"Did you realize your husband had not come to bed at any time?"

Heather Gilliland looked down as if embarrassed before looking up.

"My husband and I have separate bedrooms. He seldom sleeps in my room anymore."

"I see."

"He just. . . ." Heather did not end the sentence. She looked ashamed.

"I am sorry to have had to ask. It was routine. I did not mean to embarrass you."

Diaz sat silently before continuing.

I knew there was something wrong with his woman. By now, most wives would ask me to leave and return after dissolving in tears. This was not a marriage—at least not in the complete sense of that word. Something is wrong.

He made a mental note to check on possible affairs. Then, he remembered a story in the papers about E-Titan Energy.

"If I could ask you a couple of additional questions, Mrs. Gilliland, I will let you rest for today. To let you know, your husband's body is evidence in a murder inquiry. We cannot release it to you until after an autopsy is done. In this case, that might be some time. It looks as if this was a professional killing to me. Do you know of anyone who might want your husband dead?"

"No. I don't think so. His company has been in this lawsuit and the news recently. But I don't think that would result in a murder."

She looked down, hesitant and embarrassed. She bit her lip, looked at the detective plaintively, and said, "He . . . Well, there might be husbands or ex-boyfriends who hold a grudge, maybe. . . ." Her voice faded. Once again, that look of helpless shame.

This woman had been suffering for a long time.

"Mrs. Gilliland, I think this will be all for today. My forensics team will be here for a while longer. They will take a few things from the study—everything he or the bullet might have touched—and bag them and label them. Once the investigation is complete, we will return anything of value to you.

"One more thing. You will need to sleep somewhere else for a few days until we complete our investigation. You probably do not want to stay here in any case. We need to be sure no part of the crime scene is contaminated until after our investigation. It is standard procedure."

Heather Gilliland looked relieved. "I can stay with my sister; she and her husband live in Tanglewood, which is close."

With that, they exchanged a few pleasantries; Diaz got up and shook her trembling hand, and he left.

3

DEATH ON MOUNT BADON

THE BATTLE OF MT. BADON
NEAR MODERN BATH
APRIL 1, 647 A.D.

ARTHUR SAT ON HIS ROMAN war horse, looking downward across Mount Badon, near modern Bath. He was gazing at a small creek and the camp of Lancelot and his army beyond. He wore Roman armor left by the conquering Etruscans when they evacuated Britain. Beside him was Merlinius, mounted on a smaller horse and also dressed for battle. His garb was not the garb of the Romans but that of a Druid. His long hair and white beard waved in the hilltop breeze. This would be Arthur's greatest victory. He would defeat Lancelot, recover Guinevere, and end the wars that plagued his little realm. He would be more than just a great warrior when this day ended. He would be the King of the Britons. But, for now, he was impatient. He wanted the battle to be over.

"I hate this waiting."

Merlinius replied firmly, "I know, Arthur, but you are impetuous and like the exhilaration and danger of combat too much. You are not a petty knight. You are now a king and commander of armies—the Duke of Battles, as they call you."

"I still hate it. I sent Pelinor and his army down the hill to the left. They should be giving the signal to Gwaine on the right. I cannot see them for the trees. By now, the attack should be beginning."

If one could find the actual site today, nothing would be the same. The countryside has been turned into farm and grazing land; it is green, lush, and stretches out before the eye with hardly a tree except for boundary lines and an occasional wood. The Battle of Mt. Badon occurred long before civilization came, and people began cutting trees for lumber. In Arthur's time, that land was a great forest, dense and foreboding. To Arthur's right and left, two small paths led down the hillside to a meadow below and a small creek.

On the other side, Lancelot was encamped with his army—purchased and paid for by Arthur's enemies. It was the duty of Pelinor to attack across that creek with all the force he could muster, drawing the opposing force into the meadow on the far side. Once the battle was engaged, Gwaine was ordered to attack from the left, hidden by the trees until he emerged. Lancelot would fear neither of these attacks, especially not the first, for his army outnumbered Arthur's. Arthur was counting on Lancelot's pride and self-certainty. Lancelot would undoubtedly face the attack and join the battle.

One last element of Arthur's plan was hidden from all but Gwaine, Pelinor, and Merlinius. From the rear, Arthur's allies from the northern tribes were coming to join the battle in return for a share of the booty. Once Lancelot was committed, they would attack. With Lancelot and his army surrounded, he was doomed.

Arthur heard the beginning of the battle. In the morning fog, he could dimly see and hear activity from Lancelot's camp.

Lancelot was taking the bait and joining in the fight. Gwaine had not, however, attacked when Arthur heard and dimly perceived the attack of the northern tribes. No battle goes entirely according to plan, but this minor deviation awoke a fear in Arthur.

What if Lancelot escapes with Guinevere?

Arthur tried to control his impulse to join the battle and win it for himself. As Merlinius observed, he was impatient and missed the days when he was not the "Duke of Battles" but one of the combatants. Out of patience, he put his spurs into the horse's side and goaded the horse down the left-hand path toward the spot where Gwaine should be attacking.

Merlinius cried out, "Arthur, wait," but it was too late. The warrior's blood was up. Arthur drove his horse down the small mountain, his personal bodyguard trying desperately to keep up with their leader and not lose control of their mounts on the rocky and twisted path.

Arthur knew the terrain. This was his land. Near the bottom, the path divided into two. Gwaine would have taken one of them but must have lost his way. Trusting that Gwaine would eventually join the battle, Arthur took the other, barely visible in the morning mist. At the bottom was a small clearing. He saw one of Lancelot's knights guarding the exit, or so he thought. Arthur raised his sword and charged. The other knight seemed frightened and made little attempt to defend himself. It was no contest. Arthur slew the knight with a single blow.

Turning to be certain of his kill-stroke, to his horror, Arthur saw lovely red hair flowing from beneath the knight's armor. It was Guinevere. He dismounted and went to her, slowly holding her in his arms. She looked up.

"I was coming back to you, silly man. Now you've gone and killed me."

DUELING ANGELS
MT. BADON
APRIL 1, 647 A. D.

SUDDENLY, ANOTHER CREATURE APPEARED. ARTHUR had seen this creature before. It was a black and fiery image of Arthur himself, leering at him from behind Guinevere.

"You have done it, you fool. You killed her. I won. I have finally won!"

A black anger fell upon Arthur, already filled with all the irrational rage of battle, blood lust, frustration, and defeat. He drew his great sword, which legend would call Excalibur.

"I will kill you."

"No, you will not, for you cannot. But I *have* destroyed you. Now, kill yourself, be killed, or evermore be filled in agony and pain everlasting."

The fiery figure rose. It was tall, taller than Arthur, and strong. From its hand emerged a flaming sword, dark with fire, dark red fire like the blood of death. There was a flash of light before the fiery figure could strike a blow. A beam of pure light brighter than the sun descended from the heavens. It struck the ground between the fiery figure and Arthur, who stood in helpless grief and shock. The beam of light fixed itself on the ground and expanded until it was a tremendous white image of a human form. It began to change colors. White, then red, then orange, then the blue of the skies, then the green of the grass, the dark green of emeralds, and finally, white again.

Surrounded by the light (or perhaps better immersed within the light or formed by it), a figure, a human form dressed in white with flaming eyes and feet like bronze, could be seen. It had bright armor of the most precious gold, such armor that no knight in

Britain could afford or have made even if the gold could be found. In one hand, the creature held a flaming sword of no metal Arthur had ever seen, for it was unlike any human sword. Around his waist was a belt of platinum, as white as the sun, and on the buckle was written a name Arthur could not understand, for it was not in any language of this world. The legs of the creature were girded with bronze armor. It held no shield, but such power radiated from the sword that Arthur fell on his knees, and the fiery figure withdrew. The creature raised his free hand and spoke with a voice that shattered Arthur's ears, a voice like the raging of many waters but louder. It was a voice that could, if it desired, command all the armies of the world.

"Enough. I have seen enough. There is to be no more of this. You have done damage enough."

With that, the man (if such he was) knelt beside Guinevere and lifted her in his arms. The figure, white as a new snowfall, began to change color once again until it was blood red. It was as if all the anger and pain of the battle and death and all the battles of human history from its founding were taken into the gleaming figure. Guinevere began to move. She was alive.

"This one belongs to me. Leave this place. Your petty battle is over, Arthur. You have won the day but lost what you loved more than all."

"Where will you take my wife?" Arthur angrily demanded.

"I will take her where I will take her. But, be of good courage; you will see her again."

With that, the fiery figure disappeared with Guinevere in his arms, and Arthur Stone woke up from his dream to the sound of a telephone.

ARTHUR ANSWERED THE PHONE TO find Thomas L'Orangelo Mallory on the line.

"Boss, it's TL."

Thomas, or TL as he was sometimes known in the firm, was the associate at Winchester & Wells closest to Arthur Stone. They had met briefly years before in Memphis, Tennessee, at a Rhodes College basketball game. Arthur was in Memphis preparing for a deposition in one of his Resolution Trust Corporation cases in which what was once known as Union Planters Bank was a party. His co-counsel was a prominent local attorney who invited Arthur to go with him to a basketball game at Rhodes. During the game, there was a big fight. One of the players simply picked up the basketball from the court, walked to the center court, and sat down on the ball.

"Who is that?" Arthur inquired.

"That boy is Thomas Mallory, the starting guard. He is a great kid."

A conversation ensued, and Arthur learned that Thomas grew up in Orange Mound near the University of Memphis. It was a brutal, violent, and crime-infested neighborhood. He did well in high school and was a star basketball player. He got a scholarship to Rhodes College. He was an unusual athlete—and an even more unusual young man. He maintained an Army scholarship as well as a small basketball scholarship. As an end to his accomplishments, TL was nearly a Straight A student in the engineering school. His mother was poor but instilled a good work ethic in the boy. TL planned to serve in the Army and then attend law school.

For whatever reason, the story interested Arthur. After the game, they went to see the boy.

After a few pleasantries, Arthur asked the big question. "I understand that you want to become an attorney, but first, you must fulfill your commitment to the Army?"

"Yes, sir."

"Have you decided where you want to go to law school?"

"I think the University of Mississippi Law School in Oxford. I could watch over my mother and family that way."

"I see. You stay in touch. I think you will be admitted to the University of Mississippi and perhaps other law schools. You will have a choice to make."

Ultimately, TL fulfilled his commitment to the Army as a Ranger. He attended the University of Mississippi, clerked for a judge for a year, and then joined Winchester & Wells. Along the way, he met his wife, Alicia, who worked for Gwynn's small firm helping indigents and unwed mothers. Thomas and Arthur were very close, and Gwynn and Alicia were even closer.

Arthur returned to the present with a jolt when TL blurted out, "Brad Gilliland is dead. Your uncle heard it on the police band. He called Roger (Roger Romny, the managing partner of Winchester & Wells), who asked me to call you. He did not want to bother you with this, knowing you have been keeping a distance from this case against E-Titan."

"What did my uncle say?"

"I don't know for sure. But it looks like the death was a professional hit job. Your uncle Ben is on his way to visit the scene. (Ben Stone, Arthur's uncle, was an ex-FBI agent who owned a prominent Houston private investigating agency.) We were scheduled to take Gilliland's deposition today. The timing here is more than a little suspicious."

Arthur looked at his closet. He needed to shower and get dressed.

"I was not going to come in today because of the weather and the icy streets. But I think I will come in after all."

"You don't have to. We can take care of this."

"No, I will come in. I need to work on some other matters anyway. I will see you in a few minutes. You can give me an update when I get there. Be sure Roger is free as well. We need to meet."

Arthur put down the phone quietly. Gazing at the sleet falling outside his window, he felt the icy cold seeping like a mist through the window panes. He closed his eyes to gather his thoughts.

I have been afraid something like this could happen.

❄

Arthur could only meditate for a few moments before the phone rang again. Bad news comes in batches.

"Arthur, it's Gwynn. I hate to bother you, but we need to talk."

Gwynn DuFort was the last person in the world Arthur Stone wanted to visit at just this minute. He gazed silently at the phone receiver in his hand.

"Arthur, I wouldn't bother you, but we need to visit about Murray."

This was never the beginning of good news. Gwynn never called to say, "Everything is fine."

"What is going on?"

"Murray's grades have been terrible this semester. St. John's called me to suggest they may not be the best place for him. They feel he is disruptive and a bad influence on other students. I am worried. Very worried."

"How long have you known this?"

"Only recently. His last report card was much worse than usual. I think I sent them to you."

"You did. I was concerned. However, I was a volatile student in my high school days. Could it just be hormones?"

"I don't think so. He was sent home about a week ago, and I was asked to make an appointment to see the headmaster. That was today. I would have asked you to come along if I had known it was this serious."

"Has the headmaster given you a reason for his behavior?"

There was a silence on the line. She was carefully formulating her answer.

"Arthur, he hates both of us and everything we stand for. He said some pretty terrible things to me. He thinks that I am a whore and that you ignored me and let me get into the situation we are in today. Children in this kind of situation often act out. Sometimes in destructive ways."

Gwynn was rapidly losing her composure. "Arthur, we must do something. I am afraid for him."

In the best of times, it was difficult for Arthur to control his anger at Gwynn and Lance. He blamed them both for the dissolution of his family. He gazed out the window at the sleet slowly covering the pin oak trees in the backyard.

If this does not stop, I am going to lose a tree.

"Arthur?"

"I am just thinking. Look, I need to think more about this. It is nearly Christmas break. We can look at alternatives if the school can get him through this semester. In the meantime, what does his counselor say?" All three children had been in counseling since the divorce.

"Well, he says that it is normal in this kind of situation to see some rebellion. In this case, . . ." There was another long pause. "In this case, the counselor thinks it is more serious. Murray is showing some self-destructive behaviors. He has been self-mutilating lately."

"What?!"

"He has been scraping his lower arms with his fingernails until they bleed. He has also been sullen and withdrawn. He hates Lance. He needs to live with you for a while or go to a boarding school. I don't think I can handle this alone. I am not sure I can handle it at all."

Even through a phone line, Arthur could sense tears forming in her eyes. He never felt the slightest compassion for Gwynn these days. The only way he could keep his sanity was to drive any feelings from his mind and ignore any emotions in their relationship. When the local matrons gossiped and he learned about it, he mostly thought, *She deserves it*. Nevertheless, Murray was Arthur's child. This was no time for accusations.

"I don't know if I could give him the time and oversight he needs. Let me think about it. I could probably hire a nanny or tutor to live here. You could check in daily. I could restrain any travel unless necessary. But, if he hates me, I am not sure it would do any good. He would just be changing locations for resentment and misbehavior."

There was silence on the line, then an almost pleading response.

. "OK. But, unless I am wrong, we don't have much time to decide. It might help if you called tonight, told him you love him, and emphasized that his grades must improve."

"I will do that. Let me go now. Keep me informed. I will think about this and make some plans."

Arthur almost always adopted a strictly business-like manner in dealing with Gwynn. It was a matter of self-defense. He might scream or lash out at her if he did not. He knew this was possible because it had happened at the first. It took his brother to calm him down and convince him that this behavior was harmful to him, her, and the children.

"I will call tonight or in a day or two."

"Please, Arthur, call tonight."

Arthur put down the phone. His heart remained as cold and icy as the weather outside his River Oaks window.

4

Business Plan for Billions

DAWSON ENERGY

HOUSTON, TEXAS

SUMMER 1994

WITH INTENSE ANTICIPATION, LANCE DUFORT and his wife, Sheila, moved to Houston in 1991. Some months earlier, Lance had read about another Houston-based company, Enron Corporation, a leader in trading energy futures. The *Forbes* article praised its chairman and president as visionary businessmen and leaders. The article was filled with glowing reports of the company's financial achievements. Before new management took over, Enron had been an old-line, boring natural gas pipeline company. Enron was now seen as a new high-tech energy firm, and its shares were valued accordingly. There was money to be made in energy trading. That seemed certain. Lance DuFort was headed for Houston. He was going to grab the brass ring.

❄

When Jeff Skilling took over Enron, it was a sleepy Houston-based pipeline company. Like most pipeline companies, the business was regular, the profits stable, and the management skills required were modest. Energy trading was different. The industry is cyclical, the skills necessary to avoid losses are significant, and the ability to manage such an operation is unique. Traders were unique individuals and not necessarily an honest group. Most of them would have been right at home as professional gamblers taking advantage of marks in Las Vegas. Lance DuFort considered himself extraordinarily special. He was accustomed to thinking that he was, in his own words, "The Smartest Guy in the Room." Lance knew he could be the next Jeff Skilling—only bigger and better. He just needed to find himself the right sponsor.

When he arrived in Houston that day in early 1991, Lance met with Dobie Dawson, Jr., the owner of Dawson Corporation. His father, Dobie Dawson, Sr., had been a legend in the oil business. He was a wildcatter of the old school. He had been rich, and he had been poor. He had been so deep in debt he could not possibly dig his way out and so flush with cash he couldn't spend it all. After a few years of ups and downs, Dawson invested in Arkansas's Smackover oil field. It was the beginning of a great fortune.

In those early days, a lot of oil needed to be brought from all over to Houston, where the refining business was located on the ship channel. Dobie Dawson built pipelines. The oil exploration and refining business required a lot of equipment and new drilling technology. Dobie Dawson invested in oilfield manufacturing. There was a need for oil rigs. So, Dobie Dawson built oil rigs. He manufactured pipe. He invested in and eventually controlled many companies owning pieces of downhole technology. Ultimately, Dawson Corporation was divided into several components:

exploration and development, pipelines, manufacturing, and oil field services.

Right down at the deep, rich bottom of all this wealth was the sleepy business of Battle Mountain Pipeline Company. Battle Mountain grew out of the original pipeline Dawson built from Arkansas to Houston. Over time, Dawson had bought or built other pipelines. Some were short. Some were very long, carrying natural gas for great distances into major cities. Some of them were now a part of Battle Mountain. In good times and bad times, during boom times and bust times, the pipeline companies were a stable source of cash flow. Dobie Dawson, Sr. liked positive cash flow, just like most entrepreneurs who build a business from scratch. He watched the cash in his companies like a hawk chasing a rabbit in West Texas. Dobie Dawson liked having a lot of cash because he knew what it was like to be out of money.

Dobie Dawson Jr. was a different sort of a person. He grew up wealthy. When his father died during World War II, Dobie was barely one year out of Yale, which he entered without a high school diploma, off in Hollywood producing movies, seducing starlets, and making his fortune. World War II was a godsend for Dawson Corporation. The country needed oil to fight the war. The oil business boomed. Dobie Dawson (Junior, as the old timers called him) took over a profitable oil company, one of the nation's largest, privately owned companies. He made it into a vast integrated oil company and the largest privately held company in the world. One of Junior's first steps was to change his title from Junior to DD. He fired anyone who dared to call him Junior. Under the circumstances, Dobie Dawson, Jr. became DD within the Dawson Corporation in a very short period.

Over the years, DD developed what most people thought of as unusual habits. For one thing, he seemed incapable of a lasting relationship with a woman. The stars, socialites, and beauty queens came and went. He married five of them over the years. They eventually left him, some without much money to show for their trouble. After the first couple of wives, Junior Dawson became very good at prenuptial agreements.

DD also seemed unable to find a place to call home. Initially, he moved into his father's home in River Oaks, married a Houston socialite, and began running the family business. The marriage lasted precisely thirty-six months. His wife alleged infidelity and erratic behavior in the divorce petition. It was granted. Houston was a smaller city in those days, and everybody knew everybody. The rumors about Junior Dawson were many, varied, and lurid. In response, DD moved the company's headquarters to Los Angeles to be "closer to the movie business." That move lasted for five years and fifteen starlets.

In the early 1950s, DD developed an interest in gambling and eventually owned two casinos in Las Vegas. That being the case, he moved to Las Vegas. He spent his time dating several showgirls and married one. The marriage lasted a predictable three years. DD divorced the showgirl, who was cheating on him in any case and proceeded to Acapulco to recover from the trauma. He kept a lovely mistress from a wealthy Mexican family at the top of one of the most exclusive hotels in the city. She lasted three years. For most people, three is seen as a lucky number. DD proved otherwise.

After Las Vegas, DD developed the habit of living alone in hotel suites—usually an entire hotel floor. Although he continued to own the family home in Houston, it remained vacant and crumbling in disrepair for many years. He never returned to the family home after his first wife left him. In Houston, DD lived in hotel suites at the top of the Warwick Hotel in the Medical Center area and other hotels around the city. In Las Vegas, he lived at the top of one of his casino hotels. In Los Angeles, he lived at the Chateau Marmont. When he was in the mood, he transferred his location to Acapulco, where he kept an entire floor available at the Acapulco Princess.

This was a costly way to live, but business was good and DD was rich as an Arab Sheik—richer.

As DD grew older, he developed unusual habits. For one thing, he often refused to see people. He managed his company by telephone. He rarely, if ever, showed up at the corporate offices. He never visited the oil fields, manufacturing, or research facilities. He just sat in a hotel room and tried to manage at a distance. You can get away with anything when you have as much money as DD had.

Although it was never confirmed, it seemed as if DD might have developed a drug addiction. He also developed the habit of never cutting his hair, wearing psychedelic pajamas day and night, and neglecting his personal hygiene. By the early 1980s, the fire of his libido had burned out from overuse. He lived alone, cared for by three lovely, overpaid, and over-developed playboy bunnies, two of whom would write extremely unflattering memoirs about their boss.

DD was never much of a manager. He considered himself a visionary genius. He set the path. He did not blaze, develop, or maintain the path. Once again, if you have enough money, you can delude yourself into believing you're a genius for a long time. DD was a kind of genius. He just wasn't as big a genius as he thought he was. Plus, in business, sometimes it doesn't matter if you're a genius.

Fundamentally, DD did not like people. Moreover, he didn't have the kind of mind that focused on the details of construction projects, drilling programs, employee performance reviews, financial statements, organizational charts, pipelines, and the like. He needed someone to manage the details. After going through several chief executive officers, he finally hit upon one that worked.

Buddy Bennett grew up in the pipeline business and was a shrewd, tough, capable businessman. He had attended Texas A&M, served in the army, and then returned to Houston to work at the Dawson Corporation. When DD found him, Buddy was trapped in the middle class, a salaried employee of a giant, privately held corporation with little chance of getting rich. DD allowed him to be the chief executive officer of a large, privately held holding company at a salary and benefit level, making it inevitable he would be rich. Buddy jumped at the chance.

People liked Buddy Bennett, and Buddy Bennett liked people. Buddy even liked DD, a feat in itself. There was no problem, however detailed and complex, that Buddy Bennett would not solve. He had a good work ethic. He favored A&M graduates who had served in the army and worked hard and well with others. His formula was simple: Hire good people, treat them well, let them do their job, and concentrate on the business and whatever problems DD wanted to be solved immediately. It was a winning strategy.

Most people thought hiring Buddy Bennett was the best decision Dobie Dawson ever made. The truth was that Dawson Corporation was not very profitable by the 1980s. Years of mismanagement resulted in a decline, and employee morale was poor. When bonuses began to be cut, the best talent began to leave the company. Buddy Bennett changed all that. No one thought of Buddy as a genius, but Buddy was the best when it came to organizational charts, regular reporting, and demanding results.

BIRTH OF A DISASTER
HOUSTON, TEXAS
JANUARY - JULY 1994

WHEN LANCE DUFORT INITIALLY MET with Dobie Dawson and Buddy Bennett, the subject of the meeting was a need to finance an additional pipeline Dawson Corporation wanted to build. For a time, Lance let the conversation go on as his client anticipated; then, he began to talk about Dawson Corporation's trading operation. Like many pipeline companies, Dawson Corporation had a gas trading operation. It was a relatively small part of the business designed to hedge the company's natural gas and oil supplies for its pipelines and other functions. Lance proposed to put the trading operation into a new company so that all trading would be consolidated in one place. He further suggested that it might be possible to eventually take this particular company public and exploit the hidden value of Dawson Corporation's trading operations.

"Everyone can see that Enron has a business plan for the future," Lance told them. "Their trading operation is not a sleepy hedging operation. It's a profit center. It makes a lot of profits. Enron has been one of the most profitable companies in America in the last few years. Dawson Corporation can be just as profitable."

Lance went on to suggest the formation of a subsidiary of Dawson Corporation that would be called E-Titan Energy. The plan was to take the new company public as soon as possible. In that way, Dawson Corporation could profit from the increase in the company's value. In addition, it would take a lot of capital to build the kind of enormous trading operation that Lance envisioned. Lance didn't want just to trade natural gas and oil futures. He wanted to trade oil, gas, electricity, and anything else that could be traded in the futures market.

"If you buy into this, we can create a new kind of high-tech energy company. We don't need many assets. We just need lines of credit and a lot of very smart traders."

He could tell that Buddy was not impressed, but DD was interested.

Despite his reclusive nature, DD was an egotist. He was particularly sensitive about his leadership at Dawson Corporation and the implication that his father had been a better businessman than he was. DD thought of himself as a visionary and his father as a plodder. He sensed that many in the company and the energy business generally did not share his views. He resented his father. All his life, DD had been out to make a name for himself.

DD interjected himself into the conversation. "Tell me, Lance, what kind of return do you think we could generate on this deal?"

"DD, look at Enron and the value Ken Lay and Jeff Skilling have unlocked there. The trading operation is currently on your books for nearly nothing. It could be worth hundreds of millions of dollars. I can easily foresee the day when the value of the trading operation would be nearly as great—perhaps greater—than the total value of Dawson Corporation today."

Buddy interjected with a question of his own.

"What do you think the risks might be? Our traders are hedgers. They are not trained to be a profit center. They are hired to protect the profits of the pipeline and refining companies and ensure adequate supplies. We do not currently trade with third parties except under those guidelines. In addition, the only thing we trade today is oil and natural gas. We've never traded electricity. We don't know anything about the electricity business. As to other commodities, we've never traded one in the company."

Lance tried to look thoughtful before giving Buddy an answer he had rehearsed many times.

"That is the point, Buddy. Right now, your trading operation is a cost center. If you follow my recommendation, it will become a profit center. Of course, you will need to hire experienced traders, probably from Enron and similar companies, put them under new management, and set them loose. The older traders will either continue to do what they are already doing or gradually develop the skills and personality needed for the kind of trading operation I envision, operations that Enron and others already possess."

Buddy lapsed into silence while DD broke in once more. "Explain to me the necessity for a new company."

"You will need a new company because the cash demands of a trading operation are considerable. The trading company will require substantial lines of credit from commercial banks. In addition, you will want to be sure that no losses in the new company flow over into the rest of your empire. In the business of trading, there are wins and losses. You have to be willing to assume the risk for the ultimate payoff. Finally, unlike the rest of the business, this new entity, which I call E-Titan, will need to use mark-to-market accounting just as does Enron."

Buddy had a question, an important question. If DD had listened to the answer and thought about Buddy's objection, a lot of trouble might have been avoided. Unfortunately, DD was a proponent of the view that "greed is great."

"One of the questions people have around the industry about Enron has to do with this 'mark-to-market accounting.' As I understand it, every time Enron closes a deal, they estimate that transaction's forward profits and book those as current income. For example, recently, Enron built a power plant in a foreign country. They estimated the profits of that company for the next several years, discounted them to present value, and booked the resulting number as profit. This, even though as I understand matters, the plant has never sold a kilowatt of energy. I've been around this business a long time. I don't think you can estimate profits over three years, much less the life of a complex project in a foreign country with all the political and economic risks involved in business overseas."

Lance could feel the deal slipping away. But he had a ready answer.

"I've done some research on this. Every time Enron closes a transaction, an internal group of risk auditors verifies the transaction. More importantly, their accounting firm believes using mark-to-market accounting is justified. Most of the time, it signs off on the accounting for the deal. We will do the same thing.

"Enron has been using mark-to-market accounting for some time. They've got audited financial statements from the most prestigious accounting firm in the nation. No one on Wall Street has raised a question about their accounting practices. I think it's pretty safe to say that we won't be doing the same kind of transactions that Enron is involved in overseas. I don't intend to build power plants. This is going to be a trading operation. That's all."

Lance could tell that DD was beginning to tire.

"I am not asking you to make a decision today, but it would be nice if you could give this some thought and get back to me as soon as possible. The window of opportunity will not be open forever."

With that, the conversation ended with pleasantries.

Several days later, Buddy called Lance.

"Lance, DD's been doing nothing but talk to me about this trading company you proposed to him last week. I'll be frank: my advice has been to pass on the opportunity. Nevertheless, DD is adamant. He wants to know if you would be willing to move to Houston and take over the operation.

"DD wanted me to tell you that he will pay you generously and give you a budget for re-organizing the company and taking this thing you call 'E-Titan' public. By the way, he likes the name. He thinks using that name might mean that when you take the company public, it'll get the same kind of multiples that Enron gets, similar to multiples that fast-growing high-tech companies out on the West Coast can get on their operations."

Lance could hardly hide his glee.

"Well, Buddy, as you know, I work for a pretty big Wall Street firm. I won't be leaving here unless I get paid more than I am being paid today. With bonuses, that's in the seven figures. Of course, I expect all my moving expenses to be paid, and I'd like a generous entertainment allowance. As I said in the meeting, it's a dealbreaker if I can't use mark-to-market accounting. If I can use mark-to-market accounting, get paid fairly, and have the right to hire the kind of traders needed, then I'll come and run the operation. You just need to get back to me with some specifics."

The conversation degenerated into a long and technical discussion about the payscales at Enron, the comparable pay scales at Dawson Corporation, and the likely response of some of the existing traders to being transferred into a company run by newcomers. There would be some challenges in getting the operation set up.

Most importantly, the new company was initially to be merged with Battle Mountain Pipeline Company to take advantage of the sleepy pipeline company's considerable borrowing capacity and use its trading operation as a foundation for the new company Lance envisioned.

Within a month, Lance DuFort was in Houston as the president of E-Titan Energy, a new subsidiary of Dawson Corporation.

THE FIRST BIG DISASTER
HOUSTON, TEXAS
DECEMBER 1995

Once Lance and his wife Sheila moved to Houston, purchased a home in Memorial, and joined a local church (which Lance attended Christmas Eve and Easter Sunday when forced to do so), he began to revolutionize Battle Mountain and its new parent corporation, E-Titan Energy, Inc., into a new kind of energy giant, one less dependent upon material assets like oil and gas reserves and pipelines and more dependent upon the intellectual and trading expertise of the brightest guys in the room, whom he called his "New Supermen."

Lance raided Enron, Dynegy, and other Houston trading operations for intellectual talent and even hired a few commodity traders from Wall Street investment banks. His method was quite simple: He paid employees more for leaving than they were being paid for staying. This was a dangerous strategy because most people were already paid more than they could have earned elsewhere. Lance, never one to "count pennies," paid whatever was necessary to "buy talent," as he put it.

One of the dangers of paying someone who isn't too competent is that the person never leaves. They just stay and mess things up. This was a danger that Lance, the former investment banker, never considered. It turned out that it was easy for Lance to hire people by overpaying. It was harder to encourage people to leave.

Furthermore, Lance was not a good manager. He didn't like conflict and could never bring himself to fire anyone, no matter what they did. This encouraged misbehavior.

To make things worse, Lance instituted a bonus system based on mark-to-market accounting. Mark-to-market accounting required E-Titan to book profits on trades when they were closed. This "profit" included the estimated return on the entire transaction. In the end, it meant that bonuses to traders were paid based on the amount that looked like profit by the company in the current year. Unfortunately, the bonus calculation incentivized traders to make trades that might look good initially but not so good in the end. That's precisely what happened. And it happened fast.

During the first half of 1995, crude oil prices reached post-Gulf War highs as gasoline prices increased nearly 12 percent. The traders at E-Titan were confident the trend would continue. They engaged in a series of margin trades that ultimately bet more than the initial capital of the new entity. Unfortunately, they were wrong. Natural gas prices did rise more than eight percent for the year; in June, the price had risen twelve percent. Then, it began to fall. By the end of the year, all those "profitable" trades were seriously underwater.

Even worse for Lance was the discovery that one of the E-Titan traders, Rohan Kumar, had engaged in a series of marginal trades far over his trading limit. The losses were astronomical.

If they were reported, there would be no way to take E-Titan public for a long time. The loss put E-Titan in default on its lines of credit, which Dawson Corporation had guaranteed. Lance's dream was over unless something was done.

Lance was desperate—and Buddy was furious with Lance and the traders when he heard about the problem. This was when Buddy lost all confidence in Lance. Buddy confronted DD with the situation, took responsibility for allowing the loss, and announced that he would not stay unless E-Titan was closed and Lance was fired. DD refused to go along and chose Lance over Buddy. Something had to be done. Ultimately, what was done was to sell a profitable asset with considerable unlocked value to no one other than Buddy Bennett. For accounting reasons, the sale had to close within the fiscal year. Lance was desperate, and Buddy was willing. To solve the problem, DD decided to part with the Battle Mountain Pipeline Company, which, in any case, reminded him that most people in Houston thought his father was a better business person than he was.

Battle Mountain was the legacy pipeline in the Dawson Energy collection. The pipeline was on the books of Dawson Corporation for nearly nothing but worth more than 100 million dollars. Knowing he was losing the intercompany political battle with Lance, Buddy decided to call it quits and accepted an offer to buy Battle Mountain if he could close the deal before the end of the year. The price agreed upon was 100 million dollars. Buddy was mystified that DD would agree to such a price. He estimated that the pipeline was intrinsically worth $200 million or more— perhaps more.

Lance did not care. He just wanted to get rid of Buddy and cover the loss ASAP, and DD just wanted to cover the loss in any way possible. He did not want to face any embarrassment in the business or financial community. The result was a deal made in heaven for Buddy. The key was that the deal had to close before the end of the current fiscal year. That's where Winchester & Wells entered the situation.

It seemed like a great deal for everyone. However, it was also a seed that grew like corn in August, becoming an enormous financial problem.

❄

The year 1995 was an excellent year for Arthur Stone. In the years since he was made partner, Stone won a series of lawsuits—ten of them. Each case was more significant, complex, and complicated than the prior one. Each one was more profitable for the firm. Each one increased Arthur Stone's status as the "Duke of Texas Trial Lawyers." Arthur Stone was a good lawyer, but he had something money couldn't buy, and even brains and education couldn't give a person. People liked him, and he was lucky, very lucky.

Early in 1995, Stone won a verdict against the president and directors of a Louisiana bank, alleging that it had failed to perform on a "take-out commitment letter" on a loan that later went bad, a commitment they had refused to honor under pressure from the banking authorities. Fortunately, the bank's president had not just promised that the bank would honor the "takeout letter" but also promised in writing that he would personally see that it was taken out. This personal lawsuit against that person and the bank's directors resulted in a huge victory. The firm collected an enormous fee, and Arthur was entitled to the largest share of the cash.

As the year ended, Lance sent Buddy to talk with his "old law school friend," Arthur Stone. Stone had never represented

Dawson Corporation, and Lance saw this as an opportunity to "Throw him a bone." It turned out Lance had other ideas as well.

Today, Buddy Bennett is a wealthy man—one of Texas's two or three richest people. Battle Mountain is a public company with separate pipeline entities into which ordinary investors can invest for the cash flow. But back in 1996, Buddy was just upper-middle-class rich. He didn't have the money to purchase Battle Mountain and pay Winchester & Wells' legal fees. Therefore, Buddy suggested to Arthur that Buddy himself would give Winchester & Wells five percent of the company and pay all the firm's out-of-pocket expenses if the deal closed before year-end. On the surface, it didn't look as good a deal as it was. Buddy winked at Arthur and told him not to worry – everything would be fine. Arthur believed him.

The partners of Winchester & Wells were not anxious to accommodate Buddy, so Arthur, who immediately liked Buddy Bennett, agreed with the firm that he would receive the 5% stock instead of part of his annual cash bonus, which would have been enormous. He had already made considerable money that year, and his final distribution would already be large. He didn't need the money, so he thought he would just do a favor for someone he liked. The deal closed in record time, and Arthur Stone became a shareholder and outside counsel for Battle Mountain Pipeline.

The "Battle Mountain Deal," as it was called in the firm, began Arthur Stone's movement from being a wealthy attorney to the richest attorney in Texas.

It was also the beginning of the end of his marriage.

FUNNY NUMBERS ON STEROIDS
HOUSTON, TEXAS
DECEMBER 1998

SELLING ASSETS TO COVER LOSSES is a questionable strategy to begin with. However, things got out of hand when there were no buyers for the assets E-Titan wanted to sell at the prices needed to overcome losses. This is where Cheetah and its progeny ultimately came into play.

DD liked to think he was a great deal-maker. Because of his seclusion, however, he hardly ever closed a transaction personally. This is where Buddy had been invaluable. Buddy could close deals that DD conceived in a way that made them profitable. He had a nose for how to make things work and make money in the process. Lance lacked that particular quality. For some reason, Lance could not always see a bad deal until it was too late. His background in investment banking wasn't good training for managing a company and making deals. The oil business is not always a gentleman's business. It's rough and tumble. It takes a certain kind of strength and energy to survive. Lance was arrogant enough to think he could make any deal work. Unfortunately, he could not see through other people. He often saw only what he wanted to see. Worse, he lacked the personality to manage an organization.

In the mid-1990s, contrary to his promises, Lance decided to have E-Titan build a gigantic power facility in Honduras. (He was determined to show that he was brighter than Buddy Bennett.) Honduras has abundant natural resources, including water. In the mid-1990s, it met its basic power needs using hydroelectric power. E-Titan had done a little trading with Honduras, and Dawson Corporation had done a few oil and gas deals with them. One day, a trader at E-Titan came up with the idea of setting up a new power plant in Honduras that the Honduran government and E-Titan would jointly own, along with other international players having small interests. E-Titan traders could trade all the contracts for the energy the plants produced. (The fact that Hondurans couldn't pay for the energy and the government of Honduras was corrupt didn't seem to make a difference to Lance.) The entire deal was fraught with corruption, incompetence, and delays.

Ultimately, the plant could not produce energy at a price the citizens of Honduras could afford to pay. E-Titan had already marked-to-market its interest in the venture and booked twenty years of future profits into earnings. A crisis erupted when the Honduran government threatened to close the plant. The other partners were willing to write off their investment. However, E-Titan would have to write off twenty years of estimated and illusory profits. There were no buyers for the plant at any price which would not result in E-Titan booking a massive loss. Therefore, instead of writing off the investment, E-Titan created what is called a Special Purpose Entity. They named it Cheetah and bought its and its partners' interests in the project.

Lance knew for a long time that trouble was brewing with the Greater Honduran Power Company project. DD had been calling him for weeks, asking about the size of the write-off. Lance put him off by telling him, "We are working on it."

What he meant by that was that Brad Gilliland was working on it. Lance was not surprised when Brad asked for a meeting to discuss the matter. Unusually, Brad requested that one of his junior accountants, Benny Morelli, be included in the meeting. Brad began with a brief review of the situation.

"You guys know we have a problem with this power project in Honduras. The loss is probably in the range of $100,000,000. If such a loss is recognized, we will violate our loan covenants with the New York banks. Also, there would be no chance we would make the earnings we promised Wall Street. That will be bad for the stock."

Brad paused to let the implications sink in. Everyone's annual bonus and most of their personal net worth depended upon those earnings.

"I've been talking to Benny about this. He worked at Arthur Andersen and some New York finance companies for a time and is familiar with SPEs, which, for those unfamiliar, refers to Special Purpose Entities. I will turn things over to Benny."

Gilliland was not about to take responsibility for what he knew would happen next.

Benny Morelli looked at the group and then began his presentation.

"In my prior positions, I had the opportunity to work on creating several SPEs, including some within your industry. Special Purpose Entities (SPEs) are entities formed to develop, own, and operate a specific project while isolating financial risk and minimizing bankruptcy risk for their parent company, in this case, E-Titan. Under accounting rules (in this case, FAS 140), for SPE debt not to be consolidated with the sponsoring company, the SPE must have significant outside equity. For accounting purposes, three percent outside equity is usually sufficient."

He pulled out a chart showing the structure of an SPE called "Cheetah." It was so complicated that no one was likely to understand it.

"As you can see, E-Titan could create an SPE we call Cheetah. Cheetah would acquire the assets of the Greater Honduran Power

Company. To do this, we will need to raise about 100,000,000 dollars. The general partner of Cheetah will have to invest three million dollars in equity. That means we must borrow about $97,000,000 from our New York banks. To get that money, we will have to assure them a substantially above-market rate of return in some fashion. We can do this in several ways. Naturally, if the Greater Honduran Power Company can be sold for a profit in the future, we can use the proceeds to give the investors a return. If we can bring the company to profitability, we can generate the required return internally. Finally, if, at some future time, E-Titan reacquires the asset, our repurchase could generate the required return. The key is that we cannot explicitly guarantee the return, or the transaction will not take the current loss off E-Titan's balance sheet.

"In the transactions I have seen in the past, any guarantee-like commitments to protect the banks from a loss were oral or contained in side deals of some appropriate kind."

(Benny didn't mention that none of this was legal. No matter how you construct the transaction, no SPE can shield a loss if no risk is being shifted. They were never intended to be used to shield losses. They were created to allow assets that generated cash flow but required borrowings to be placed off the books of sponsoring corporations.)

At this point, Morelli had recommended fraud, but the point was lost in the conversation due to the complexity of the diagram and the impenetrable language of accounting. In the end, DD spoke to his friends in New York, and the transaction went forward. Lance could honestly say he did not know precisely what was said.

As it was finally structured, the transaction involved two E-Titan employees, Benny Morelli and Marjorie Melton, as co-general partners of Cheetah. Each borrowed $1,500,000, which they contributed as capital. This allowed Cheetah to borrow $97 million, secured by its assets and treasury shares of E-Titan worth $25 million. E-Titan booked a gain on the transaction and avoided a loss for the year on its financial statements. No one ever asked where Melton or Morelli got the money. No one asked about any side deals. No one questioned anything.

The problem was that no one in his right mind would invest in the "Greater Honduran Power Company." No bank would loan money for the assets being transferred without some kind of assurance. Solving this problem required a lot of creative accounting and what courts or bank regulators might consider banking fraud. Once again, no one asked the kind of questions that were needed. The issue came to light as Brad Gilliland investigated how to account for a management-created financial problem. It was too late when what had actually transpired came to light.

❄

The Honduran power company deal would have been bad enough. Unfortunately, Cheetah and its progeny became a kind of dumping ground for questionable E-Titan transactions. Worse, it became a dumping ground for questionable transactions involving the Dawson Corporation. Dobie Dawson figured out that he could sell underperforming assets at an appraised value to E-Titan, get the cash, and then E-Titan could put that same asset into a Cheetah after raising even more money, entering into more loan agreements and making more side deals with bankers. Eventually, there were Cheetah 1, Cheetah 2, Cheetah 3, Cheetah 4, a Cheetah for every year. Lance began using the Cheetahs to massage the numbers he needed for Wall Street. But that was all in the future for now. Now, everyone was making money. Big money. Money like there was no tomorrow.

5

BETRAYAL

ON THE ROCKS
HOUSTON, TEXAS
1997

GWYNN AND ARTHUR STONE COULD remember the exact moment their marriage began unraveling. Trying ten major lawsuits in a decade is a time-consuming and exhausting business. Becoming a large, successful, influential law firm's chairman is hard work. By 1997, Arthur was a legend; like all legends, he was extremely attractive to the members of the opposite sex inside and outside the law firm of Winchester & Wells. Gwynn's decade had not been glamorous, but it had been just as important. Gwynn and Arthur Stone had three children: Murray, the eldest boy and the most like his mother; a daughter named Margaret, or Maggie; and Stephen, the youngest and the most like his often-absent father. Gwynn's priority had become the children.

Gwynn maintained a small law practice, focusing on family law and representing battered women. She also served on the Houston Symphony board and in the leadership of several other charitable organizations. She was busy, socially active, and a much sought-after celebrity in Houston society. She also had no end of admirers. She was considered the most beautiful and desirable matron in the city. Gwynn was also increasingly irritated at Arthur, who seemed so focused on his career that he ignored his wife and children.

Even in a city as large as Houston, the social circle at the top is relatively small. The DuForts and Stones frequently saw each other at charity events. Lance was consistently charming, and Arthur was unfailingly tired and bored.

Closing the Battle Mountain Pipeline transaction allowed Lance to contact Arthur for a celebration. They met at the Houston Country Club, where Lance was a member. The Stones belonged to River Oaks, near their home on Avalon near downtown.

It so happened that earlier in the evening, Arthur and Gwynn quarreled. A certain coolness had descended on the couple when they arrived for dinner. Arthur was withdrawn and brooding. On the other hand, Lance was smiling, charming, and confident. Interestingly, Sheila, his wife, seemed depressed and withdrawn. The result was a wonderful evening for Lance and Gwynn and a not-so-wonderful evening for Arthur and Sheila.

When they arrived home, Arthur and Gwynn quarreled again. During the weeks and months that followed, the quarrels became more frequent. Then, one Saturday, while Arthur was out of town on business, Gwynn ran into Lance at Neiman Marcus. It was a fateful encounter.

It is not helpful to go into the details of the affair. Gwynn divorced Arthur, Lance divorced Sheila, and when the marriages were over, Gwynn married Lance. It was not long before Gwynn

Ever so slowly, Gwynn DuFort began to lose weight until she was skin and bones. A haunted look was often seen in her eyes. Before, she had been beautiful and voluptuous. She was still lovely, but the beauty had a harsh, lean, stark, terrible hardness. She was always as cheerful as she could force herself to be around the children, but at night, alone in her bed, she cried and stared at the ceiling for hours, thinking to herself, *How in the world did I get here?*

BOYS' NIGHT OUT
LOS CABOS, MEXICO
DECEMBER 2000

As with Heather Gilliland, Gwynn's breaking point came with the publication of the article in *Texas Quarterly*, a glossy magazine found in every doctor's office in Texas and read religiously by everyone who matters, at least all of the intellectual and social elite, who think they matter. *Texas Quarterly* is not a scandal rag by any means, but it was largely critical of big business, especially the big oil business, conservative politics, and traditional religion. It serves what is sometimes called The New Texas.

In late 1999, Lance decided to hold an "officers" retreat and "planning session" in Mexico at Los Cabos on the Mexican West Coast. The given reason was to plan for 2000 when it was anticipated that E-Titan would have its best year ever and celebrate the accomplishments of 1999. The primary emphasis was on raunchy, drunken celebration. The retreat involved a little business and a lot of tequila and whores. Someone present had a camera, and the pictures were bound to sell magazines in Texas. They sold the story and pictures to *Texas Quarterly*. The headline for the

Texas Quarterly article was "E-Titan Retreat Turns into Deadly Frat Party."

Before the retreat was over, the body of one of the women involved washed up on the coast near the resort. She appeared to have been violently assaulted before being dumped in the ocean. One of the pictures published by *Texas Quarterly* showed the woman on Lance DuFort's lap. The young lady was identified as Javiera Velasco Dominquez, the granddaughter of Javier Velasco, known as El Halcón, or The Hawk. The Hawk was a former high official in the Mexican government with friends in very high places all over the world. He counted former presidents among his confidants. El Halcón was aged and in ill health, having been injured in a bombing many years previously. The incident made him a bitter man. He had always been a dangerous man to cross in business or politics. Now, he made it his crusade to see that justice was done.

By the time the body washed ashore in Mexico, Lance DuFort and the other E-Titan executives were safely back in Texas. Nevertheless, statements under oath given by Lance, Gilliland, and Marjorie Melton, the sole female on the weekend, all stating that Javiera left the party alone. The three testified that they had retired to Lance's suite for drinks and some business conversation before leaving for their rooms. One of the things Gilliland's deposition might have revealed was that that was not exactly true. Gilliland and Melton had left Lance's room for his, where she spent the night.

Marjorie Melton was known within E-Titan as "M&M" because she resembled Marilyn Monroe, the movie star, and her status as the executive suite's chief eye candy. M&M began her career at the company as a former Las Vegas showgirl, whom DD wanted to employ as a personal assistant. At the creation of E-Titan, she moved to Lance's office as a personal assistant, then to Brad Gilliland's office, where she became an Executive Vice President for Shareholder Relations and Hospitality. Finally, she became one of the executives running the Cheetah partnerships. No one in the company knew precisely what M&M did at any point in time, but she had a vast expense account and frequently traveled with DD, Lance, and Gilliland.

Heather Gilliland was particularly interested in the article because the same picture showing Javiera on Lance DuFort's lap showed M&M on Brad Gilliland's lap with his hands in an immodest position relative to her skirt. Heather put two and two together and recognized that she had been a fool. Nothing Brad Gilliland could say, and no story he could concoct, changed her opinion about what was happening.

Gwynn DuFort was also less than convinced by Lance's insistence that nothing had happened.

What began as an executive retreat rapidly turned into an international incident. The original plan was to take all E-Titan senior staff to Los Cabos for five days to consider the future. It turned out that "Thinking about the future" really involved five days of partying. Each morning, there was a short meeting around 9 o'clock. By 10 o'clock, the day's activity had begun. The day's activity might be parasailing, deep-sea fishing, or riding motorcycles in the desert. It always involved something fun and a good bit of drinking. After lunch, there would be another short meeting. Then there was personal time from about four until six. At six, the group had dinner and then revelry.

Brad Gilliland was not sure it was a good idea, but Lance sold him on it.

"Look, it's going to be great. We're going to go and have a lot of fun. Sure, we're going to have to talk about a little business. We will talk about long-range plans, company, values, and other things we won't pay much attention to when we return. But people will have fun and return even more committed to the company than before. Besides, I need to get away from here. Gwynn and I are going through a troubled patch. I just want to get away."

Gilliland had his reasons for thinking a trip to Los Cabos would be fun. He and Marjorie Melton were deep into an affair. His home life was, if anything, worse than Lance's. Heather was frequently hurt and angry. He could not be sure, but he thought that she guessed he was having an affair. But she could not know with whom. Of that, Brad was confident.

In the end, the top twenty officers of E-Titan made the trip to Los Cabos, San Lucas, for the Retreat and Long-Range Planning Conference. The people selected to go met two criteria: They were essential for the future of E-Titan and were likely to do whatever Lance wanted. At the time, the trip seemed to be everything they could've wished for. It wasn't until the very end that things went wrong. But when things did go bad in the end, they went very bad indeed.

The final day started just like every other day. It was a lovely, warm day on the Baja Peninsula of Mexico. The sand was white. The breakfast was an excellent buffet. The conversation was full of laughter. Everyone seemed to be having a good time. Lance had picked up a local girl the night before, and she joined them at the table. She was with them most of the day. Her name was Javiera, and no one thought to ask about her last name or who her family might be. That was a mistake.

Everyone went out and rode mountain bikes together. Marjorie, who didn't like physical exercise of any kind, insisted on staying at the hotel. Brad claimed that he needed to look at some financial statements that would be due when they returned. Everyone else went out to ride. It was a long, exhausting, and sometimes dangerous day. At least one executive fell and had to be carried to the hospital. It was a sign of things to come.

When they returned, there was just enough time for a shower and dinner. Javiera joined them for dinner. After dinner, they went to the bar and partied until around 10 o'clock. Around 10 o'clock, Brad Gilliland and Marjorie announced they were tired and decided to go to their rooms. Taking Javiera by the hand, Lance asked her to have another drink with him in his room. Javiera refused, and Lance and she argued briefly. Javiera walked out of the bar. The new threesome of Brad, Lance, and M&M left for Lance's room. When all hell broke loose the following day, everyone testified that they didn't know what happened after Lance left. Brad, Lance, and M&M testified Javiera was never with them.

The following day, the authorities arrived to interview the group about a missing girl. Everyone recounted more or less the same story, ending with Javiera's leaving alone. The threesome of Lance, Brad, and M&M testified that they went up to Lance's room, had a drink, and then broke up for the night. The authorities did not require that they stay in Los Cabos, and that afternoon, the group hurriedly flew back to Houston in the same private jets that had brought them.

Unfortunately, neither the Mexican authorities nor El Halcón ultimately believed the story told by the E-Titan executives. In particular, El Halcón, who was close enough to authorities in the United States and Mexico, did not believe the story. Javiera was his namesake and favorite grandchild. He was determined to bring someone to justice for her death—and high on the list of potential "someones" was one Lance DuFort.

THE MORNING AFTER
HOUSTON, TEXAS
JANUARY 2001

WHAT AM I GOING TO *do? What am I going to do? What in the world am I going to do?*

Gwynn Murray DuFort had always thought of herself as a capable person. In her legal practice, she found it easy to make decisions. As an associate at Winchester & Wells, she could always think clearly about the future, even when millions of dollars were at stake. But now, there didn't seem to be any future at all. Worst of all, her old decisiveness seemed to have disappeared. She didn't know what to do. And so, she repeatedly asked herself, *What should I do? What should I do? What am I going to do?*

The night before, Lance came home very late—in fact, it was early in the morning. He smelled of alcohol and perfume, which she could smell on his clothes the following day. They had quarreled violently after the *Texas Quarterly* article was published. Lance, with what he thought was a look of innocence and what she thought was the look of an arrogant adulterer who believed his wife was a fool, denied that anything was going on.

"Javiera was a pretty girl. She attached herself to our group. When that picture was taken, she sat on my lap. After the picture was over, she got out of my lap."

Gwynn didn't tell Lance that others on the trip had a different memory of the events. She was friends with several angry wives. Lance was prone to forget that Gwynn was an experienced divorce lawyer. She had heard a lot of stories. Many of them were fairytales told by a guilty spouse. She remembered her father telling her, "Don't believe half of what you see and nothing of what you hear." It was good advice she never forgot. Lance might wish that she would forget, but she would not.

Another one of her mother's sayings, often repeated, was a piece of simple advice: "It doesn't take very long to get into trouble. It takes a long time to get out of trouble. The best course of action is to stay out of trouble." Like many children, Gwynn forgot to pay attention to that advice when she met Lance. She wasn't inclined to ignore the advice again. It hadn't taken long for her to get in trouble, and it wasn't going to be quick to find a solution to the problem.

Initially, she tried the advice of friends from a local Bible study she sometimes attended. Their strategy was to forgive, forget, and rebuild the relationship. There was only one trouble with this advice: it takes two to repair a relationship. Lance wasn't even trying.

As hard as it is to believe, Gwynn initially thought something was wrong with her that caused her not to be the wife Lance needed. She tried changing. Unfortunately, no change made any difference in Lance's philandering. When she reached the end of that line of thinking, she realized that she had become like her mother. Her mother had initially blamed herself for her father's affair with a Houston Oilers cheerleader. She wasn't beautiful enough. She wasn't young enough. She wasn't something enough. Her mother made many excuses for her father's behavior before she finally realized that there was no excuse. What her father was doing was wrong.

It helps to see the truth. Eventually, Gwynn recognized the truth: Lance's actions were wrong. *Nothing I do can make them right, and nothing I have done can justify them. So why do I think there must be something wrong with me?*

This was the beginning point for the next stage of Gwynn's healing. With the realization that nothing she had done could excuse Lance's behavior came another realization: No excuse she could give could justify her behavior. It was at that moment that Gwynn confronted another stark truth about herself. She had secretly blamed herself for her father's infidelities at the end of her parents' marriage. Somewhere deep in her wounded heart, she felt that what was happening to her now was some kind of justifiable punishment for her past.

Around that time, she attended a little ladies' Bible study in her neighborhood. It happened in a strange way. She didn't intend to go. She had forgotten the Bible study was meeting. She did not regularly attend. She was too busy with her law practice, children, and many social activities. Out of nowhere, one of her neighbors called and asked her if she would like to come. She said, "Yes."

The text for the day happened to come from the New Testament. It was from a familiar passage in Second Corinthians: "If anyone is in Christ, they are a new creation! The old has gone! The new has come!" Gwynn did not feel very new. She felt lost and tired. She felt used up. So, she asked the group a question.

"I'm not sure I feel like a new person. I feel like past mistakes continue to haunt me. Worst of all, they haunt my children. I don't know what to do."

This led to a long discussion about confession, forgiveness, and grace. It so happened that the lady who sponsored the Bible study had been divorced in the past. She wasn't the least judgmental. She was filled with a kind of luminescent love for Gwynn. It streamed out of her eyes, and it was evident in the compassion she showed. After everyone else left, they had a chat.

"The whole point of the New Testament is that we are not perfect people. We make mistakes. Some of our mistakes are deliberate. Some are accidental. Sometimes, we violate God's will knowing precisely what we are doing. Sometimes, we act out of ignorance. Christ was revealed to us to show us that we can live free of our past mistakes no matter why they occur. We can't always escape the consequences. We rarely escape the immediate consequences. But we can decide to accept the love of God in the form of his merciful forgiveness of our past. When we do that, we are new people. Once again, that doesn't mean we don't have the same problems we had yesterday. We do.

"When my first husband divorced me, I had had an affair. It was the senseless act of a young, self-centered, and foolish woman. My parents had warned me I was too young to get married. I paid no attention. My friends warned me that the man I was marrying was not a good match. I ignored them. I might have blamed my first husband if I wanted to, and I did for a while, but the genuine fault was mine. I could have found another way out of the situation without doing something that left me feeling used. I didn't.

"One day, I went to a Bible study just like this one. It was out in the Bellaire area where I was living at the time. It so happens that the verses we were studying were similar to those we studied today, and I had the same questions you have. It was a story from the gospel of John about a woman who had been caught in adultery. The people wanted to stone her as was recommended by the laws of their day. The teacher reminded us that the woman was caught in adultery. That means the man was seen as well.

The people wanted to stone the woman, but the man was not mentioned. In the end, Jesus picks up the stone and says to the crowd, 'If any of you are without sin, let that person cast the first stone.' Everyone dropped their stone and left. Then, he looked down at the woman and said, 'Go home and don't sin anymore.'

"I went home from that Bible study and got down on my knees. I asked for forgiveness. To be quite frank, I didn't feel very forgiven in the beginning. I had to live into my forgiveness. Today, I'm happily married. I have a great family. I have good friends. I have a great life. It didn't happen overnight, but it did happen."

Gwynn didn't go home that night, get down on her knees, and pray. But she did think—a lot.

6

BUSY DAYS

AT THE FIRM

HOUSTON, TEXAS

FEBRUARY 15, 2001

THE FIRM WAS OFFICIALLY CLOSED because of the icy, cold weather. Nevertheless, when Arthur arrived, most of his team, including his assistant, were there. Everyone knew it was going to be a busy day. Shutting himself up in his office, he made a list of things to do. First on his to-do list was calling his brother. As he expected, his brother's secretary answered the phone.

"Annie, this is Art. Can I come by and see Johnny later today? I want to talk with him about some personal matters. I'd be able to be there by about 6:00."

"John has someone with him, but I will ask him as soon as he gets free. Either he will call you back later today, or I will."

"That will be fine. If I am in a conference, you can leave a message with my assistant."

As Arthur hung up, Roger Romny, the firm's managing partner, walked in the door to see him. It was a rare day when Roger and Arthur did not spend time together. Roger, a corporate lawyer, had been Arthur's supervisor when Arthur was an associate. Roger had been seriously injured in a bombing that killed a partner in Winchester & Wells—Stephen Winchester, Ahn Winchester's husband. Roger walked with a noticeable limp and had nerve damage to some of his facial muscles, which gave him an odd look. His mind was not affected by the incident.

Before the tragedy, Roger and Art had not been close. Roger did not like Arthur and intended to oppose Arthur's becoming a partner in the firm. However, for some months after the incident, Arthur had been assigned to cover for Roger. Romny was much changed when he returned to the firm, and they became friends. As Arthur became more prominent and the firm's chairman, he made it plain that he did not wish to be the managing partner when Patrick Armbruster retired. When Armbruster retired, Roger became managing partner—a job that suited his personality and abilities. They were a perfect team. Roger was an unfailing realist in contrast to Arthur's occasional misplaced idealism.

"Do you have a minute or two?"

"Always when it's you, Roger."

"First, I'd like to discuss <u>Battle Mountain Pipeline Company vs. E-Titan Energy, Inc</u>. You already know about Brad Gilliland. His deposition was important to the case. My guess is it will be some time before his replacement is chosen. Lance will want to keep things as opaque as possible as long as possible. Even when a new chief financial officer is selected, you can be sure that their deposition will only be a recital of 'I wasn't around then and have no personal knowledge.' We will have to get evidence of the facts that we expect some other way."

Arthur agreed. Lance was slippery as an eel. He would use the death to delay the litigation if at all possible. However, Arthur and his clients did not have time to waste. Arthur believed that E-Titan and Lance DuFort were hiding massive losses from trading operations. Increasing numbers of short sellers were betting against E-Titan's stock. Arthur wanted a settlement or a judgment before E-Titan's house of cards fell. He did not want to be dragged into a bankruptcy proceeding.

"Battle Mountain vs. E-Titan" or "The Case" was the most interesting case in which Winchester & Wells and Arthur Stone were currently involved. When Buddy Bennett purchased Battle Mountain Pipeline Company, he did so near the end of a fiscal year. The purchase price was somewhere in the neighborhood of $100,000,000. Buddy did not set the price. Lance DuFort and Dobie Dawson set the price. Buddy simply agreed to the purchase and was chosen because he knew the asset, would have to do little due diligence, and could close before year-end. Perhaps, just as importantly, Lance wanted to get rid of Buddy, and Buddy wanted to get away from Lance and E-Titan.

Buddy never then or later suggested that he had been given a "sweetheart deal." He was way too street-smart for that. However, soon after his acquisition, Buddy took Battle Mountain public to raise cash to purchase other pipelines. Battle Mountain was valued at substantially more than Buddy paid for it in that offering. DD and Lance had deliberately or accidentally sold Battle Mountain for less than it was worth. Buddy Bennett was now one of the wealthiest people in Texas, and the foolishness of Lance DuFort and Dobie Dawson had made his fortune for him. (Coincidentally, Arthur Stone's interest in Battle Mountain more than doubled in value. He was now a very wealthy man.)

Eventually, E-Titan shareholders (or lawyers who saw an opportunity to make some money) sued E-Titan, alleging a breach of fiduciary duty by E-Titan in the sale. In his typical way, Lance began to issue press releases claiming Buddy had cheated E-Titan and announcing E-Titan was ready to sue Battle Mountain if necessary.

The implications were not lost on the management of Battle Mountain. Buddy feared he would become embroiled in an expensive litigation in Houston. Battle Mountain was headquartered in San Antonio, where Buddy preferred to live. After consultation with Arthur, Battle Mountain filed a lawsuit in San Antonio alleging that E-Titan, through its president, Lance DuFort, had published injurious falsehoods and slandered the title of Battle Mountain to its original pipeline properties. Slander of title is a common law tort involving a false statement published by a third party or entity that disparages a person or entity's title to the property and causes financial harm or loss to the offended party.

The elements of the lawsuit were pretty straightforward. First, Battle Mountain had to prove that E-Titan, through its officers and directors, made false, disparaging statements about Battle Mountain, which statements were published to third parties (in this case, the *Wall Street Journal* and other media). The second element was that E-Titan made these public statements with malice and reckless disregard for the truth.

This is where Gilliland's testimony was crucial. He was in a position to testify that Lance knew all along that Battle Mountain and Buddy were guiltless because the plan was Lance's, not Buddy's. It was also pretty straightforward that E-Titan should have known or recognized a third party might rely on such a statement and cause financial harm to the plaintiff because the stock price of Battle Mountain had fallen to lows never seen before the press releases and interviews with the financial media.

Buddy wanted the case tried in Bexar County (San Antonio) because he felt the courts would be more favorable to

Battle Mountain there. Arthur agreed both because of Buddy's wishes and because he and Gwynn had a verbal understanding that, for the good of the family, he would avoid being involved in litigation against Lance. Therefore, while Winchester & Wells was on the pleadings, a local San Antonio firm, Morales & Nichols, was hired as lead trial counsel. Eddie Morales was an experienced trial lawyer and long-time friend of Arthur. They worked together for the Texas attorney general years before. Morales & Nichols was a boutique litigation firm known throughout Texas. It did not have the size and employees to manage the discovery in such a large case. Therefore, Winchester & Wells was hired as co-counsel. Thomas Mallory was designated as Winchester & Wells' chief attorney assigned to the case. Behind it all was the strategic genius of Arthur Stone.

Arthur Stone's second call was to Eddie Morales, who had already called him. After pleasantries, they got down to business. Eddie began.

"This death of Brad Gilliland leaves us with a hole in our case. To prove our claim against E-Titan and Lance, we must prove that Lance knowingly made statements to the press that he knew were false when he made them. Brad Gilliland attended all the meetings with Lance and DD when Battle Mountain was sold. He knew it was Lance's idea, and DD and Lance set the price. Gilliland knew firsthand that the claim that Buddy defrauded them was false. Lance and DD have different memories. With Gilliland dead, we need additional proof regarding this element of the case."

Arthur interrupted. "Yes, I have been reading our memorandum about this aspect of the case. Of course, we have Buddy's testimony concerning the meetings. But the jury might not believe he was speaking the truth. Lance and DD will deny everything, as they did in their depositions. We need concrete and undeniable evidence that Lance lied to the business journal in his statements to their journalists."

The conversation went on for some time about details of Texas law, precedents, and the likely rulings of the judge during the trial. Then, the conversation turned to other matters. Morales was concerned.

"Arthur, we need to be careful. There is enough money here that it is not beyond imagination that someone knew about Gilliland's likely testimony. If they would kill Brad Gilliland, they might kill someone else."

Arthur was quick to reply.

"Yeh, I know. I will have my uncle's private investigation company work on this. Give me a few days. Since the standard of proof is high, we have not joined the business journal as a defendant in the case. We don't think we can prove their malice. Nevertheless, on your end, I think you should rattle their cage just to see what happens. On my end, I will see what we can turn up here."

With that, Arthur said goodbye and made his third call—this time to his Uncle Ben.

"Uncle Ben. This is Arthur. Do you have a moment to speak to me?"

"Always. Is this about our case?"

"Partially. The strictly business part of this is pretty straightforward. We were going to take the deposition of Brad Gilliland today. As you know, he was shot and died last night. Gilliland was an essential witness for Battle Mountain because he did not want to lie, and we were certain his testimony would establish that Lance knew his statements relating to Buddy's activities in the Battle Mountain acquisition were false. Without that testimony, we are 'up a creek without a paddle' on that part of the case. I want to know more about the death."

Ben had a quick reply.

"Art, here is what I know. I spoke earlier to the lead investigator on the case. This was not a suicide. The authorities believe Gilliland was shot with a high-powered sniper rifle during a snowstorm at some distance—across a small lake. It was almost certainly a professional job. Thus far, the police have not ruled out anyone as a suspect as to who might have ordered the hit."

This was news but not surprising in the least. Arthur had a request to make.

"Can you see the widow to see if she heard anything that might be entered into evidence? Because it would be an admission against interest, it might be admitted into evidence at trial because Gilliland is dead. I would also like to know if we can get our hands on any papers he had at the house. He was to be deposed today, and I would bet good money he was getting ready last night.

"Also, I have a personal favor to ask. Could you contact our friend in San Miguel de Allende and ask him to conduct another investigation for us? It is not unrelated to the case exactly, but I want to pay for it personally."

"What kind of investigation?"

You remember that *Texas Quarterly* article about E-Titan and its executive retreat involving misbehavior and the death of the young girl?"

"Sure."

"I have been thinking about that cover picture in Los Cabos. You know, the one with Lance, holding the girl that turned up dead on his lap, and in the background, Marjorie Melton, an executive with E-Titan, on Brad Gilliland's lap. Several things about that picture interest me. First, the girl involved was the granddaughter of someone we both know is a very bad person. If Lance has got himself tied up in some way with El Halcón, he is in big trouble.

"In addition, Marjorie Melton, an executive at E-Titan, was on Brad Gilliland's lap. She might have information she received from Brad Gilliland. If they were having an affair, there may have been pillow talk. I would like to know if the people in Los Cabos can give us any information. Eventually, I want to take her deposition, but I'd like to know what she might know before I do. We will review the records here to see if she might help our case.

"I don't want to do this through ordinary channels. This situation involves Gwynn, her marriage, and our children. Given the character of Javier Velasco, international drug smuggling could be involved. If E-Titan is involved in something like that, the lawsuit we are currently engaged in is the tip of a massive and dangerous iceberg. I wouldn't imagine Lance would want our lawsuit to last much longer if he thinks we know something.

"I'd like our friend, Juan Bardero, to visit Los Cabos. While he's there, I would like him to stay at the very same place where the E-Titan people stayed. I'd like him to interview as many people as possible connected with the crime. He might also talk to the local police. I'd like a clearer picture of what happened on that trip. I'm not interested in Lance's shenanigans. I'm interested in what happened, why Gilliland died, Gwynn and the children, and our case.

"Be sure to handle this delicately. We do not want to put Bardero at risk. He may need to take an associate to contact the local police and get their information."

Ben was quick to agree.

"Gotcha. By the way, are you going to the Hill Country soon? I might tag along to see my brother!"

"I will talk to my brother tonight about just such a trip. If we go, we will surely invite you to come along."

With that, they signed off.

E-TITAN OFFICES
GALLERIA AREA, HOUSTON, TEXAS
FEBRUARY 15, 2001

LANCE WAS A PROPONENT OF what he liked to call Hard/ Soft—Hands On/Hands Off Management. In practice, this meant bullying people he could bully, staying as far away as possible from details of any kind and most difficult decisions, and remaining intentionally ignorant of circumstances of dubious legality. Despite the warm comments by business journals, with employees fighting tooth and nail for bonuses and positions in the company, Lance created an emotionally deadly and immoral culture at E-Titan. He did not care for anyone but himself—and no one else did either.

During recent weeks, as the litigation with Battle Mountain reached a critical stage, and his traders were driving up gas and electric prices for Texas consumers through a variety of strategies prudently referred to as "Strangulation" and "Pay or Freeze," Lance had been "Hard" insisting that the cold weather was a once in a lifetime opportunity for huge profits and "Hands Off," insisting that Brad Gilliland take care of the Battle Mountain litigation and the shareholder derivative suit issues. He had been Hands-Off by staying as far away as possible from the trades and avoiding managing the company's most crucial litigation. He was Hands-

On by insisting that people do dubious things. At the company, most people referred to Lance's management style as "If anything goes wrong, you're the fall guy."

Today, however, the chief executive officer of E-Titan had to be just that. Brad Gilliland was dead, and there was no dodging the problem. His first call was with DD, who was safely ensconced in a hotel in Acapulco, far away from the cold weather and difficulties of E-Titan, which he was rapidly wishing he had never agreed to form. Lance could tell DD was upset.

"I just heard that Brad Gilliland killed himself. Is that true?"

"No. It is somewhat more complicated than suicide. He was shot at long range during an ice storm by a sniper. I don't know much, but one of our lawyers talked to a friend in the police. The investigators suspect a hit."

"I see."

DD wanted Lance to understand the implications if he had not already figured them out.

"It will not be long before they learn that Brad was to testify today in a deposition. You can bet that opposing counsel in the Battle Mountain litigation will plant the seed that someone with a connection with E-Titan hired the killer."

Lance had already considered the possibilities.

"There are many other possibilities. He might have a gambling problem, or he might have gotten on the wrong side of a jealous husband. I don't know. There have to be other possibilities."

"This deposition—were you worried?"

"Frankly, yes. Brad oversaw the accounting for the Battle Mountain sale, how that sale was connected to other E-Titan transactions, and the financial reporting for the year in question. He was present during the negotiations when we sold Battle

Mountain to Buddy. He knew most of the facts. Since recent events, I've had my fears that Gilliland wasn't as loyal to us as he once was. I know, for example, that his attorney has met privately with the attorneys for Battle Mountain. I have no idea what they talked about. However, I'm concerned. As you know, some aspects of the transaction might be embarrassing.

"More problematic is the potential that he would be asked about other similar transactions. Of course, I was never directly involved in creating the Special Purpose Entities or their accounting. Remember that I am a lawyer and investment banker by trade. I left the accounting to Brad. Nevertheless, any discovery could complicate the shareholder lawsuits and our discussions with the SEC.

"Gilliland, in his heart, was a Boy Scout. He introduced us to the people who designed the Cheetah transactions, but he was not deeply involved most of the time. He knew nothing about any side deals. Nevertheless, he was an accountant. He could have testified about matters that might hurt us."

DD could see that the Battle Mountain situation was dangerous.

"Look, Lance, I don't want to tell you how to manage your company. However, we are in a difficult spot. Rumor has it that the SEC is considering ordering us to restate our financial statements. If E-Titan is forced to restate prior years, I'm not sure the New York banks will stay with us. They might call the loans. If that happens, E-Titan might not survive, and Dawson Corporation will have a big financial problem. I don't want to become involved in that kind of thing. You need to do something."

Lance was already well aware that he needed to do something.

"I'm not sure what I can do right now. Our attorneys believe that Battle Mountain will have difficulty proving its case. At this point, we are in a pretty good position. However, as long as this case is in the news and Arthur Stone is on the other side, the *Wall Street Journal* and the other financial press will make this a story. Excusing the pun, as far as the press is concerned, this is a Battle of Titans."

DD knew this.

"That's part of what bothers me. I notice that the short sellers are piling up against E-Titan. It's gone beyond just a few specialty shops. Some of the New York investment banking firms have been making negative trades. More troubling, some London, Paris, and Berlin-based traders are betting against the stock. If this continues through this year, we will have trouble with the banks.

"You know I have friends in the intelligence agencies. Dawson Corporation has done a lot of favors for the intelligence community by allowing them to use some of our assets overseas as cover. We've always been friends. I called one of my friends the other day. He's particularly concerned that one of the short sellers is known to be extremely well-connected politically. He's not just connected with our government but with governments worldwide. He's also known to have shorted currencies, commodities, and stocks. When this guy gets involved, he's capable of causing the result he wants. We don't want this to go on much longer. We need some good news."

DD had said his piece. Lance was quick to understand.

"If it's who I think it might be, he is real trouble. When I was on Wall Street, he was known to be a vulture. I agree we need to do something. It's early in the year. We have ten months to do some transactions that will make our financial statements look strong by year-end. Right now, this cold weather is driving up the prices of natural gas and electricity. Our traders are riding the wave. We'll come out of this winter in pretty good shape."

DD was one step ahead.

"I agree. However, it would be best if you were careful. I don't know what your traders are doing, but if it becomes public that you were driving up the price of gas and electricity during a cold wave, you'll get a lot of bad press. Old people and poor people die in this kind of situation. The press love those kinds of stories. Don't get too close to the traders."

"I won't."

DD had one more sensitive piece of business to talk about.

"I'm worried about one more thing. This girl who died in Mexico. Her grandfather is a pretty wealthy and powerful man. He has a lot of friends. Some of those friends have very powerful connections. His connections run all the way to the White House. I'm told that he believes you were involved somehow in the death of his granddaughter. We don't want this guy on our tail.

"For your information, Javier Velasco is friendly with the very person who's been shorting the E-Titan stock. Their business relationships go back a long way. It would be best if you were careful. We all need to be careful. I am powerful but not as powerful as some of the people involved."

This was news to Lance.

"I will be careful. As Brad, Marjoric, and I have all testified, I had nothing to do with the girl's death."

DD put one more shot across Lance's bow before hanging up.

"For your sake, I certainly hope not."

DETECTIVE LIEUTENANT RICO DIAZ HAD been a cop and detective since returning from Vietnam. He had investigated a lot of cases in his day. This morning, he was studying the file on Brad Gilliland's death. The police had not made a lot of progress in solving the case. It was evident that the crime was a professional hit. But why and ordered by whom? As he was pondering his next move in the investigation, there was a knock on his door, and another detective came into the room.

"We have a coroner's initial report."

"Don't tell me; he died of a gunshot wound fired from a sniper rifle."

"Yes, that is what he died from. But there is more."

"More?"

"Yes, more."

"Gilliland had a case of sepsis when he died. Further examination showed poisoning consistent with the use of human feces."

Diaz made a face.

"I'm not sure what that adds. He died of a gunshot wound."

"There is more. We checked the cup of hot chocolate we found spilled in the study. The residue showed signs of contamination by human feces.

Diaz leaned back in his swivel chair.

"Well, Well, Well. I think we had best interview the grieving widow again. In addition, I want her bank records and any other information that might tell us if she hired the assassin."

"Do you want to interview her today?"

"Not right now. Let's do our homework first. We want to know if there are any suspicious checks from any of the Gilliland accounts and if there is anything incriminating in the house—like dried feces. Get a warrant, but tell Mrs. Gilliland that this is just a routine search to see if we have missed any evidence."

After the detective left to get started, Diaz took out a legal pad and began doodling. *We may have just solved the case. She was having trouble killing her husband with poison, and so she hired a hitman. Case solved.*

Not long after that, there was another knock on the door. It was his chief assistant.

"Hey, boss, do you have a moment for an update on the Gilliland killing?"

"Only if you have some light to shed on it."

"I do."

"Come right on in."

A young police officer assigned to the case stepped into the room.

"Here is what we know. I checked to see if a .300 BLK, with a Swiss-made B&T USA .300 SPR Pro, was purchased recently. I got an interesting reply from an all-night pawn shop. A man entered an all-night pawn shop near midnight and pawned such a weapon. The owner was able to give a pretty good description. He said the man was Eastern European, tall, and well-dressed. He wore an expensive Italian suit and spoke good English with an accent.

"Interestingly, there was almost no haggling. The man took the first offer, though it was low. He said that he was getting a divorce and needed money. This particular pawn shop is near Intercontinental Airport."

"Did you get the gun?"

"Yes. A test of the rifle and the spent round recovered from the scene of the crime matched. The shop clerk's description of the man who pawned the rifle and a check of the gate personnel at the airport showed that a person matching that description boarded a flight to Atlanta shortly after the gun was pawned. Unfortunately, the identification presented by the person turned out to be forged. Additionally, he apparently changed both his passport and looks before leaving Atlanta for unknown points. We can't trace him further. But I will bet he is now spending his money somewhere in Eastern Europe."

Rico pondered this information.

"Do you see Heather Gilliland as capable of hiring such a person?"

"Actually, no. This is not a case of 'I have a buddy who knows someone who can handle your problem.' This person was a highly-trained, high-priced professional. If we are correct, he lives in Eastern Europe. Such people don't come cheap and are known only to a restricted number of people, usually criminal syndicates and intelligence agencies. Lance DuFort might be able to hire such a person, but one doubts that Heather Gilliland would even know where to start.

"More importantly, this was not a $500 job out of the barrios. This guy cost thousands of dollars. We checked Heather Gilliland's accounts as we know them, and there is no check of five figures, much less such a check to a foreign account or even to a United States account that is not shopping or household expenses."

Diaz considered the news.

There is something deeper going on here.

"I understand that Ben Stone has been nosing around."

"Yeh."

"I would like to visit with him. Can you get him in for a talk? He might know something."

"Sure. I talked to him earlier today. Ben is reliable. He is working for Winchester & Wells, which means silk stocking stuff. When Gilliland was killed, that firm was going to depose him for a big case the next day. I don't think they are happy about the death. Ben believes the firm was confident that Gilliland's testimony would help their case. If they can prove that E-Titan Energy had anything to do with Brad Gilliland's death, it would probably win the case for them. I would bet that's the angle Stone is investigating."

"See if he can come by this afternoon."

At precisely 3:00 that afternoon, Ben Stone entered Diaz's office. Stone was a short, stocky, good-looking man of medium build. He did not look like a man in his early 80s. Like his brother and nephew, he had been an athlete in high school and attended college on the G.I Bill after the Second World War. As always, he was dressed impeccably, a habit he had formed in the FBI and continued in his much more prosperous retirement. His son now ran the detective agency. His wife had died a few years before. After she died, Ben just kept on working. He had good genes. He looked and acted about 70.

Rico looked up, smiling.

"Ben, it is good to see you. How are the children and grandchildren?"

The small talk continued for a time as the two caught up. Finally, Rico got to the point.

"Ben, we know you are snooping around looking into the Gilliland murder. What can you tell me?"

"Not a lot. You probably know all that we know and more. My client finds it suspicious that Gilliland was killed in what must have been a pretty expensive hit the night before he was to be deposed."

"We find that unusual as well. We are looking at several possibilities but are focused on the wife for now. Do you know anything?"

"I am going to visit with her sooner or later. However, frankly, I would be amazed if she were the killer."

Rico did not want to give away his theory of the case.

"We are going to interview her in a few days. We would prefer you wait for us to interview her before you go by. We will let you know if we find anything important involving your client. You know about the *Texas Quarterly* article. She had reason to be jealous."

Ben saw where the conversation was headed.

"Gilliland was a wealthy guy. Divorce is a lot cheaper and a lot less risky than murder. They had nothing when they married, and Texas is a community property state. She would have received half of everything Gilliland had. Why murder someone when there are other ways to get even? I have seen murders in this kind of situation, but I have seen a whole bunch more divorces."

Rico was inclined to agree.

"You will let us know if you discover anything?"

"You know I will if I can without compromising a client."

Ben then asked his questions.

"What exactly do you know about the actual murder?"

"Gilliland was killed by a single shot through the head fired by a .300 BLK outfitted with a Swiss-made B&T USA .300SPR.

The gun was later pawned near Houston Intercontinental Airport, and a man fitting a description given by the person working at the pawnshop boarded a plane to Atlanta. We think he was Eastern European. He must have changed identities in Atlanta. But we don't know where he went. We cannot track him."

"Too bad."

"We also have no financial information indicating that Mrs. Gilliland hired a paid assassin. We do have an indication that she was planning to harm her husband using poison."

"Poison is a woman's weapon. Swiss-made sniper rifles usually are not. Have you found any evidence that would implicate E-Titan or any of its officers?"

"No. However, we are looking into the possibility."

With that, the conversation returned to children and grandchildren before Stone left.

7

Waking Up Alone

QUEEN OF LONELINESS
HOUSTON, TEXAS
JUNE 2001

GWYNN DUFORT WOKE UP ALONE with a small child crying in the next room. She awoke from the fog of a forgotten dream into the exhaustion of her current situation. It took a few moments for her to realize she was alone and glad to be alone. She often woke up with Lance beside her, sometimes with the scent of another woman on his pillow. She had grown accustomed to the experience. For the 10,000[th] time, she asked herself the question.

How in the world did I get here?

In the beginning, Lance DuFort had been a knight in shining armor, loving and rescuing a deserted and depressed wife from the endless boredom of raising children and trying to keep up a career with a spouse who was often absent and, if present, constantly preoccupied. It was not until after the affair, after leaving Arthur, and after marriage to Lance because she was carrying his child that Gwynn realized the awful truth: Lance DuFort was a confirmed narcissist. He might even be a sociopath. She realized that Lance had married her just to take her away from Arthur and conquer Houston society's most beautiful and desirable woman. Once he had accomplished his goal, he lost interest in the woman he had conquered. Now, she regularly caught the scent of other women on his clothing. She saw the lipstick on his shirt. She sensed their emotional distance. He always had an easy excuse if she pointed out the lipstick and perfume.

"Don't be paranoid. It was a hug after a meeting at the office. You know how some women are huggy."

No, she did not know. *I was a fool,* she thought.

After looking in on her youngest child comforting her, and carrying her back to the bedroom, she picked up the phone and dialed a number she knew well.

"Ahn?"

"Yes."

Ahn recognized the voice.

"It's Gwynn. I need to talk to you. Can you meet this afternoon? I have a pre-trial appearance this morning related to a divorce I am handling, but I can be free by 2:00 this afternoon. Can I just come by and talk?"

"Yes. Please come by at 2:00. I have a meeting in the evening but am free all afternoon."

"Our little talk won't last beyond about 3:30 or so."

"I will be here. You can have all the time you need."

Gwynn went downstairs. Her meeting at school was about Murray, her now 14-year-old son by Arthur, a meeting with a local charity, a need to go by her office, and finally, a dinner engagement with Lance, who was flying in from out of town to go to a gala. Now, part of her afternoon would be spent talking with Ahn, whom she trusted and whose advice she desperately needed to hear.

The life of a working mother.

Unlike most working women, who must personally care for children, get them up and ready for school, and deal with the confusions of child-raising with minimal help, Gwynn had an au pair from Eastern Europe who lived in the garage apartment. The au pair drove the children to and from school, caring for them whenever Gwynn was occupied. It was one of the benefits of being wealthy and having had two wealthy husbands.

She wandered downstairs, took out frozen waffles for breakfast, and went back upstairs, knocking on doors and letting the children know it was time to get ready for school. Claire was crying by now, so she held their two-year-old briefly, changed a diaper, and wandered back downstairs. Melena (the nanny) was sitting at the counter drinking her coffee.

"Good morning, Mrs. DuFort."

Gwynn handed the baby to Melena.

"I've told you a thousand times, just call me Gwynn."

"OK, Gwynn, good morning. Tell me about the day."

"It is complicated. I will run the carpool this morning. However, you will need to pick up the children. Margaret has a dance class after school. Stephen has karate lessons. Murray can probably get a ride home, but you must be sure. I have a meeting with Ahn Winchester this afternoon, and Lance and I have a social engagement this evening. I must be in my office a good bit of the morning. If you need me, you can always call."

"I will be fine."

One of the best things about Melena Babiarez was her self-sufficiency. Her parents had been Communists, who did not fare well after the fall of the Communist regime in Poland. Melena had become a Catholic in the religious fervor that followed the fall of Communism and the national pride that accompanied the papacy of John Paul II, the former Karol Józef Wojtyła, a prominent Polish priest and the first non-Italian pope since Adrian VI in the 16th century. She was now in her late 20s, still beautiful as many Polish women can be. Her naturally blond hair and full figure drew many stares, including from Lance DuFort, for whom Melena seemed to feel nothing but disdain. She was close enough to the family to know the truth.

The Stone children drifted downstairs. Stephen, the younger brother, arrived first. He was a light sleeper and early riser gifted with seemingly endless energy. Margaret was next, dressed in her school uniform. Murray was the last to come downstairs. At fourteen, he was a bit unkempt, hostile, and awkward.

Gwynn tried to make small talk. Stevie and Maggie gladly joined in. Murray sulked.

"I am going to drop you guys off this morning. Melena is going to pick you up this afternoon. I will be at the office this morning and with Aunt Ahn this afternoon for a couple of hours. It has been a long time since we chatted. I will see all of you this evening. Lance will be home at about 6:30, but we have a Houston Symphony fundraising event tonight. Melena will be with you most of the day and tonight."

The children nodded, and Murray made a face and grunted.

"Just one big happy family."

Gwynn ignored the comment, kissed all of them, picked up the baby, and announced, "I am going upstairs to dress. I will be back in just a minute to take you to school. Try to be ready."

As promised, Gwynn showed up at Ahn's condominium in River Oaks promptly on time. Ahn had acquired the apartment after Jackson Winchester and his mother both died. Ahn decided to sell Arthur and Gwynn the house she and Stephen had lived in on Avalon in River Oaks and buy Jackson's condominium from the estate. It was a win-win situation. The house was too big for Ahn, and Arthur and Gwynn needed a home near downtown. Ahn was the principal beneficiary of Jackson Winchester's estate. Even after the legal costs and the settlement of litigation resulting from the closure of Marshland Savings, of which Jackson had been chairman, it was a considerable estate.

"I do not need the house anymore," Ahn had remarked. "You and Gwynn need it for your family. You buy my house, and I will buy Jackson's condominium from the estate." She completely redid the entire condominium, including having a Catholic exorcist cleanse and bless the apartment. (Jackson had not been one of her favorite people.) The apartment, as she redecorated it, was nothing like Jackson's bachelor's pad.

When she arrived, Ahn welcomed Gwynn at the door and showed her into the living room, decorated with Vietnamese and Texas furniture. The furniture reflected her dead husband and honored him as much as her taste. Gwynn got down to business after some small talk and catching up on the children.

"Ahn, I understand you firmly opposed my divorce and thought I was being a fool to marry Lance. You were right. Now, I need advice from someone whose wisdom I trust.

"I love our child, but our marriage is a disaster. Lance is never at home. I have every reason to believe he sees someone else. I should say 'someones else' because the perfume on his clothing is seldom the same for very long. I don't know what to do."

Gwynn, who hated showing emotion before others, began to break down and cry. Ahn sat silently, watching for a moment before responding.

"I don't know where to begin. This is such a complicated situation. You know I am close to Arthur, who is still angry and has never recovered from you or the divorce. On the other hand, I have always understood that there was more to the divorce than Arthur's friends believed. It takes more than one person to create marital problems unless one person is a saint, and few people are.

"Why don't you begin by telling me what you have learned while pondering this situation."

Gwynn took a deep breath.

"I have been in counseling. I am seeing the very person you recommended. I have talked to friends in the neighborhood. It has been a journey. I came from a broken home. My father left my mother for a much younger woman when I was in my teens. I saw the pain my mother endured. I never dealt with that emotional brokenness before Art and I married. In some ways, Arthur was like my father. He was not an intellectual. My father was successful in the oil business, as Art is in law. He was attractive to women. To some degree, I think I feared that my handsome husband would leave me just as my father left my mother.

"However, there is more. Before we married and had Murray, I was on a career path in law. Once Murray came, I shortened my hours, worked from home, and developed a different practice, primarily family and estate law. I did divorces and child custody cases. Arthur was building his career. Quite unexpectedly, he became hugely successful. He was even becoming nationally known. He took exciting cases from all over the place and was gone a lot of the time. I think I resented him. By the time we had three children, I was in over my emotional head.

"When Lance began his seduction (and that is precisely what it was), something inside me snapped. You and others tried to warn me about Lance. I paid no attention. It was like another person had taken over my mind and will. I could not help myself, or at least I thought I could not help myself.

"Later, when the womanizing began, I started to come to my senses. I do not know what would have happened if it had not been for your advice. Now, I see that this cannot go on. I cannot go on like this. I have become a recluse. I am chronically lonely. I have lost weight, and I don't have any appetite at all. I have very few friends. Something has to give.

"Unlike Arthur, who always shared difficult problems with me, Lance does not share anything. Nevertheless, I can tell that Lance is also coming apart at the seams. He yells at the children and me at the slightest provocation. Sometimes, he almost seems possessed. It is like there is another person in the room—someone I don't know at all."

She stopped before continuing.

"He . . . can be violent. Not often, but sometimes."

Ahn was alarmed.

"Gwynn, you know that I am a devout Catholic. I do not believe in divorce. But, if he can be violent, if he could hurt you or the children, then you must, for your safety and the safety of the children, get away, at least until he has some counseling."

Gwynn looked down. To Ahn's eyes, she also looked like someone who was being emotionally abused. Then she spoke.

"I have given the same advice to hundreds of women who come to my office. It is easy to give such advice to others, but hard to take it. The problem is that I also don't want the children injured any more than they already are. Murray is having trouble at school and is showing signs of drug use. He blames Arthur for what happened in our marriage. Stephen and Margaret are younger and a lot easier for me to handle, but they know enough to start to blame me. Then there is Claire. She is too young to understand exactly what is happening—but it won't be long before she does.

"I know from experience that it is tough to be a single mother, and having four children is more than most women can handle alone, especially with a career to manage. I'm losing my family. I've lost Arthur, and I don't want to lose the children."

Ahn interjected with an obvious point.

"You are not just any woman. Arthur is wealthy. He has provided for you and the children. Your father was wealthy, and you inherited a part of his estate. Your mother is still alive, and you will receive more of his estate when she dies. Finally, Lance is pretty well off. He will have to pay child support. I think if you separate, you will be fine."

Gwynn nodded.

"Maybe the truth is that I am afraid to be seen as the fool that I certainly am,"

Ahn said nothing. After a bit more conversation, Gwynn left. She looked utterly hopeless and abandoned.

PRINCE OF EMPTINESS
LOS ANGELES, CALIFORNIA
AUGUST 2001

LANCE DUFORT WOKE UP SLOWLY, gazing lazily at the woman he had picked up the evening before who was lying naked at his side.

Jesus, I can't even remember her name.

As was most often the case, he woke up thinking about his business problems. He had been a lawyer and then an investment banker. Before Dobie Dawson hired him to run E-Titan, he had never managed anything, not even been on a management committee. DuFort always enjoyed the thrill of the hunt, cutting the deal, making the commission, and moving on to the next deal and the next commission. Lance did not enjoy the day-to-day discipline of actually managing a company.

He had tried to make E-Titan a thinly disguised energy investment bank, taking positions, trading natural gas and electricity, making deals, banking profits, and moving on. The problem with management was that there was no moving on from the endless day-to-day grind of personnel issues, financial statements, SEC filings, meetings with analysts, wining and dining commercial bankers, and increasingly dealing with problems mounting at E-Titan. On top of that, he had to keep his mind on investigations in Washington, lawsuits in Texas, and a stock market that was moving in the wrong direction.

Damn it. I should never have let Brad talk me into Cheetah in the first place. He was forgetting that Cheetah had been his idea. It actually happened in a slightly different way than Lance wanted to remember.

One day, when considering how to hide some losses after the Battle Mountain deal, Brad and he talked about the mounting losses on a power plant that E-Titan had financed, built, and entered into long-term energy contracts in Honduras. Unfortunately, the Hondurans refused to buy power once the plant was constructed unless the deal terms were changed. Since E-Titan had already marked-to-market twenty years of future profits, changing the deal would mean restating financial statements. A significant loss would result. Any restatement might draw attention to other accounting issues with other E-Titan contracts. Then, Lance remembered something from his past.

"You know Brad, years ago when I was a young investment banker, a guy here in Houston, Jackson Winchester, had an idea of how to get underwater real estate out of savings and loans. His idea was to put everything into a big, publicly traded limited partnership. The deal never closed because the Fed closed the S&L, but the idea was actually brilliant. Could we do something like what Jackson Winchester tried?"

Brad, who worked closely with bankers, thought for a few moments.

"Lance, there is a similar thing called a Special Purpose Entity. Banks and other financial institutions use SPEs to move assets and liabilities off the balance sheet. Often, SPEs are used with car loans, student loans, commercial loans, and the like. The institutions form a limited partnership with someone or some entity as its general partner. Under accounting rules, the general partner must have at least a three percent capital interest in the transaction. That is to say, there must be some indication that the SPE is actually assuming risk."

Lance had effectively planted the seed, which he wanted to be Brad Gilliland's idea.

Gilliland described SPEs as those that Enron, a local competitor, had used.

"Enron and perhaps a few other energy traders have used the SPE concept. I was talking to one of their financial folks the other day. He described SPEs as a great way to get assets and debt off a balance sheet. Many banks, insurance companies, car manufacturers, and other businesses use the device. As you said, SPEs are mostly used to transfer income-producing financial assets and related liabilities in order to manage earnings and cash flow more effectively."

Lance's mind was made up.

"I want you to have your people put together a memorandum describing a transaction in some detail. I want the Honduras deal included in the SPE. We need to look carefully at the assets and liabilities of E-Titan to see what we can do to get both some assets and liabilities off our balance sheet."

With that, the conversation ended, and Cheetah was born. It was never Brad Gilliland's idea—it was Lance's, just like selling Battle Mountain had been Lance's idea. Lance was a fountain of complicated and ultimately complex and difficult business strategies.

From the very beginning, Cheetah had been a problem. One problem was that to get $100 million of assets off the balance sheet, someone had to be a general partner and come up with $3,000,000 in capital, something no one in the organization wanted to do. In the end, Dobie suggested that Marjorie Melton and the accountant in charge of Cheetah be the General Partners. She was loyal and would do anything for Dobie, for whom she had worked, and Brad Gilliland, whom she very obviously liked. Benny Morelli was chosen since "it was his idea anyway." Getting the two partners the money required a complex combination of bonuses and loans to be paid out of Cheetah's earnings.

The second problem was Dobie Dawson. Once DD understood the strategy, he insisted on putting underperforming assets into Cheetah and taking out cash in the form of debt assumed by the limited partnership. One of the assets was an older gas field that Dawson Energy owned. It was contributed at a value established by an in-house appraisal. Unfortunately, soon after closing the deal, Lance discovered that the field had substantially fewer gas reserves than the mark-to-market appraisal assumed. The result was another hidden loss.

The third problem ultimately became the biggest mistake of all. To make the transaction work, and for the banks that provided the loans to Cheetah that enabled E-Titan to take the assets off its balance sheet, the lenders had required that E-Titan put up shares of its stock as collateral as well as the assets of Cheetah. The loan agreements obligated E-Titan to contribute additional shares to the collateral pool if the value of Cheetah's assets, including those held as collateral, fell in value by a certain amount. This was a hidden time bomb in the loan documents. Ultimately, E-Titan would be caught in a perfect financial cyclone. Lance was worried.

The body next to him began to stir.

"What is wrong? You seem troubled," a smooth and sultry alto voice intoned.

"Nothing. I am just thinking about business. Last night was fun, but I have to get to our office in Los Angeles, meet, and catch a plane back to Houston."

In precisely twenty minutes, Lance was out of the apartment. He never did figure out the woman's name.

On the plane to Houston, Lance tried to get some much-needed sleep. As was increasingly the case, he had difficulty sleeping. Even before Mexico, he sensed problems in the Cheetah transactions might become unmanageable. If there were restatements of the E-Titan financial statements caused by unwinding any of the Cheetahs, the banks might declare a default. Just as dangerous was the possibility that the banks would demand additional capital in the form of stock. If that happened while the stock was falling in price, E-Titan could enter a kind of death spiral. The banks would request more collateral, diluting the value of the outstanding stock. This would cause the stock to fall further in price. The banks would require even more additional capital. The stock would fall again. Once it started, the end of the game was bankruptcy.

I have to find a way out before that happens.

Then there was Javiera. DD had warned him about Javier Velasco. It was a name Lance already knew from the past. If Javier decided to get rid of Lance, one way or the other, he was a dead man. It might not be a physical death. But his career would be over, and he would be penniless. More than likely, he would be dead.

Finally, there was his marriage. He could tell that Gwynn was well aware of his dalliances. She was no fool. He really couldn't remember why he started the affair. *Probably just to prove I could do it.* Sheila, his first wife, had not been high maintenance. She had been a pretty good person.

Most importantly, she put up with him most of the time. Of course, he never loved her. He just desired her.

I'm just like my father. I seduce women. Some of them have children. I ignore the children. I ignore the wife. I seduce other women. But in the end, I'm empty.

That was the first honest thought that Lance DuFort had had in years. It wouldn't last long. Lance was the kind of person who had no real human feelings for anyone or anything. His life was about personal pleasure, positions, and power. That's all he cared about. Of course, like most people in the situation, he couldn't confront himself with that fact. Instead, when faced with reality, he saw another woman, got another job, and achieved more power. But Lance DuFort never changed. In his heart, he believed he never would.

There has to be a solution to all this, a way out. I just need to find it.

Unfortunately, Lance Dufort's current problems were different. They were not the kind of problems that could be ignored. They were not the kind of problems that could be solved by finding another woman. They were not even the problems that could be solved by getting another job. These were problems that would follow Lance DuFort no matter how far he ran.

NAKED EMPEROR
ACAPULCO, MEXICO
SEPTEMBER 2001

DOBIE DAWSON WAS LYING IN his hotel suite in Acapulco, simultaneously getting a massage, taking a hit of cocaine, and looking at the latest financial statements of Dawson Corporation and its publicly traded affiliated corporation, E-Titan. He did not like the reading. He always felt his companies were well-run when Buddy Bennett was at the helm. In the beginning, after Lance DuFort came on board, he had been spellbound by the promise of vast and unending profits and the potential for his name to outshine his father in the business annals of Houston and beyond. Then came the first trading disaster, the Battle Mountain sale, the loss of Buddy Bennett, and Lance's increasingly erratic performance. Worse, DD had never been able to replace Bennett as the steady hand over all the other Dawson companies. He felt naked and alone.

DD had insisted that Marjorie Melton be made corporate secretary of E-Titan and a senior vice president partly to keep a watch on Lance, whom he had not entirely trusted from the beginning. He had insisted that she be made a general partner of Cheetah. She was supposed to report anything unusual to him.

He and Marjorie went back a long way. She had been one of his girls, showed her brains and loyalty, and been richly rewarded. M&M was loyal.

Unfortunately, she fell for Brad Gilliland, and DD began to doubt her loyalty to her old boss. Then came Cheetah and all the Cheetahs that followed. DD arranged for her to be the co-general partner despite her lack of financial experience. He could control her. M&M made a lot of money with Cheetahs, and her loyalty was further compromised.

DD had been surprised when she called the evening before.

The conversation began as hundreds had in the past, reminiscing of old times. *She is buttering me up,* Dobie thought. Then, she began to get to the point.

"DD, I have been thinking about things. Maybe it's Brad's death. Maybe it is the stock market, but I am not as satisfied here at E-Titan as I have been. I know you think you need me here, but with Brad gone, Lance out of the office more often (who knows where), and the pressure of running the Cheetahs (there were now more than one), I just think it is time for something different."

Marjorie sees the light of an oncoming train at the end of the tunnel. Dobie was worried.

"I don't know, Marjorie. I need someone to look after things for me at E-Titan. Lance and I get along fine, but we are not friends or long-time colleagues like the two of us are. He is just another employee. You and I go back a long way."

"Yes, I know. Maybe that is why I need to return to Dawson Corporation."

"It would be hard for you to leave just now. The stock price has been falling. Some analysts don't like the complexity of the E-Titan balance sheet. They don't understand the Cheetah transactions, and we are getting bad press due to the situations at other energy traders. Then, there are these litigations and investigations. Frankly, I don't have anyone to take your place. I can talk to Lance, but I don't think he will want you to leave just now. Honey, I would love to have you back with me, but this might not be the time."

Marjorie knew she was stuck. She decided to move the conversation along.

"DD, how familiar are you with the Battle Mountain litigation, the surrounding shareholder suits, and other transactions?"

"As familiar as people have wanted me to be. Probably not as familiar as you are. Frankly, I don't think any attempt by us to regain Battle Mountain will be the least successful. Buddy is now one of the wealthiest, best-connected, and politically influential people in the pipeline business. He is well thought of in Austin and Washington. We all know that Lance dreamed up the transaction. Buddy saw a good deal and a chance to escape Lance and his plotting and deal-making."

Marjorie understood the situation.

"Brad was worried before he died, I can tell you that. He did not think it wise to sue Buddy. He felt it opened up a can of worms. Before he died, Brad told me that Lance had 'stepped on a rattlesnake' when he sued Buddy. I don't think that the rattlesnake was just Buddy. It was the way analysts looked at the suits and began to ask hard questions. In suing Buddy, Lance was bound to face Arthur Stone, who despises Lance. By the time he was killed, Brad was a shell of his old self."

"So, what would you recommend?"

"We need to settle the lawsuit with Buddy as soon as possible. Lance would go along. He can see that the suit is not good for the stock price, which could impact other things."

"OK, I will talk to Lance. Is there anything else on your pretty mind?"

"Just one more thing, and it's personal. Like I said, I am worn out. If possible, I'd like to take a few days and stay in your rooms in Las Vegas. I need to chill out and get some perspective on things. Can you let me have it for a few days? After all, you are in Acapulco."

"I sure can. When do you want to go?"

"Next weekend."

"That will be fine. One last question as long as you are on the line. What do you hear about the investigation of Brad's death?"

There was a long pause.

"What made you bring that up?" Marjorie knew that this conversation involved a trip into dangerous territory. Dangerous for DD and unsafe for her.

"Nothing. I was just wondering. I get the impression that it is a cold case."

"Months ago, the police interviewed me. They wanted to know about my relationship with Brad, when we last saw each other, and who I thought might have him killed. I believe that they are working on a theory that, somehow, his wife had him killed.

"Ben Stone of the Ben Stone Detective Agency came by and asked the same questions. Then, the police came around a second time. This time, it seemed that they were interested in Lance. But nothing came of that either. Since March, no one has contacted me—and to the best of my knowledge, no one has contacted anyone else at E-Titan since then. Nevertheless, I worry about the police and Ben Stone. Ben is a wily old coyote. He fought in World War II; he was with the FBI for many years. He has had his own agency in Houston since. He is also Arthur Stone's uncle. He could be real trouble."

"I know. Well, like I said, I was just asking."

After they hung up, Marjorie wondered why he had asked.

Later in the day, DD called Lance.

"Lance, old friend, tell me how you are doing."

"Fine."

"I hate to bother you, but I wondered how you were doing. I know that you are under pressure. I hope our recent conversations haven't added to your worries."

He tried to sound genuinely interested in Lance, which he was not.

"DD, I am fine. I am a bit worn out. I need more time to think just now. E-Titan is now a big operation, and I don't have time to run its day-to-day operations. We are at an inflection point. We just need to get through the fourth quarter this year with good profits. We had huge profits last winter during the cold wave, but there have been trading losses since then. The traders will just have to make more deals. Finally, this new chief financial officer is just not Brad. She is not nearly as creative."

"I see. How is Marjorie doing in her role? Does she seem happy?"

"I think so. She might not have been the best person to put in charge of the Cheetahs. Bennie Morelli thinks she is lost in the accounting. She is a smart girl, but her financial background is all learned by experience. She struggles with concepts. You already know the stock price has been weak. She is in charge of investor relations, and she has to answer an awful lot of questions. I think it is wearing her down. She just called to tell me she was going to Vegas for a few days to rest."

"Yes. She asked to use my rooms in Vegas for the weekend. Since I am here, she can have them for as long as she needs."

DD paused just long enough for Lance to think he had another idea unconnected to M&M.

"Lance, I have been thinking about this Battle Mountain lawsuit. The longer it goes on, the worse our stock price will be. I just think that we should try to settle it. Make it go away."

Lance thought for a moment, then gave his best reply.

"I agree that the case needs to be settled. However, it cannot look like a defeat for E-Titan. We need the markets to see this as a positive for our stock. I will talk to our lawyer."

"I would appreciate that, Lance."

After Lance hung up, DD put on his bathrobe and went out onto the balcony to think. He had been doing a lot of thinking on the balcony lately.

8

COLD CALLS

A BROTHERLY CONVERSATION
HOUSTON, TEXAS
FEBRUARY 2001

AFTER 5:00 THAT COLD FEBRUARY evening, Arthur left the firm, got into his car, and drove from downtown to 5300 South Main Street to the First Presbyterian Church of Houston, located in the Rice-Medical Center area of Houston. The temperature had never exceeded freezing during the day—a rare occurrence in Houston. The road was treacherous for drivers unfamiliar with ice and snow, so Arthur drove slowly.

The First Presbyterian Church had originally been downtown, but after a fire, it was moved under the leadership of Charles L. King, perhaps its most famous pastor. There are and were innumerable stories about the character and leadership of Charlie King. One of his legacies was the Georgian sanctuary set back from Main Street. For years, it had been a force in Houston and beyond. Many of the Presbyterian Churches in Houston owed their existence to the insistence of Dr. King that the First

Church lead the way in new church development. Houston was growing, and the church needed to meet the needs of the city. The Synod's camp, Mo Ranch, near Hunt, Texas, had been arranged to be purchased under his leadership.

Dr. King developed a generation of leaders, some still active in the congregation as late as the turn of the century and the beginning of a new millennium. One of them, Warren Bellows, owned the construction company that built the beautiful, stately sanctuary. A feature that Arthur loved most was the legend that the two marble pillars at the front of the narthex were left over from the building of the Supreme Court building in Washington. They were found and bought by Bellows, who, with the architects, incorporated them into the structure.

After Dr. King's successor, Dr. Lancaster, retired, a period of instability ensued. In the end, Arthur's brother, John Stone, was called as pastor. John had spent most of his career in the East and Southeast. His parents were getting older and needed care, and he was ready for a new challenge. He accepted the call to be the senior pastor of one of the most important churches among the Presbyterian churches in America. It was every bit as big a challenge as he thought.

Arthur parked at the rear of the church in a parking lot that no longer exists and entered the building from the southeast side. It was a short walk to the reconfigured office suite, where his brother was the only one left.

Arthur knocked on the door, stuck his head in to see if John was busy, and was enthusiastically welcomed. Until recently, the two brothers had not been close since Arthur left for college. The joint task of looking after two aging parents, one of whom showed signs of early dementia, had drawn them together. Arthur took care of any legal or financial matters, while John focused on supporting the parents emotionally, particularly his mother, who was now a caregiver much of the time. Whenever Arthur could, he attended services at the church.

After a few pleasantries, John asked Arthur the purpose of his visit.

"I have two purposes, one about Mom and Dad and one personal. Let's save the personal for last. I want to bring you up to date on Dad's will and his estate planning. As you would guess, Dad is leaving everything to Mom in what is called a "Living Trust." You and I are its trustees and the executors of Dad's estate. It is not as small as you might guess. Dad has his pension, and Mom will receive about two-thirds of its current amount if Dad dies. She also gets his Social Security. Miraculously, Dad saved a lot during his lifetime and invested conservatively but wisely. They still have Grandpa's ranch and its value increases as the Hill Country becomes more populous. Mom is going to be OK.

"Mom will have the ranch to live in during her lifetime, which is the asset I want to visit with you about. Dad insisted on dividing his estate evenly between us, even though I am somewhat better off financially than you. Recently, an adjoining property—a larger ranch of 1500 acres with some frontage on the North Fork of the Guadalupe came on the market. When Mom and Dad told me about it, I purchased it. A fine old limestone farmhouse on the property has more rooms than I will ever use. I will use it as a weekend place and perhaps run a few cattle. It is also a good hunting property, though I don't hunt much. This being the case, Dad will give you the family ranch. This means you will have a retirement place if you want to live near Kerrville in the Hill Country. The only restriction on the property is that I can buy the family ranch if you ever want to sell. Dad does not want that property he loves so much to leave the family if possible."

With that, Arthur stopped and looked at his brother for a response. It was precisely what he expected.

"Arthur, this is just fine. I appreciate you and Dad making provision for me. I do think we might retire there. It is only a few miles from Mo Ranch, which Jane and I love. Our church goes there annually, and we sometimes sneak up for a retreat or a weekend there. It would be wonderful if we could become neighbors. I am sure your kids are going to love the Hill Country."

The conversation lasted a bit longer before Arthur got to the second reason for his visit.

"The second reason for my visit is personal. You know that I have had dreams of a spiritual nature. You also understand that the divorce was tough on me. I would like to believe that my anger and rage at Gwynn had dissipated after all these years, but I am not so sure. For one thing, it is all we can do to have a conversation without me blowing up at her.

"Last night, I had what you will think is a ridiculous dream. I was King Arthur before his most famous battle at Mount Badon. I was anxious about the battle, which in my dream was to recover Guinevere from Lancelot. It was a blood battle to the end. In the end, I charged from my observation post into the battle. On the way, I encountered a knight. In the blood rage of battle, I killed the knight, who turned out to be Gwynn. At that moment, the fiery dark demon from my prior dreams, about which you are aware, appeared to declare victory. I was again enraged enough to attack it. However, an angel of light appeared between us to stop the fight. This angel took Gwynn in his arms, healed her, and took her away from the battle. At that point, I woke up.

"I know that those past dreams and this dream could be nothing more than disturbances in my psyche. I also know I could be subconsciously battling my false self. I need to talk to someone."

John listened intently. Arthur knew that, while his brother was primarily a teaching pastor, he counseled people occasionally and was pretty good at it. In addition, one of his accomplishments at First Presbyterian was opening a spiritual direction and counseling center on campus. After thinking and praying for a few moments, John began to talk.

"Arthur, one of the most essential things about dreams is that they are usually about the dreamer, not the actual objects of the dream. I don't think the dream is primarily about Lance or Gwynn. Most likely, it is about you.

"I have felt for some time that you have not recovered from the divorce. For one thing, you are the most eligible bachelor in Houston. Despite small affairs and the energetic attempts of many women your age and younger to enchant you, you never really connected with any of them. Every relationship, however promising, eventually ended, usually with hurt feelings. A few of these women have been part of our church.

"My first question is, 'What is happening or not happening inside of you?'"

Arthur, never one to reveal his feelings, sat staring at the wall momentarily.

"Johnny, I am not sure. It is true that I simply cannot find any woman about whom I feel the way I felt about Gwynn. That is a big problem. On a deeper level, I have friends who divorced and remarried, and I know there are typically tensions between the two families. I cannot be a good father to even one family, much less take on another. Finally, there is this feeling of failure. You know I like to win and would not like to fail at another marriage.

The way it ended with Gwynn left feelings of emptiness and humiliation. I don't seem to be able to get by them."

John thought carefully, pondering his words.

"Art, when I counsel people, I try not to give too much advice. This is your problem. As much as I would like to tell you what to do next or wave a magic wand and take away all the pain, I can't. We can't change the past. One thing is sure: Marriage is not a game one tries to win. I encourage you not to think about your prior marriage in terms of winning or losing.

Marriage is a relationship that two people must nurture and grow. We sponsor marriage seminars for our members, but here is the truth—there are no sure ways to have a good marriage. Every marriage is different. No marriage is perfect. You were not an ideal husband, and Gwynn was not a perfect wife. In the end, you were just not able to make it work.

"I know enough about Lance DuFort's reputation to believe that Gwynn made a tragic mistake. The mistake probably did have something to do with you being busy with your career and reputation as the 'Duke of Litigation.' But there had to be more. She came from a broken home—and broken homes often cause children emotional pain. She might have had issues she needed to face before marrying. However, the two of you were so much in love that I don't think she had the time or took the time. You can't completely ignore your role in that problem: You were also caught up in a big romance."

Arthur looked at his hands folded in his lap.

"You know she was pregnant when we married. But that is not why we married. Months before, I had decided I wanted to marry Gwynn and was just waiting for the right time to ask. The baby was just the moment I asked. Maybe I pushed too hard, too fast."

His brother agreed.

"Maybe. Dad and I did the wedding. We did not have time for counseling, at least not a normal or recommended level of pre-marital counseling. Neither Dad nor I put you through all the pre-marital questionnaires, readings, and counseling sessions we normally would. That part of it is our fault."

Arthur quickly interjected, "It was not your fault. It was mine if a mistake was made. I was so confident and sure that I knew more than you, Dad, or anyone else that I would not have listened. Perhaps I should have, but I would not have."

John tried to comfort Arthur. He was having a hard time. His brother was a wounded man.

"Right now, Arthur, as hard as it is, I think your dream is encouraging you to let go of your anger—your anger against Lance and especially your anger against Gwynn—and love her unconditionally. Deep inside, you know that your anger is both unwarranted and counterproductive.

"Try always to do what she needs you to, expecting nothing in return, and let your psyche heal. The marriage is over, but your life is not over. I cannot say what the future will bring. Perhaps you will never remarry. However, if you can let go of the anger and pain, forgive, and love Gwynn and the children unconditionally, you at least will be spiritually and psychologically whole. That is more than most people achieve."

Arthur immediately knew that his brother's advice was sound. He also thought that it was consistent with how his dream ended.

"I don't want to let go of the past—I know that—but I guess I have to."

"I think so."

There was a bit more brotherly back and forth, but the evening was getting late. John needed to get home to Jane, and Arthur also needed to get on. He had a fundraiser to attend. The meeting broke up.

GUILTLESS GUILT
SANDLEWOOD SUBDIVISION
MARCH 2001

FOR THE PAST MONTH, HEATHER Gilliland had been living a nightmare. She was not surprised when the police asked to see her again, showing up with a police warrant to search her home. She was also not surprised that they dismantled her kitchen, searched her pantry, and asked for all her personal checkbooks and financial records. She was also not surprised when, several days later, Rico Diaz asked to see her with another detective. She was astonished when they took the opportunity to remind her of her right to remain silent and to have an attorney present during her questioning.

"So I need an attorney?"

"We cannot decide that for you, but we have some questions about your husband's death."

"Well, you might as well go ahead and ask them."

Heather Gilliland had already spoken with an attorney. She knew when to stop the interview and ask for counsel to be present. For now, she wanted to appear cooperative.

"First, we want to review the sequence of events with you again. If we understand matters, on the night your husband was shot, you came to his study around 10:00, brought him some cocoa, and said goodnight; he remained in his study."

"Yes."

"As we understand matters, you went upstairs, took a sleeping pill, and did not hear anything until you woke up the next morning."

"That is correct."

"Are these the sleeping pills that you took?"

Heather put on her reading glasses and looked at the bottle's label, responding, "They appear to be."

"The next morning, you awoke, looked in your husband's bedroom, came down the stairs, entered the study, and found your husband. Is that correct?"

"That is correct."

"You've stated that you were in shock and sat in a chair in the hallway for a few minutes before calling the police. Is that correct?"

"Yes."

"Did you touch anything in the study before you called us?"

"I don't think so. I may have straightened up a few things, but I don't think so. There was blood everywhere. It was. . . . She shook violently. "It was terrible."

"Mrs. Gilliland, your husband was killed by a gunshot from a sniper's rifle. A professional did it. Under the circumstances, we would not usually anticipate finding poison on the premises or in the deceased's body. In this case, we found sepsis in your husband's body. In the residue of the hot chocolate, we found evidence of human feces. The autopsy indicated the beginnings of a massive infection from an undetermined source. Can you explain this to us?"

Heather Gilliland bowed her head and began to tremble and cry.

"I did not mean to kill him. I did not kill him. I would never kill Brad. However, I was so angry after the *Texas Quarterly* article that I had to do something to get even. He humiliated me in front of the entire state of Texas."

"So you admit to poisoning your husband?"

Heather nodded her head, sobbing.

Rico went on.

"You realize that you have just confessed to attempted murder?"

"I told you, I never intended to kill him. I just wanted him to be sick. I did not try to kill my husband."

"Well, if you are indicted, that will be for a jury to decide."

Heather Gilliland looked up, this time with a tinge of anger in her voice. "I told you, I did not attempt to kill my husband. I loved him . . . at least until. . . ."

At this point, she broke down entirely.

The detectives waited patiently for her to regain some self-control.

"We are sorry, but we must ask you a few more questions. You will understand that we now know that you had a motive for killing your husband. He had humiliated you. We can understand that. What we want to ask you is this: Did you order the murder of your husband?"

Once again, Heather's voice showed apparent anger and hurt.

"I did not. I would not do such a thing."

"That is all our questions for today. I appreciate your cooperation. We need you to come to the station and make a complete statement. You will want your attorney to be present."

With that, the interview ended.

❄

On the long drive back to the station, the two detectives were silent for a long time. Rico eventually asked his assistant what he thought about the interview.

"I can't say. Frankly, I don't think she contracted for the murder. We cannot find such a payment in her checkbooks, records, or their joint accounts. They lived well, and she is a spender regarding clothes, food, and entertainment. But there are no records of any payment near what a hit on a prominent businessman would cost. I think we are back at square one. We can indict her for attempted murder or a lesser charge based on the chocolate, but I am not even sure a jury would convict. I don't like the 'Terrible and Unfaithful Husband Defense,' but juries buy it all the time."

Rico shook his head in agreement.

"We need to follow up on this. She did have a strong motive. But I am not sure about whether she had the means. As to opportunity, of course, as a spouse, she did, but nothing points to her as the person who contracted the killing."

With that, their conversation turned to the Astros.

LONELY REVELATION
HOUSTON, TEXAS
MARCH 2001

BEN STONE WAS THOUGHTFULLY DISTURBED. Something did not add up about the death of Brad Gilliland. The police had given him the details of what they knew. The way the killing was accomplished indicated a sophisticated killer. The police might suspect that Heather Gilliland had ordered the death of her husband, but the idea did not seem plausible to Ben. Rico had let him know that his people were also dubious. Ben also knew that their investigation of Lance DuFort had not revealed a single financial transaction that might have involved a killing for hire.

In Ben's mind, Lance was the most likely candidate. He had the motive, the means, and the opportunity—in fact, he had more than one motive. Gilliland might have given very, very damaging testimony in his deposition.

One more thing bothered him: for some time now, he had been followed. Someone wanted to know if his investigation was making progress. He was being tailed at this very moment. Months of observation cost money that only governments, large businesses, or wealthy individuals possess. E-Titan and Dawson Corporation were big businesses. Lance and DD were wealthy. In any case, someone was watching.

As he drove into Heather Gilliland's West Houston neighborhood, he noted the new guard building (a result of the murder), the new security cameras, and other indications that the residents had taken note of the Gilliland murder. He had done his research. The neighborhood had become a favorite of wealthy foreigners. Its seclusion, lake, and amenities made it an attractive address. Not every resident had a business that justified the address. There was clean money and dirty money in the neighborhood.

Houston has been changing for a long, long time. It is not the Houston my children grew up in. It is a huge, multicultural, multi-ethnic nexus of international businesses of all kinds, not all of them legitimate.

❄

He drove into the circular driveway in front of the Gilliland home, exited his car, and walked to the front door. He noted security cameras in the eaves, trees, and other locations. *Mrs. Gilliland is scared,* he thought to himself.

Heather Gilliland opened the door in her dressing gown. It was obvious that she had been crying.

"I apologize for not being quite ready for your visit. Come into the living room. I will be down when I get my face on in a few minutes."

Ben nodded and entered the living room, which opened into a den. The living room's back wall primarily consisted of windows overlooking the lake. The den was filled with precisely the kind of books that one might expect from an accountant: a few business books, some books about famous financial scandals, mysteries, and spy novels. He noted there were security cameras there as well.

Mrs. Gilliland does not want to be surprised.

It was not long before Heather Gilliland reappeared in slacks, a top, and tennis shoes. In her mid-forties, she was an attractive woman. The outfit showed off her figure.

She will not be single longer than she wants to be.

Gilliland had left her a good bit of money. From Ben's investigations, he knew she had placed her money in a local trust department, which insisted on diversifying her portfolio. She was not exposed to a decline in E-Titan stock. This girl was no fool.

At Heather's invitation, he sat down on the couch. She took a chair across from him. The maid brought a pot of coffee and a few biscuits. They made small talk before Ben announced the reason for his visit.

"You know that the investigation into your husband's death has stalled. We know there was a professional killer involved. We believe the killer was of Eastern European origin. We believe he returned home to Europe through Atlanta. From there, the trail is cold. We do not have sufficient facts to identify or find the killer."

Heather nodded.

"You know you have been on a list of suspects. Right now, the police have no evidence that you were involved."

"That's because I wasn't. I've admitted to trying to make my husband sick. That is as far as it goes. I did not kill my husband. I was not trying to kill my husband."

"Mrs. Gilliland . . ."

"Heather."

"Heather, I believe you. I think the police believe you. However, that leaves us with the question, 'If Heather Gilliland did not order the killing, who did?' I don't want to go over the facts again with you. The police have done that several times, and I went over them with you early on when I came by to visit. I want to know if you can think of anything we have missed. The police have searched this house and every piece of evidence they could extract. They have nothing to go on. Did your husband have any other place he might have put personal records?"

"The police already asked that question. We have a lake house on Canyon Lake near New Braunfels. It was my parents' until they grew older, and we bought it from them to keep it in the family. I have good memories of water skiing there as a teenager. The police visited it and searched it. My understanding is that they found nothing of interest to their investigation."

"Is there any place else you can think of where he might have kept records or papers that could shed some light on why he was killed and by whom?"

"No."

Then, she stopped as if thinking. She wondered if she should reveal some secret she was not supposed to know. Ben was an experienced investigator. He knew when to push and when to wait patiently for the facts to come out on their own. This was a time for silent waiting.

Finally, she looked up. *Lovely eyes,* Ben thought.

"By now, you know that my husband was having an affair with Marjorie Melton. I think the boys call her M&M because she is, among other things, eye candy. Her rise to the top at E-Titan was no accident. My friends tell me that she was one of the many women that DD has paid and pays to 'keep him warm.' Marjorie was more intelligent than most of them. She made herself useful to DD, who responded by giving her responsibilities in his companies. My friends think DD made her Secretary and a Senior Vice President of E-Titan to keep an eye on Lance. It is rumored that she and DD had a brief affair. Eventually, she seduced my husband."

She looked down in embarrassment before continuing.

"DD keeps a suite of rooms in Las Vegas in a hotel he owns. Once in a while, he moves there for a few months. Most of the time, the suite is empty. My husband and Marjorie spent time there on 'business trips.' I think she goes there alone on occasion."

"Can you give me the name of the hotel?"

Ben wrote down the name.

"I will check it out. Unlike you, M&M has not been particularly helpful in my inquiries. Do you know for certain if she still visits the hotel?"

"Actually, I do. When I became suspicious about my husband, I hired a private investigator. M&M traveled to Las Vegas with and without Brad. Since Brad's death, I have had no reason to pay the detective. But I suspect that she still visits Las

Vegas. It is in her blood. While I was paying my detective, he let me know that she always makes her reservations through a travel agency owned by the daughter of one of the high-level executives at Dawson Corporation. It might be hard to get a list of visits, but I think there will be records."

Before it was over, Ben Stone regretted knowing this information. But for now, it was the best lead he had. It was time to say goodbye.

"Well, thank you, Mrs. Gilliland. As I mentioned before, I can't speak for the police, but in my mind, you aren't the kind of person to order a killing. I was an FBI agent for thirty years and have owned my own agency for a long time. I've seen a lot of terrible things. If I were you, I would try to put this in the past and continue my life. You are an attractive woman and about half as old as I am. You have a lot of years. Don't waste them."

When he returned to the office, he arranged a break-in at a local travel agency.

9

*V*ISITATIONS

MEETING AT A MONASTERY
SAN MIGUEL DE ALLENDE, MEXICO
MARCH 1990

ACROSS A SMALL VALLEY FROM a small monastery near San Miguel de Allende, the abbot was sitting in a posture of peaceful tranquility, praying silently next to a relatively short, powerfully built, late middle-aged man with a well-trimmed beard and wearing an expensive guayabera shirt. Even in prayer, there was a sense of barely suppressed energy in the man's demeanor. This was a man of action, or at least he had been at one time.

The period of quiet prayer lasted twenty minutes as the two meditated together. The abbot taught all those who came to him for direction this practice. At its completion, they recited the Lord's Prayer and sat quietly, slowly returning to their everyday worlds. Then, the monk spoke to his companion.

"Bardero, you have been with us a long time. I notice that you have been busy in town. Have you any plans?"

"I think so."

"I gather you will not be joining our order. You have been an oblate of our order for a long time. If you were called to become a Benedictine, God would have made it plain by now. Don't be afraid to tell me your thoughts. I have suspected them for many months."

"I am glad that you brought this up, Father. I have been meaning to visit with you. You know I have a small investment in a hotel in San Miguel de Allende owned by Texans from Houston. I run the hotel for them. You also know I opened a small taxi service for those who wish to be picked up in either Leon or Queretaro—and even as far as Mexico City and Monterey. My businesses have done well."

"I have heard of your success in these businesses. Yet, I do not think you are satisfied."

Bardero nodded.

"Father, do you see that small farm across the valley? I recently bought it. I intend to renovate the hacienda and surround it with a vineyard. When it is done, I will move to that home."

"I see."

The small farm ran from the crest of the hill down into the valley until it met the monastery's property line. The hillside was perfect for a small vineyard—just large enough to break even. With care, it might even make a little profit. The small farmhouse was made of concrete and tile with an arched porch on all four sides. The abbot could see that construction had already begun on the improvements. It would make a more than adequate home for a single businessman.

"Have you prayed about this decision?"

"Yes, Father, I have. When I came here, I was a fugitive. I was tempted to become one of your monks for a long time. I know how the order struggles to attract young men these days. Yet, inside of me, there was an inner hesitation. My past experiences, abilities, and talents make me more suited to serve God outside the church's orders. I intend to remain an oblate and live according to the Benedictine Rule as it applies to oblates. But I also hope to be married one day and have a family. During my years in the Special Forces, I did not think it fair to have a wife. I saw the difficulties in the marriages of many of my friends. We were sometimes gone for long periods. That's not easy on a young man or woman. I did not want to be an unfaithful husband, and I did not want to deal with an unfaithful wife.

"I saw how hard the separations and anxiety were on wives and children. Not all of us came home from every mission. I have sat on a couch and comforted more than one young widow. Those women were sometimes left to raise a child without a father. I decided to wait until I retired to have a wife and family."

Bardero smiled wryly before continuing.

"I did not know I would have to die and be reborn a different man before that could happen."

The abbot smiled knowingly.

"Are you sure this is the correct course of action? You know that you will never be completely safe, nor will you ever be completely free of the past. It has a way of visiting us when we are least prepared. The men you defeated are not the sort of people to forgive and forget."

"No one can completely escape their past. For good and for ill, it shapes us all. Yet, I have learned that we cannot let the past and fears about the future keep us from following our dreams. In my prayers and dreams, I am assured that my life of action is not over. The death of Stephen Winchester was never solved. The dark forces previously at work in my former country are still at work. They may become more powerful than they were before.

Nevertheless, I can only wait and watch for now—remember, I was a Watcher, and patience is needed when watching a dangerous enemy. Someday, I think the time of waiting will end.

"In the meantime, I must go on with life. None of us can see the future. Perhaps the future I fear might come will never come. Possibly, enemies of the past will find me in this place, and maybe they will not. Perhaps if we must meet again, I will defeat them. Possibly, I will not. The future is not disclosed to any of us. I have seen good men turn to me in a jungle to talk about a restaurant we would visit on our next leave and die in that instant. No man's fate is easy to discern."

The two sat silently for a few minutes longer. Then, Bardero spoke again.

"Do you remember the woman I brought here to meet you some time ago?"

"The oriental widow of this man Winchester?"

"Yes."

"I remember her well. She made a very gracious contribution to our building program and continues to send us contributions from time to time. She has also visited and contributed to our sister house in New Mexico. She is a generous woman of deep faith."

Bardero continued.

"She is one of the hotel's investors. She comes occasionally to visit me. She is still searching for her husband's murderer. She does not think that the person who ordered the death of her husband was the person ultimately responsible for his death. She believes there were other forces and other persons at work. She is devout and prays for hours daily. Her eyes see beyond the horizon of this life. She also believes that I should not take vows but remain a layperson. Perhaps she is merely being selfish and irrationally hoping to find out more about her husband's death, but I do not think so. There is more.

"I am not the least bit interested in this woman. She is many years my senior. More than that, I sense that she will never forget her husband, Stephen Winchester. He must have been quite a man. I wish I had known him."

The abbot nodded.

"For all these reasons, I must bless you in your decision. I think I best also pray for your protection. I think one day you will need it."

The priest set his hands upon his disciple's head and said a long prayer of blessing, ending in silence.

"You will come frequently to see me?"

"I will."

NEW FRIEND
SAN MIGUEL DE ALLENDE, MEXICO
FEBRUARY 2001

IT WAS A COOL, DRY, and lovely winter day in San Miguel de Allende. It had been years since Bardero sat on the hillside above the monastery and prayed with the abbot. Those years had been good to him. He was still in good shape. His athletic body was aging, but much more slowly than the bodies of most other men. He was in what he knew was the prime of his life. He still had his energy. He also had experience in business and life. He was at the peak of his powers. The fates had been good to him. His businesses had been successful. The little vineyard had grown into a lovely and profitable enterprise. He had almost everything he had ever wanted.

The sky was deep blue and clear, so clear that one felt that if one had eyes to see, one could see to the end of the universe. His office was well-furnished, functional, and full of Mexico's history and furniture. Juan de la Cruz Bardero sat at his desk, reviewing the hotel's business results for the past month. There were no real surprises. Business was good. There was a quiet knock on the door as the manager entered the room.

"A young lady in the lobby is asking to see you."

"You know I do not see guests or those looking for work."

"Yes, Sir. However, this lady says you are expecting her. She has a letter from Mrs. Winchester from Houston that she was asked to deliver to you."

The manager knew "Mrs. Winchester" very well. She spent several weeks in the hotel each year. Perhaps more importantly, he knew she owned part of the business.

Bardero nodded.

"Bring her in."

The manager disappeared briefly, then returned with a slightly built, pleasant-looking woman in her 30s. Her dark, intelligent eyes seemed to take in more than the surface of things. She sat down.

"You have a letter for me?"

"Yes."

"Can you give it to me now?"

"Certainly.

She handed the letter over to Bardero, who opened it and read its contents several times.

Dear Juan:

    Greetings from Houston. I have received a request from one of our friends here in Houston to contact you.

It involves a matter of some delicacy. Some months ago, Texas Quarterly magazine ran an article about an executive retreat at a resort hotel in Los Cabos involving executives of E-Titan Energy. There was a good bit of misbehavior associated with the trip. Most unfortunately, a young Mexican lady disappeared and was later found dead. This young lady, Javiera Velasco Dominquez, was the granddaughter of Javier Velasco, a name you will remember from the past.

Recently, an executive was found dead in Houston in what appears to have been a contract killing. This person was involved in the misbehavior in Los Cabos. The husband of the ex-wife of a mutual friend is pictured on the cover with Javiera on his lap. The executive killed was about to testify in a significant lawsuit our friend is handling. His testimony was critical in establishing an element of the case. His death was highly suspicious.

Our friend is concerned about two things: First, on a strictly business level, he would like to know if anything occurred during the Los Cabos trip that might shed light on the killing in Texas. Second, knowing the family's character, he is concerned that his ex-wife and their children might be embarrassed by future disclosures or even be in danger. He wishes you to look into this matter while you are in Los Cabos.

You will be compensated for this trip, and your expenses will be paid. When you go on this trip, our friends think it might be wise to take along another person with the same abilities you possess.

Maria Mendoza, who is conveying this message, is an accountant at Worthington Hunt, the accounting

*firm I use. While she is with you on vacation, I would
like you to give her a tour and show her the books on
our businesses in San Miguel de Allende. We might as
well use this as preparation for your annual review.*

*I send my regards and hope to come and visit you
in the near future.*

Very truly yours,

Ahn Winchester.

When Bardero was finished, he folded the letter and put it into his coat pocket. He smiled at the young woman.

"It says here that you are Maria Mendoza from Houston, Texas. How do you know Mrs. Winchester?"

"It is a long story. My father was killed in a plane crash in Texas some years ago while returning from a business trip to Mexico. I met a young lawyer at his funeral who has since become well-known in Texas. This young lawyer was instrumental in uncovering some of what had occurred, though no one was ever apprehended for the crime. Since that time, he has been very kind to me. When I first met Arthur Stone, I was a school teacher. After a few years, I decided to follow my father into accounting. I have a knack for numbers.

"After the plane crash, a trust was set up by a third party to compensate victims and help them recover from the deaths involved. Ahn Winchester and Arthur Stone, the young lawyer, were involved in setting up the trust. It helped my mother get back on her feet after the death. She remarried some years ago. When I decided to go to school to become an accountant, the trust helped me. A local Houston firm hired me when I graduated, and I have worked there ever since. Though our firm is small, we work for some significant Houston families and small businesses."

She paused, noting that Bardero was taking things in and even seemed to know some of what she would say before she said it. He responded quietly.

"Mrs. Winchester is an investor in this hotel, and we admire her greatly. I believe she lost her husband during the unfortunate affair in which your father was killed. Arthur Stone, as you probably know, is also an investor. They are both fine people."

"Yes. Ahn has never remarried. Her husband must have been quite a person."

Bardero looked at the kind face before him, with its darting bright eyes and smiling lips.

"You never married?"

"No."

Maria looked down.

"Some years ago, I was involved with someone. It did not work out. Nevertheless, I was left with a child, Manuel. He is the light of my life, but most of my life has been spent working and caring for a child. Manny is eleven now."

"And the father?"

"He deserted me shortly after Manny was born. I have not seen him since."

"I am very sorry."

There was an awkward silence. Then, Bardero spoke with the authority of someone who had decided what to do.

"Your client has asked me to do her a favor. I must let you go to your room. We have reserved one of the best rooms in the hotel for you. Tomorrow or the day after, I must leave on a trip for a few days. I would like you to dine with me at the hotel tonight. It will not be a late dinner, for I live in the country outside of San Miguel, where I have a small farm."

Maria agreed to dinner. The two said a few pleasantries, and the manager came in to take her to her room—one of the best in the hotel.

✳

When Maria was gone, Bardero sat back in his chair for several minutes, gathering his thoughts and thinking about what to do. He read and reread the letter until he had it memorized. Then, as was his habit with such letters, he shredded it. Bardero and his friends in Houston were careful about their relationship. Not many people knew of it.

There were several parts of the letter he found disturbing. In the fourteen years since the events that surrounded Maria's father's death, no similar request had ever been made.

Something must be involved in this Los Cabos trip, or she and Arthur Stone would never have asked me to expose myself in this way.

After the death of her husband and the probate of his estate and that of his brother, Ahn had contrived a vacation to San Miguel de Allende, where the two of them had activated the trust she had created in Houston by her lawyers. While there, she decided to make an offer on the hotel where she stayed, which was on the market for purchase. On paper, Bardero was the majority owner of the hotel. Like Arthur Stone, Ahn Winchester owned 24 percent through a Texas company. They were investors when he formed his taxi service and a small private security firm. Ahn came to San Miguel annually for a week or two. She loved the ambiance of the city. Arthur had brought Gwynn a few times but had not visited San Miguel since his divorce.

More troubling than the request to go to Los Cabos was that Javier Velasco was involved. If El Halcón were to discover his identity, nothing good could come of it. He would trade that information to the United States government or the drug lords in Mexico in a second. He was a close friend of the leaders of Mexico and the United States. He had connections with intelligence services all over the world and with the drug cartels in Mexico. This trip would put Bardero at risk.

I will take someone else along. Jorge will do. He was in the special forces in the Mexican Army. If trouble occurs or hard questions need to be asked, Jorge will do it for me.

Because of past events, Arthur Stone and Ahn Winchester were careful about communicating with Bardero. It was always done obliquely, usually connected to a trip to San Miguel by Ahn. It was rarely necessary to speak, but they did not want to expose a connection between Juan Bardero and any events of the past for fear that someone would connect Juan Bardero with John Mirador, who was officially dead. Arthur had covered his tracks here. He had chosen to contact him through Ahn so that his fingers could not be seen. (It was even more complex: Arthur asked Ben Stone, who had requested Ahn Winchester to write the letter so that not even Ben Stone's investigative firm could be seen as interested in the events at Los Cabos.)

I might just as well get this over with.

After a few more moments of silent meditation, Bardero made a few calls. The following afternoon, he and Jorge would travel to Los Cabos by plane. At the airport, they would separate. Both were checked into the resort but under separate company names. Bardero was a hotelier from San Miguel interested in improving his customer service. Jorge was a security specialist from San Leon on vacation for a few days of fun, food, and sightseeing.

That evening, Bardero met Maria in the hotel restaurant. In its nearly 300 years, the hotel had been a nunnery, a private home, and now a hotel. High ancient stone walls surrounded the buildings that made up the hotel. The hotel restaurant was in one of the buildings that had been a stable when the hotel was a private home. The kitchen was a modern rendition of the original, separate building from the nunnery and the then-private home.

When Maria arrived, they were seated outdoors in a leafy, lantern-lit courtyard surrounded by lush vegetation.

It was a cold evening by San Miguel standards. Bardero apologized.

"It is cool this evening. I am sorry for that. San Miguel is known for its temperate and delightful climate. I apologize for the cooler-than-normal temperature you may have experienced today."

After a short conversation about the weather and the recent terrible cold spell in Texas, Bardero and Maria discussed their life experiences. Bardero was careful to disclose nothing except that he was a devout Catholic and an oblate in the Benedictine Order which had a mission near his home.

"I came to the monastery and San Miguel at a challenging time. Many things had gone wrong. In my prior life, I was a thrill seeker, loving danger and never staying in one place for long. I lived in southern Mexico—a poor and drug-infested area where there was little opportunity. When I arrived at the monastery, I found a home. For a time, I thought I might become a monk. Ultimately, I decided I was best suited for a secular occupation. Just about that time, your client offered me the opportunity to manage this hotel. She, too, is a devout Catholic. In the end, I was offered a percentage of the hotel. Now, I am interested in a few other businesses related to the hotel. We provide drivers and security for some of our guests if they ask for it. I own the company we generally recommend. (He did not mention doing discreet investigations for his investors.)

"But you never married?"

"I never quite met the right person. As a 17th Century Spanish poet wrote:

I have no taste for beauties that decay and are the spoil of ages as they flee, Nor do those riches please me that betray;

Best of all truths, I hold this truth to be: Cast all the vanities of life away, and not your life away on vanity."

Maria interjected, "You have read Juana de Asuaje y Ramírez de Santillana?"

"Yes, there was a book of her poetry in the monastery's library. I read it while I was living there. The abbot is a man of great learning. He even studied in Rome in his early years, writing a dissertation on angels.

"The poem expresses my current way of life. I wasted much of my life seeking adventure, men's praise, and beautiful women's love. In the end, that life disappointed me. I am not attracted to most of the women here. I have never found a woman with the values of my mother. My mother was a simple person filled with love for her husband and me. We were a happy family. I have never wanted less for any children of my own."

Bardero moved the subject of the conversation to Maria.

"You know Juana de Asuaje y Ramírez de Santillana?"

"Yes. My father insisted I study Spanish in high school and college. I was already fluent by the time I entered college. I took several courses at the Master's degree level at the University of Houston. I read Juana Inés de la Cruz (her more famous name) and many other Spanish and Latin American poets during those years."

"Do you keep up with this study?"

"Oh, no. I am now a busy mother and accountant. Occasionally, I find a book from my undergraduate days on a bookshelf and read a few lines. This just happened to be one of my favorites. Not many people read her today."

"Yes."

Afterward, Bardero never fully understood why he reached out and touched Maria's hand lying on the table. For the rest of his life, he would remember that one second in which he felt the small, brown hand of Maria Mendoza with her long and elegant fingers. When she looked down, he expected she would pull her hand away. Instead, their dark brown eyes met, and in an instant, a connection was made that was not merely physical but deeply emotional, even spiritual. He felt the touch of her hand throughout his entire body, and there was a tingling in his mind for just a second. From the look on her face, he was sure she felt the connection. She smiled a timid and disarming smile, immediately followed by his equally timid and disarming smile.

A new friendship had been birthed, more profound than either suspected.

For the rest of the meal, their conversation went from Spanish poets to the intricacies of Mexican politics, her job in the United States, and his tiny home surrounded by a vineyard and lavender plantings. Before they knew it, the night was gone. Bardero was reluctant for the evening to end, but finally, he suggested he walk her back to her room.

"Tomorrow, I must visit the West Coast of Mexico on some hotel business. I shall be gone for several days. I hope that you will be here when I return. I will take you to see my little hacienda."

At the door, he kissed her goodnight. She did not resist his kiss.

A SAD GOODBYE

LOS CABOS AND SAN MIGUEL DE ALLENDE, MEXICO
FEBRUARY 2001

THE TRIP TO LOS CABOS WAS tedious. Traveling in Mexico is rarely easy. In this case, Bardero had to travel first to Santiago de Queretaro and then to Mexico City on a full and uncomfortable Aero Mexico flight. Changing planes in the busy and overcrowded Mexico City Airport, he flew to Cabos San Lucas, ending at the San Jose del Cabo International Airport. He arrived tired and hungry from the journey.

Bardero was a private person. He was wary of being in situations where one of his old military comrades from the United States might recognize him. For that reason, he did not like visiting a resort. One of the things he always did was closely examine the bookings in his hotel. If there was any possibility he might be recognized, he worked from his hacienda, avoiding San Miguel de Allende. Juan Bardero did not look much like John Mirador, but Bardero was not a man to take chances. When he arrived, after he checked into his room, he made a quick trip around the lobby to see if he could see any familiar faces. There were none.

Then, he called the manager, introducing himself as Juan de la Cruz Bardero, a San Miguel de Allende hotel manager. He explained that he was in Los Cabos to look at more prominent and luxurious hotels. The manager quickly agreed to meet the following day. Then, Bardero called several other local hotels, including the one where the E-Titan executives had stayed, and made similar appointments. Anyone checking on him would find confirmation of his identity and reason for the trip.

The next morning, he woke early, ready to begin an exhausting two days. The hotel manager had graciously agreed to meet him for breakfast. Before the breakfast was over, Bardero considered the trip a success. He had learned a few new ideas for his hotel.

❊

At the second hotel, Bardero asked the same questions as at the first hotel, beginning with questions about advertising, following up on visitors to confirm they had a positive experience, staffing issues, and issues related to the hotel restaurant and bars. The last set of questions was on security. Bardero spoke about his security operations and then asked for suggestions.

"It is interesting that you should ask. We recently changed some of our policies and procedures due to an incident."

"Tell me about the incident and if you think it could happen at my hotel."

"The exact problem could not occur at a hotel not located on a beachfront, but a similar situation might. We hosted a corporate retreat for a sizeable Texas-based company. Frankly, things got out of hand from the beginning. There was a lot of carousing and misbehavior. On the last night, there was a genuine catastrophe. The group had been drinking heavily. There were prostitutes and others present.

"Unfortunately, the granddaughter of a prominent Mexican family joined the celebration. We do not know what happened exactly. However, the body of the young lady washed up on a nearby beach dead a few days later. It appeared that she had been strangled, taken out to sea, weighted, and dropped off a boat. Her grandfather is a wealthy and powerful figure and has been hounding us and doing his own personal investigation. In response, we are more careful to see that people do not drink so much, and we have asked the waiters and bartenders to be very observant. No one here saw or knows what happened to the girl. The Texas executives swear that she was not with them after they left the bar. I don't think El Halcón believes them."

"El Halcón? I have heard of him. That is not a person I would want to cross."

"Exactly."

The conversation went on a bit longer. To avoid suspicion, Bardero avoided asking additional questions and learned little more of help, except that the president of the Texas company seemed to be most taken with the girl.

At the third hotel on Bardero's list, the subject of the death came up again. This hotel had heard of the problems involved in the death of Javiera Velasco Dominquez. As expected, few people in Los Cabos believed the story of the Americans.

"I have heard that one of the executives called an associate late at night and that a Mexican who worked for the company helping with the retreat's recreation made a late-night trip to the hotel. Our hotel now insists we know all the entertainment and consultants hired for any retreat. This particular associate runs a company that provides dune buggies and other special vehicles for competitions among guests of several hotels. I am not sure this person has a good reputation. He is an American expatriate, known to take drugs, and came to Los Cabos under suspicious circumstances. I have heard that El Halcón will have this man tortured and killed eventually, if necessary, to learn the truth. I believe he will do so no matter what. Everyone involved is living on borrowed time. Sooner or later, El Halcón will call the loan. Our hotel does not want to be involved in anything like this in the future."

By the end of his two days, Bardero and his associate had a relatively clear picture of the incident. They flew separately to Santiago de Queretaro and then drove together to share information. By the time Bardero returned home, he had a relatively clear understanding of what was known about Javiera Velasco Dominquez's death.

When Bardero returned to San Miguel, he immediately wrote his report. In his report to Ahn, Bardero made the following points.

There is no question but that Lance DuFort was taken with the girl, who had a reputation as being the promiscuous member of a rich and powerful family. She felt she could get away with anything because of her grandfather's power. The girl was with DuFort for most of the evening. At least one bartender thinks they left together at one point. He does not remember when.

The coroner determined that the girl had been strangled before she was put in the water. She did not drown. Interestingly, the coroner believes the girl had intercourse shortly before her death.

After leaving with or without Lance DuFort (memories differ on this important fact), the girl was never seen again. Whether they went for a walk on the beach or to his room is unknown. It is unclear if DuFort saw the girl again after he left with Gilliland and Melton, if their testimony is to be believed. The police in Los Cabos have no reason to think she went to any other bars later in the evening. Her friends testified that she never returned to their hotel rooms that evening. They assumed she was with a man.

El Halcón is aware of the facts and determined to investigate further. He does not accept DuFort, Gilliland, or Melton's testimony as accurate. He believes that they are covering up something.

The person who arranged the daily executive activities has left Los Cabos allegedly on a vacation trip to Brazil. It will be interesting to see if he returns. He appears to be hiding.

There was little more to report as a result of the visit. Bardero himself did not believe the story told by the E-Titan executives. However, he kept it to himself in the report.

❄

When Bardero arrived in San Miguel de Allende, he was saddened to discover Maria Mendoza was planning to leave. The next morning, they had a short conversation before she left, during which he gave her a sealed envelope to be delivered to Ahn Winchester upon her return.

"My son, Manny, has become ill, and my mother is distressed. Therefore, I must leave. I am not finished reviewing the books. If Ahn wishes, I will return to finish this project when possible. Perhaps I can finish from Houston."

Bardero chose his following words very carefully.

"I am very sorry to see you go. This envelope contains a memorandum for Ahn. I would appreciate it if you could deliver it to her as soon as possible."

Handing her the envelope, he paused before continuing.

"I very much hope that you can return. I would like to invite you and your son to visit. I can assure you that I will be more available to show you our lovely city and the surrounding area, including my vineyard."

Their eyes met one last time before an awkward goodbye. Bardero was doubtful he would see her again.

Some things are possible, and some things are impossible. It is best not to dwell on the impossible.

For her part, Maria Mendoza thought to herself, *What a nice man! It is too bad we live hundreds of miles apart in different countries.* Years of loneliness had hardened her to illusions and disappointment. She had a child to care for and needed to get home.

144

(10)

FUNNY NUMBERS

FIRST FATEFUL STEP

HOUSTON, TEXAS

SEPTEMBER 1995

JUST AFTER E-TITAN WAS FORMED, and while it was registering a public offering to raise money for expansion, Lance had been faced with a crisis. He originally had been an investment banker, not a manager. He had never actually been a trader, having moved from law school to a large corporate law firm in Houston. During a break late one evening at a printer in Houston, waiting for the final proof of a prospectus to return, an investment banker from New York remarked on his understanding of the deal and asked a fateful question.

"Have you ever considered changing sides and working on Wall Street? Someone with your background and ability would find Wall Street a lot more fun and profitable than repeatedly churning out legal documents for similar transactions. I make more money in my annual bonus than you make in a year."

They began to talk. Lance revealed that his father had worked for a large French oil company. His family had lived all over the world, including Texas. He was fluent in English and French and knew a little German and Italian. Lance had never really liked Texas, but he got into the University of Texas at Austin School of Law, made Law Review after his first year, and graduated with good grades. His best of several job offers at significant firms was from Vinson & Elkins in Houston. His parents were living there at the time. He took the job almost without thinking. It is what successful law students do.

The investment banker listened intently, seeing in Lance someone he could use. Even then, Lance exuded a certain amoral flexibility that some people find useful. Finally breaking in, he suggested a way forward.

"Lance, when I return to New York, I will talk to the executive committee. If they agree, I will send you an offer. You can take it or leave it."

The offer was for more than Lance had made or would make for some time practicing law. Lance accepted the offer and moved to New York.

Because of his Texas background, he was often assigned to projects in Texas. He had worked on various oil- and gas-related projects, insurance, and other areas. Lance knew Arthur Stone from law school. Both were on Law Review. The urbane Lance always felt superior to the likable son of a small-town pastor, with his friendly smile, outgoing personality, and tendency to prefer poker to studying for exams. They met again when Arthur, after a stint clerking for a federal district judge and working for the Texas attorney general, ended up at Winchester & Wells working on the infamous "Marshland Transaction."

The transaction, conceived near the end of the Texas banking crisis of the 1980s, involved merging two savings and loan associations and forming a public partnership to dispose of unwanted properties. At the time, it was one of the most complex securities transactions ever conceived. Interestingly, a former Wall Street investment banker dreamed up the deal.

The Marshland Transaction never closed (costing Lance's investment banking firm a considerable fee), but somehow, Arthur Stone emerged unscathed and respected by the partners of Winchester & Wells. Within just over a year, he was a partner, married to Gwynn. From the first moment he met Gwynn Stone, Lance wanted her. It was not until she was his that he understood he just wanted to defeat and humiliate Arthur Stone.

In any case, not long after forming E-Titan, Lance began to realize that his fateful mistake had been moving from investment banking to management. Investment bankers put together deals, make a fee, and move on to the next deal. Managers are stuck with the reality of the business they create, own, or manage. Mark-to-market accounting worked fine in the banking and investment industries, but it was flawed as a measure of profit in an operating company. It did not take long for Lance to realize that he lacked the temperament to run a large and growing company. It took a lot longer for him to realize that his entire business plan was fatally flawed. By then, it was too late.

DuFort vividly recalled the day Brad Gilliland walked into his office to discuss a trade E-Titan called "Tarantula." Tarantula was conceived as a bet on declining gas prices in the northeast. E-Titan had contracted to supply gas to the northeastern utility at a fixed price sure that the price of gas would fall. Surprisingly, the price rose—significantly. E-Titan had already "marked-to-market" the contract and booked years of unrealized and potentially nonexistent profits. Under the same accounting principles, it would need to book five years of losses at current market value. The considerable loss was more staggering because a trader had exceeded his authority and magnified the loss.

"Lance, I have to visit with you about Tarantula. The news is bad. The losses in Tarantula cannot be overcome this year. We will have to book a loss, and the loss is going to be over $100,000,000. The losses previously reported to you were understated. Rodion Morozov, one of the traders hired last year, engaged in a series of margin trades that vastly increased his losses and ours. He was not the only person involved."

Lance grimaced.

"That can't be true. Please tell me it is not true."

"It is true."

"How could that happen?"

"Lance, I don't want to seem critical, but the truth is, our systems and controls for trader fraud prevention are not adequate, and the 'pit bosses' that run the trading operation are not enforcing them. The so-called Risk Management Team lacks your authority and backing to say 'No.' The result is that the traders are running wild. This is not the first time this has happened. In the other cases, the losses were small, or there were later profits, and the violator actually got a bonus for breaking the rules. There needs to be a change."

"OK, I will look into it."

This was Lance's typical response when he intended to do nothing. Lance was not nearly as self-assured as his exterior demeanor indicated. His father had been harsh with him. He avoided confrontation and did not know how to confront people needing to improve in the quiet way good managers always adopt.

Gilliland continued.

"This loss will have terrible consequences. As you know, our trading operation requires extensive lines of credit. A loss of this size will trigger defaults in most of them. Frankly, it could easily take E-Titan under. If we cannot borrow, we cannot trade. If we cannot trade, we cannot earn money and overcome this loss. It is that simple."

Lance looked down, then asked his question with a desperate look.

"What can we do?"

Gilliland looked down. He did not like suggesting what he was about to suggest.

"I've looked at our assets. When DD allowed you to form E-Titan, he put several legacy assets of Dawson Corporation into the new company. One of them, Battle Mountain Pipeline Company, is on our books for next to nothing. It was among the first pipelines that DD's father built. It is worth well over $100,000,000—a sum we cannot get in a quick sale before year-end. Buddy Bennett is anxious to get out of E-Titan and the Dawson Corporation. He is tired of the internal politics and having to ride herd on you. He will buy Battle Mountain, which will generate a gain large enough to overcome the loss. Our assets will fall, but not enough to bring us into any default on our lines of credit for trading. It is the only way out of the problem I can see."

Lance went into crisis mode. The traders worked overtime to minimize the loss, but the loss was too significant to cover with profitable trades. Then, Lance convinced DD to sell Battle Mountain Pipeline to Buddy. The gain on that sale covered the loss for the fiscal year in question.

Unfortunately, the transaction with Buddy led to the bad habit of covering losses by selling assets.

THE YEARS BETWEEN 1995 AND the end of 2000 were some of the most exciting years in Houston's business history. Houston had been deeply wounded by the real estate and savings and loan crises and the collapse of most of its major banks. A lot of business moved elsewhere. In particular, the banking business, the circulatory system of any economy, was no longer run from Houston but from California, New York, Illinois, North Carolina, and other places.

Financially, Houston became a bit of a backwater. First, the oil business recovered from its doldrums, and new companies were formed and grew. The emergence of companies like Enron and E-Titan changed everything. All of a sudden, the old Texas swagger was back. The times were good. People were making money. Bonuses were big. Expense accounts were liberal. A new Texan with West Texas swagger was in the White House.

Unfortunately, no one was paying much attention to where this was all leading. In this enthusiasm, accountants turned a blind eye to lousy accounting that did not reflect reality. Analysts on Wall Street ignored difficulties in financial reports. Money center banks loaned money for marginal transactions. Lawyers created vehicles for transactions that lacked financial reality. This was especially true at E-Titan. Lance used his contacts on Wall Street to grow E-Titan at astronomical rates—growth rates that no serious investor should have believed. But they did. Everyone forgot the old maxim, "If it is too good to be true, it isn't."

Years later, one of the architects of the final growth of E-Titan (its lead trader) put it this way:

"Postmodernism is popular on college campuses these days. One principle of postmodernism is that human beings can and do create reality through language. That is what we did at E-Titan. Accounting rules and financial statements involve the language of mathematics. We made the mistake of believing that we could just create our own reality and that whatever that reality was would one day be real. We didn't stop to think that it would come crashing down on us all since it wasn't true. The question was never 'if.' The question was always 'when.' We were just too arrogant to see it coming.

"I remember Brad Gilliland telling me one day, as we created another Cheetah and took more assets and debt off our balance sheet, 'I think we might be forgetting that when Judgment Day arrives, everyone will have to go to cash accounting. That includes E-Titan.' I didn't remember Brad saying that until Judgment Day arrived—at least as it pertained to E-Titan.

"We thought we were supermen. We were making all these trades, and we were making big money. Our bonuses were huge. Who cared about the accounting? Who cared about the financial statements? Who cared about the pension plans investing in our stock or the fate of those leaving E-Titan stock to their aging spouses? Somewhere along the line, we lost our moral bearings.

"After a time, we began believing our Lance DuFort-created false reality. We came to believe that the illusions created by mark-to-market accounting were true. (Or, maybe we just wanted to believe it was true, or we would not have been able to live with ourselves.) Here is the bitter truth: after E-Titan failed, and the bankruptcy lawyers and managers reconstructed and restated all the transactions, they became convinced that E-Titan never made much money on a continuing basis. It was all smoke and mirrors."

The financial merry-go-round went on for almost a decade. Every quarter, E-Titan produced astounding results on paper. Using its magical accounting, E-Titan earnings-per-share grew and continued to grow. DD and Lance were darlings of Wall Street. On paper, DD was one of the wealthiest people in the world. Lance was considered a financial and business genius. Correspondingly, E-Titan's stock price rose to unsustainable levels, fueled by an expectation of enormous future growth. Trading in gas and other forms of energy, including electricity, became an utterly amoral free-for-all—a free-for-all in which those with the most creative and devious minds made the most money.

The bonus structure at E-Titan was designed to take full advantage of human greed. Every time a deal was closed, it was marked to market. That is to say, a deal that might take five years to pay out was marked-to-market so that all the profits were recognized on the front end. Bonuses, including Lance DuFort's bonus, were based upon this mark-to-market accounting. Benny Morrelli remembered it this way:

"We might close the deal on Monday, which would involve providing energy to a city for over five years at a fixed price. Built into that was an expectation that we would make a specific rate of return. We just marked that rate of return to the market, discounted it for present value, and booked it. At the end of the quarter, I got a big check. No one stopped to wonder whether or not this was all going to work out in the end. Most of the time, not surprisingly, we overestimated the profits.

"No one cared where this would all end. Everyone was making a lot of money. Some of the traders were retiring early. They were the lucky ones. They had their stock. They had their cash. What happened next was none of their business. At least, that's the way the traders and senior management looked at it. They never considered the investors, the widows whose husbands left them E-Titan stock, the pension plans that invested in E-Titan, or even E-Titan employees, who had most of their retirement tied up in its stock. After all, they were Supermen (and Superwomen). They didn't have to play the rules.

"Lance was mesmerizing. He'd been a lawyer, and he'd been an investment banker. But he didn't understand business. He didn't have the kind of mind that thinks beyond the current deal. He didn't have any capacity to think about where all this was leading. He was incapable of creating a disciplined trading structure. He just cheered the rest of us on. And we wanted to be cheered. We did deal after deal, some good and some bad. If it was a good deal, we made money. If it was a bad deal, we moved it into a Cheetah; it didn't matter. We always made money."

JUDGMENT DAY BEGINS
HOUSTON, TEXAS
JULY 2001

THE BEGINNING OF THE END arrived inauspiciously. Certainly, no one expected what happened to occur, which, as with most tragedies, is why it was able to happen in the first place. One Monday morning, when there was not a lot of news, the *Wall Street Journal* decided to publish an article revealing that Wall Street banks were concerned about the exposure of certain companies to restatements of the financial results of certain SPEs in the event of a recession. This was hardly news. Every bank worries about exposures "in the event of a recession." Near the end of the article, the editors mentioned that banks were especially concerned about their exposure to certain unconventional SPEs related to the energy business in Texas. This meant E-Titan, among others.

Deep in the bowels of investment firms specializing in short trading, a few skeptics began looking into the fine print of the companies' financial statements, including E-Titan's. They did not like what they found. One analyst put it this way:

"When I began to dig deep into E-Titan's financial statements, I found that they did not make much sense. In particular, they seemed to have been written not to disclose the reality of its financial situation but to hide it. It was virtually impossible to understand what was happening in the business."

Then, one of the most respected short-sellers on Wall Street took a position and issued an analysis critical of E-Titan's accounting. Other short-sellers began shorting the shares of E-Titan. Ever so slowly, the shares started to decline in value. In response, the banks asked for more E-Titan treasury shares to be put into the collateral pool, which E-Titan quietly did. This, however, could not continue forever. Fortunately, E-Titan had a good quarter; the shares went back up after a dip. However, at a management meeting, one of the traders asked, "What happens if the shares fall too much?"

That got a few insiders thinking.

E-Titan may have to issue more shares to collateralize loans, which will cause a price decline, which might require more shares to be deposited, which would cause a price decline. If this goes on too long, the company will collapse.

Insiders began to sell their shares. This is never a good sign.

In London, one of the most famous hedge funds, a firm owned by a mysterious person who had often brought down currencies and companies, began to short E-Titan's stock on a much larger level. Lance, for his own reasons, viewed this as a betrayal. Publicly, he pumped the stock:

"E-Titan has never been stronger than it is today. Our trading markets are unparalleled. Our profit-making capacity is greater than any company in our industry. Next quarter, we will report even larger profits than in the past."

The only problem with his public statements was that they were not entirely true. Inside E-Titan, even the traders, usually the most confident group in the company, began to wonder where this would end. Lance himself did not seem to believe his bluster. He began to drink more heavily. He spent long periods out of the office and out of Houston.

E-Titan shares had a pendulum-like cycle for the next few months. The shorts had the advantage for a time, and the stock declined. Then Lance announced a new initiative or deal, and the stock increased for a while. This see-saw effect had some positive results—the smaller short sellers lost money during the upturns, and some stopped shorting the stock. This eased the pressure on the company.

The second event would also have been minor under most circumstances. Benny Morrelli began demanding more compensation and power within E-Titan "because of the risks I am taking." Some of the newer financial people started to wonder what those risks might be. Brad Gilliland was forced to review the Cheetah transactions to ensure he understood them. (It was a matter of common knowledge on Wall Street and within E-Titan that no one understood its capital structure or financing, least of all the Cheetahs). Brad did not like what he saw.

One night, while he was with Marjorie on a trip to Las Vegas, he voiced his concerns.

"I was uncomfortable when Benny first came up with this, but others in the industry were doing it. Arthur Andersen was signing off on a similar structure at Enron, and it seemed that we were complying with the letter of the rules that govern SPEs. Nevertheless, I am worried that the entire thing might collapse and take E-Titan with it if things get bad enough on Wall Street or with our banks."

M&M, who did not like to talk business in bed, shrugged her smooth, round shoulders, leaned over and kissed him, and told him not to worry. Gilliland looked at her and decided not to think about E-Titan until morning.

"Don't worry, honey. DD has this under control."

On that particular trip, Marjorie left Las Vegas a day earlier than Gilliland, who was partially there for a meeting of accountants and to get some continuing education for accountants. He decided to attend a session on SPEs. He listened quietly in the back of the room. As time went on, his fears began to subside until the speaker mentioned the three percent capital requirement.

"There have been rumors that certain companies have tried to avoid the capital requirements by arranging for loans to fund the general partner's interest. In some cases, sponsors have arranged this with participating banks. In at least one case, there are rumors that the money to repay the loan was distributed to the general partners shortly after the SPE was formed. Naturally, any such activities would cast in doubt the independence of the SPE and might require the debt of the SPE to be reflected on the parent company's balance sheet."

Gilliland made a mental note to check up on this. When he did, he realized that Benny and Marjorie had borrowed most of the money for their initial capital contributions and almost immediately received distributions from the Cheetahs greater than their original investment. He also heard rumors about side deals. One of E-Titan's bankers let the existence of the side deals be known.

"We are not worried because Dobie and Lance have guaranteed we won't lose money and will make an outstanding return no matter what happens."

That slip of the tongue was the last straw. Gilliland now believed that the SEC would demand a restatement if ever there was trouble. His rough calculations showed that the restatement would almost certainly take down E-Titan unless DD invested a massive amount of his net worth.

Gilliland thought to himself, *We are not in "the strongest position ever," as Lance proclaims. Instead, we are a house of cards.*

11

ROLLING THE DICE

ROULETTE IN LAS VEGAS

LAS VEGAS, NEVADA

OCTOBER 2001

AFTER HE LEFT HEATHER GILLILAND'S home, Ben Stone began having his employees watch Marjorie Melton. Of course, it would have been entirely illegal to tap her phone, but interestingly enough, Ben arranged to have access to transcripts of her phone conversations. After all, this was a murder investigation with international repercussions. His friends were delighted to help.

In September of the year, he finally hit pay dirt. He was not surprised when it was reported that M&M had arranged to spend a few days in Las Vegas. As she explained to the in-house travel agent, "It has been a busy time at the office, and I couldn't get away when I wanted to, but now I have a few days and just want to get away from Houston—besides, I have some business to take care of."

Ben called his son, who ran the detective agency, and asked if he could use one of his contractors for a few days. The young man, who had been in the special forces and was now involved in the security business, was delighted to spend a few days in the world's gambling capital.

Ben spent the first few days in Las Vegas asking questions. He learned that M&M had been a showgirl who caught Dobie Dawson's attention. This was back when Dawson was a little bit less addicted to drugs and a bit more presentable. M&M sensed the potential for money. Big money. Her sugar daddy had arrived. She and Dawson became an item. DD recognized that Melton had brains and began using her for special projects, especially those where he needed a man to comply with his wishes. She was very successful. Over time, she became his confidante.

Even after there was nothing romantic about the relationship, Marjorie Melton was influential in the universe of Dobie. M&M became something between an ex-wife, a personal assistant, a troubleshooter, and a go-between, and the daughter DD never had. People who worked for his companies never fully understood the exact nature of their complex relationship. DD eventually brought her to Houston, where she became a top executive in the Dawson Corporation. M&M made a lot of money from her relationship with Dobie. She did not even have to marry him to do it. Majorie Melton was a girl who knew how to capitalize on her assets.

The little group of investigators had been watching M&M for a few days when she arranged to see her banker to empty a safety deposit box. They managed to listen in on the conversation.

"I don't get here often, and I need to move the contents of my safety deposit box from Las Vegas to Houston. I wouldn't say I like getting on an airplane to get something I need in Houston. I would like to close this account with the bank."

The bank agreed.

❄

On the morning in question, Marjorie got up, put on her very best outfit—the one most likely to charm any bank official—and went to the bank. When she arrived, she talked with her bank officer, signed a few documents, went to the safety deposit box, and studied its contents.

This all needs to go away when I return to Houston.

After reviewing the documents, she emptied the safety deposit box into an elegant, expensive, feminine leather suitcase she had brought, said goodbye to her banker, and walked out the front door. Ten steps down the street, she was hit from behind by a male running at top speed. The male expertly grabbed the bag and continued running. Marjorie ran after him, but he was gone when she turned the next corner.

M&M filed a police report, returned to her apartment, and called Dobie Dawson.

"Dobie, something has happened. I have a safety deposit box here in Las Vegas. The contents are mostly personal, but some items relate to the Dawson Corporation business, including E-Titan. I decided I wanted to move the box to Houston. I went to the bank this morning and emptied the contents into a suitcase. As I was leaving the bank, it was stolen. Frankly, I don't believe it was an accident. The person who stole it simply disappeared. I think this was a professional job. The person was probably just after the money and jewels, but I cannot be sure. The police are looking for who did this, but my guess is they will not. I think I need some help."

There was silence on the other end of the line.

"Darling, I'll contact my friends in the Las Vegas police department. I also have a detective agency I use in Las Vegas. I'll look around. Now, tell me, exactly what was in that satchel?"

M&M was not anxious to answer this question.

"As I said, some of the contents were personal. Letters. Some of the contents were business documents that I thought should be kept for a time. . . ."

There was a pause before she went on.

"DD. Some documents concern my relationship with Brad Gilliland and what transpired in Los Cabos."

"I see. It would be best if you flew to Mexico as soon as possible. We need to talk."

"I will grab the first flight in the morning."

She hung up and began making arrangements to fly to Acapulco.

DD, despite his oddities, was not stupid. He went out on his balcony, thought long and hard for a few minutes, and then made a few phone calls.

It was late the next day before M&M managed to arrive in Acapulco. A driver picked her up at the airport and drove her to the hotel. She was shown to her room, showered, dressed, and went to have dinner with DD. Conscious of her looks and the power it gave her over men (even older men in poor health), she wore a light blue, floral Mexican sun dress with a plunging neckline. The lipstick she chose was a deep red.

It was bittersweet to be with DD. They had a fling when she was still a showgirl in Las Vegas. After a time, his unusual habits annoyed her enough that she gradually moved away from DD on a personal level while managing the delicate task of becoming one of his trusted assistants. She eventually accomplished the impossible. No one ever had as much influence with DD as Marjorie Melton, not a wife, not a movie star, no one.

M&M lacked a professional degree in business and long experience, but she had a quick and unusually mathematical mind. DD came to rely on her. After a while, their relationship was almost like that of a father and daughter or brother and sister. DD was unable to have a healthy relationship with a woman, a fact of which he was blissfully unaware. However, DD was human. He needed human relationships. So, he bought them. Only two of them amounted to anything. Buddy had been one until he left the company, and M&M was another. Beyond Buddy and M&M, DD had employees and servants. He did not have friends.

Usually, DD ate on what might be called "DD Time." He would call room service at any time of the day or night. Since he owned the hotel, he was always accommodated. He never dressed for meals. It was a testimony to his feelings for M&M that, when she entered his apartment and was shown to the dining room, he was clean and showered, his beard was trimmed, and he was dressed in a tuxedo with a Stuart-plaid cummerbund. He looked as good as a seventy-five-year-old drug addict could look. He smiled and showed her to the table. After a few minutes and hors d'oeuvres, the real conversation began.

"Marjorie dear, tell me exactly what was in your safety deposit box and what happened."

"As I said on the telephone, I have had a safety deposit box in Las Vegas for many years. The box contains a bit of jewelry, my will, and personal items, including letters and memoranda. Some of them, I don't think anyone else should see."

"Does any of that have anything to do with me or Dawson Corporation?"

"Not directly." (This was not strictly true.)

I need to give him a version so close to the truth that he will not be suspicious that I am lying.

"There were some letters in the box that Brad Gilliland wrote to me."

She looked out the window just long enough to decide what version of the truth she needed to tell. DD would catch a lie. A half-truth was different.

"Brad and I were lovers. He wrote me letters. Most of the contents are private, but some contain comments about E-Titan's business. For example, Brad was worried about this litigation with Buddy. He did not think we would win and was concerned it might harm the company. He was also worried about the way the Cheetahs were structured."

DD nodded. "I am worried as well."

"At the time Brad died, our relationship was not good. Initially, he would talk about leaving Heather and the two of us being together. After Los Cabos, things changed. The death of that girl, Javiera Velasco, changed him."

"Is the death of Javiera Velasco referred to in those documents?"

"Not directly."

There was another pause. M&M had hoped to avoid the subject of Javiera.

I need to be careful.

"The night Javiera died went down differently than Lance, Brad, and I told the authorities. We were all three in Lance's suite, talking and having a few drinks. Javiera was not with us. That much is true. After a time, Lance decided to go to bed. Brad and I left. Then, in the middle of the night, Brad got a call from Lance. He got up and left. He was gone for a long time. I went to my room. The following day, Lance announced that Javiera was missing and the group would return to Houston. I could see that Brad was tense when we left. Lance was very upset—almost irrationally frantic.

"The deal is, we do not know where Lance was all night. I don't know where Brad went when he left the room. All I know is that we left in a big hurry for fear of harassment by the Mexican authorities, or at least that's the reason Lance gave."

DD looked troubled.

"This is not good news. Javiera's grandfather is a very powerful person in Mexico. His influence is felt in Texas, Washington, DC, and beyond. He has vowed revenge on whoever killed his granddaughter. He is more than capable of reaching Lance, you, or me."

M&M sat in silence, hoping DD would end this time of disclosure. She felt DD was getting too close and already knew too much. M&M was fearful that there was more to his silence than she wished to know. They were close, but nothing was closer to DD than his money and Dawson Corporation.

What if, after Brad and I left, Lance reconnected with Javiera? What if she resisted his advances, and he ended up strangling her? What if Brad, Lance, and the guy from the rental company ditched the body in the sea?

The thought only had to go through M&M's mind once before she thought, *I'll bet that's what happened.*

It was a while before DD responded.

"I said I would help, and I will. I have been in contact with the police in Las Vegas. They have no line on the bag. The jewelry was fenced within hours. The other contents might have simply been put in a trash bin and are now under a pile of garbage in Las Vegas. Unfortunately, another possibility is that someone has that information. If they do, you can expect to be contacted. If you are contacted, please call me. There is one last possibility—that is that this is tied up with Gilliland's death. There are several people, including El Halcón, who have an interest in the death of Brad

Gilliland. I am told that Winchester & Wells is looking into this. I wish to God that Lance had never gotten us into this.

"Stay here for a few days and relax. We will see each other again. When you return to Houston, do not tell anyone you have been here, but stay in touch."

M&M nodded her thanks. She did stay a few days. She and DD did talk again, and when she returned to Houston, she said nothing.

INTERESTING INFORMATION
HOUSTON, TEXAS
OCTOBER 2001

AFTER SNATCHING THE CONTENTS OF the safety deposit box, Ben Stone and his associates boarded an airplane to Houston in less than six hours. First, the bag's contents were dumped into a backpack, and the bag was destroyed. The jewelry they found was discreetly fenced to ensure this would be considered a robbery. No one would trace the bag or its contents. Ben was concerned that DD was wealthy and well-connected enough to access the flight information about every person who took a flight from Las Vegas to Houston that day. Therefore, Ben Stone returned to Houston through Denver; everyone else went through another city, Dallas and Kansas City. Everyone traveled on false IDs. There wouldn't be much to tie them together. But that did not help in the end.

When Ben arrived in Houston, he went home, took the contents from the backpack, and began studying them. It wasn't long before he whistled.

This is going to be big. It is going to be big on several levels.

The following day, he went into the office and copied the contents of the safety deposit box. He kept one copy, put a second in his safety deposit box, made a third copy for Roger Romny, and created one last copy for the police.

Arthur was funny about certain things. Ben knew Arthur to be something of a Boy Scout. He didn't want to show Arthur the contents of the safety deposit box in Las Vegas before he talked to Roger Romny. He made an appointment to see Romny. It was just after noon before they were able to meet. Arthur was out of town on another case. That was fortunate. He would have asked too many questions.

He was shown into Romny's office, just down the hall from Arthur's. Roger was a functionalist and a minimalist. The office contained the minimum amount of furniture and artwork necessary to be seen as the office of the managing partner of an important firm. The chairs, desk, and seating were strictly modern and functional. They sat at a small, circular conference table sufficient for no more than three or four people.

"Roger, I wanted to come and see you about some information that I've come into that pertains to your Battle Mountain litigation and other matters. I can't tell you exactly how I got it, and I'm not able to allow you to show it to anyone else. It can't be delivered as part of a court filing. However, when you read these documents, you'll see a way for Battle Mountain to win its litigation against E-Titan."

Roger held out his hands.

"I assume you came to see me because you didn't want to involve Arthur in this."

"That is correct."

"I assume you didn't show these to Thomas Mallory because you know he would show them to Arthur."

"That is correct."

Roger nodded and shuffled his way through the documents. Once or twice, he stopped to take one of the documents out of the stack and look at it more closely. Finally, he looked up.

"I do not know what to tell you. The information certainly is relevant to our litigation involving Battle Mountain. Some might best be sold to a scandal rag like the *National Enquirer*. Unfortunately, some of the information is relevant to a murder investigation. I think you will have to find a way to get it into the hands of the police. And, under no circumstances will you involve Winchester & Wells or Arthur Stone in this."

"I know."

"Exactly how do you intend to get this into the hands of the authorities?"

"I'm going to take a trip to New York City. When I get there, I will mail an envelope to the police in Houston. They will be able to explain how they got it if they must. In any case, no one will know they got it from me. Even then, they will not be able to use the evidence.

"The more complex question is how you will use the information that indicates malice and deliberate deceit were involved in E-Titan's filing of its litigation against Battle Mountain?"

Roger nodded. He did not like it when he had to keep things from Arthur, nor did he like being in the position he was in—and not for the first time.

"I will have to give this some thought. We cannot enter into evidence information that we received illegally. It is best if you take the information you have provided me and put it into your safety deposit box."

"OK. Can we keep this between ourselves just for now?"

"For now."

After Ben left, Roger closed his door and thought for a long time. When he finished, he picked up his phone.

"Penny, can you see if Thomas Mallory can come and visit me for a few minutes? I need someone to do some research. When Thomas entered the room, Roger asked him to sit down.

"TL, I have an unusual request. Please do a bit of research for me. This does not need to involve anyone but me. As you know, we have been investigating the possibility that Lance DuFort or someone at E-Titan might have been involved in the death of Brad Gilliland. If we discover information relevant to the murder inquiry, what are our obligations to disclose what we have learned to the police? Is it enough to see that the information reaches the authorities, or must we disclose it ourselves?"

TL thought for a moment.

"Roger, from my time in the JAG Corps and law school, I think that attorney-client privilege protects the confidentiality of communications between clients and their attorneys. It allows clients to confidently share sensitive information, knowing that these communications cannot generally be disclosed to others without the client's consent. However, attorney-client privilege has its limitations. It doesn't protect some conversations, for example, if you plan to commit a crime or voluntarily share the information with a third party." TL paused a moment. "In this case, is the source of the information a client?"

"No, it is an independent contractor we hired to investigate the potential that a crime was committed by a company we oppose in litigation."

"I don't think we need to disclose the information we received from a private investigator working for the firm, but I will confirm it."

Roger was pleased by the information.

"If you can confirm this, I would appreciate it."

"I see. I will look into it. Do you know if the crime we think may have been committed is likely to be committed again?"

"No. But, I would not think it likely."

"That is good news. Things might be different if we thought a crime might be committed in the future."

The conversation continued long enough for Roger to ensure that Arthur did not need to know about the research. It was a private inquiry. As it turned out, it might have been better if Arthur had known.

FRIENDLY ADVICE
HOUSTON AND SAN ANTONIO, TEXAS,
OCTOBER 2001

WHILE BEN STONE, THOMAS MALLORY, and Roger Romny conversed, Arthur Stone was having lunch with Patrick Armbruster at the Hallmark near Houston Galleria. Presbyterians built the Hallmark with the help of a legendary Houston real estate investor, but it was open to all. It was known to be one of the finest facilities in Houston, especially when someone needed special care. Patrick's wife had needed special care when they moved to the Hallmark, and when she passed away, he stayed.

Elderly men are at a premium in such facilities, and Patrick became a favorite. He played a mean game of bridge and was a much-sought-after bridge partner for many a widow. Patrick no longer got out much, so he and Arthur ate in the Hallmark dining room. Eventually, the conversation involved the firm, in which Patrick had an undying interest.

"So, how are things going with the firm?"

"Houston has recovered from the big crash of the 1980s, but there is a lot of competition. Most of our competitors have grown, merged, or opened new offices. I have been fighting it, but I don't know for how long. We regularly get outbid for talent."

"That is interesting, but I was thinking about this Battle Mountain case."

"Why Battle Mountain?"

"Frankly, I am hearing things. I am an old man, but I have a few contacts left, even at my age. You would be surprised what I learn over a few drinks at the Hallmark—and occasionally elsewhere."

Arthur smiled indulgently. "So, what have you learned?"

"This fellow, Lance DuFort, I think he is 'moving too fast in the passing lane,' as they say. He is headed towards a head-on crash with reality. I know you still care about Gwynn, even if you try to hide it by being mad at her most of the time. Lance is a big lady's man. My experience in business is that if a man cheats on his wife, he will cheat on you.

"Rumors are Lance is cheating on Gwynn, using 'creative accounting' to massage his income statements, and cutting corners to show profits for Wall Street. I have sold all my stock in Enron, E-Titan, and other energy traders. I cannot understand their financial statements, nor can my broker. If I can't understand it, I don't invest—especially if I dislike management. Between you and me, I don't like the management of some of these companies."

Arthur looked down before speaking.

"Patrick, as you know, one of our clients has personally sued E-Titan and Lance, claiming he has been disparaging our title to Battle Mountain. In connection with that litigation, we have made some interesting discoveries. We are also now co-counsel for a group suing E-Titan, alleging their public filings are inaccurate and misleading. I stay in the background for the sake of Gwynn and the children. We have a non-Winchester & Wells lead counsel for the litigation in San Antonio. There is another lead counsel in Delaware in the securities litigation. However, you can bet I keep informed."

Patrick decided to get to the point.

"Arthur, you know that, for years and years, I was all in at the firm. I thought we were building something meaningful. I also felt I was doing something important and building an important reputation. I rarely worked less than seventy hours a week. For many years, I never even took a vacation. The law was my life.

"I realized I was mistaken when Jeanie got sick so soon after I retired. The firm was important, but Jeanie and the children were more important. She rarely complained, but everything we planned to do in retirement never happened. I had my priorities mixed up.

"You have been far more successful than I ever was. You are known throughout the nation. Most people think you are Texas's best litigator and corporate attorney. It makes me proud every time I hear your name. But you are fifty now. Soon, your children will be grown. As you have said, the law is changing, and there is every possibility that what we know as Winchester & Wells might not survive the changes. I would hate to see you at seventy alone and thinking, *It was not worth it.*

"I am an Irish Catholic. I still go to mass once a week. Our priest uses a message from St. Augustine in sermons at least once a year. It is about disordered love. Augustine felt that human beings love as primary, what are secondary things like power, success, possessions, and pleasure. In the process, we make love for God and other people secondary. Most of the world's problems come from loving the wrong things too much or the right things too little.

"I would hate for you to chase crown of victory after crown of victory for another twenty years or so, only to end up alone and empty. Plenty of men and women do. I did. Your family is more important than winning another case or even 100 other cases. You are a wealthy man and do not need to show how good you are to anyone ever again. Right now, your family needs you.

"I did not ask you to come and see me for no reason. What I hear about Lance's character is not good. You know better than me that E-Titan is a flaming missile. It remains to be seen whether it blows up or goes into orbit. My current bet is 'blows up before reaching orbit.' Your former wife and children could get hurt in the crash."

Arthur looked just as disturbed as he felt. He tried to tell his old friend as much as was prudent.

"I cannot tell you any details, but proving a case is more difficult than figuring out what is happening with a big, complicated company like E-Titan. People at the firm and experts have studied its financial statements, and I think I understand what has been happening, but I cannot be sure. More importantly, we currently lack enough proof that any massaging of financial statements was intentional or that Lance deliberately lied about the sale of Battle Mountain to be sure of victory at trial. We need more evidence."

Patrick, as always when giving Arthur advice he did not necessarily want to hear, was not to be put off so quickly.

"You need to think about Gwynn and the children. They are more important than this case. If what I hear is true, Lance is not a good husband, and it cannot be good for your children to be in that household more than necessary. It would be best to consider whether letting this situation continue without change is wise."

Arthur cut Armbruster off in mid-thought, something he rarely did.

"I agree. But Gwynn is a good mother. We talk. Even if I slowed down, I would still need a lot of help with the children. Gwynn would have to be involved a good deal."

Patrick was undeterred.

"This Gilliland murder is something to consider. I understand the police originally thought it was the wife, but they no longer believe she was involved. Others might have a motive, opportunity, and means. However, Lance DuFort is certainly a primary suspect. You haven't told me anything about the case, but it does not take a genius to ponder who might have paid for a hit the night before a deposition."

Arthur was a bit put out at Armbruster by now. He was going beyond the boundaries of "Old Business Friend and Colleague."

"Patrick, I am not a fool. From the beginning, I suspected Lance might be behind the killing. We have people working on that angle. Thus far, however, we have found nothing. Nothing."

Armbruster was aware that Arthur was tiring of his advice. He decided to retreat with honor.

"You have always had good judgment, and you have always put others before yourself. As successful as you are, you might have been even more successful if you were a bit more ruthless. It is an admirable quality. Just be careful. I don't trust Lance DuFort—and I don't trust Dobie Dawson, Jr. Never did. You shouldn't either. Be careful."

Arthur smiled.

"I will, old friend, I will. And, as soon as I decide what to do with all this good advice, I want you to come down to the firm and have lunch."

"I will be glad to come and see my old friends and make some new ones."

The conversation ended there. Arthur excused himself, but his drive back downtown from Tanglewood was troubled.

Patrick is right. I must do something to protect Gwynn and the children.

12

MANY MEETINGS

OFFICE OF THE HEAD OF THE MIDDLE SCHOOL
HOUSTON, TEXAS
NOVEMBER 15, 2001

YOU CAN PUT OFF DECISIONS, BUT the consequences are usually worse than if you dealt with a problem at the beginning. Old problems grow generally worse. There are exceptions to the rule, but ex-wives and children are not two of them. As time passed, Murray's behavior and Gwynn's concern worsened. Arthur, always inclined to make decisions at the last moment, waited and watched, hoping things would get better, all the while watching them get worse.

Complex litigations are notoriously slow. There are endless means of delay for a party inclined to delay. There are endless depositions that might be taken. There are endless motions to be argued, even occasionally an "interlocutory appeal," which means an appeal of a trial judge's ruling before the case is heard. In the case of <u>Battle Mountain Pipeline Co. vs. E-Titan Corporation and the Dawson Companies</u>, all of these factors and more came into play. Frankly, E-Titan and Dawson had little hope of success on the merits but needed time to cover other problems. These events and delays tested even Arthur's customary good humor.

It was an unusually frigid November morning when events came to a head, at least as far as Murray was concerned. Arthur was sitting in his kitchen having his usual breakfast of cereal and fruit when the phone rang. Outside, it was cold, humid, and raining hard. Gwynn, usually a model of grace in any crisis, was crying.

"Arthur, I need to see you today. Or rather, the principal at St. John's Middle School needs to see us today. They are going to expel Murray. He has been arrested."

The school had previously threatened Murray with expulsion, which was bad enough. An arrest was much, much worse. Knowing Gwynn was upset, he tried to keep his response calm.

"Tell me what happened."

"Apparently, Murray has been supplying drugs to his fellow students. He has been charging them, not just providing them drugs. Yesterday, an undercover policeman working at St. John's caught him in the act. He was arrested."

"He is fourteen."

"That did not seem to matter."

Gwynn stopped for a moment and then went on.

"The principal called me this morning. It is the school's policy to expel any student under these circumstances. I do not think we can talk them out of it."

"No. I doubt if we can. We are going to have to find another school."

"Finding another school will not be easy. I don't think any of the private schools in Houston will do it—not Episcopal School,

Kinkaid, the new Presbyterian Middle School, Second Baptist, or River Oaks Baptist. I cannot think of one, Arthur."

"I don't suppose they would consider delaying this until after the semester?"

"No."

Arthur was almost out of ideas.

"There is the Texas Military Academy in San Marcos and the Marine Military Academy in Harlingen. Frankly, none of them sound like Murray. What about the public schools? Don't they have to take everyone? Under the circumstances, it might be best to put him in public schools. A local school near my home might be a good choice. He could attend Lamar when he reaches high school."

Gwynn liked the last option on several levels. One excellent reason was that Murray would be living with his father. Arthur also thought of that, remembering his conversation with Patrick Armbruster. They agreed to meet at the principal's office at 11:00 and have lunch afterward in Arthur's office, where they could have privacy. Arthur made arrangements for lunch before he left for the meeting.

The head of middle school at St. John's was a nice-looking man in his early thirties. He had been a Latin and Classical Languages teacher before becoming head and had a doctorate in education. He seemed genuinely concerned about Murray. After introductions, he got down to the problem at hand.

"As both of you know, your son has had issues for some time. He has been difficult for his teachers. This is too bad because he is highly intelligent and would easily make outstanding grades even at a school as competitive as St. John's if he applied himself.

I have had many opportunities to meet with Murray. He is fundamentally a good kid. Unfortunately, he is not responding to our attempts to help him. Now, he has done something we simply cannot accept.

"We were happy when you had him begin seeing a counselor. Counseling does not always work, but it is an excellent place to start. Whatever happens, he should continue getting professional help. Both of you know he was the most injured by your divorce. He blames both of you for different reasons. Unfortunately, he blames Arthur the most, and a boy this age needs a good relationship with his father.

"Notwithstanding our feelings for him and your family, we must expel him after yesterday. I have confirmed this with the headmaster and the board as late as this morning. The fact that he was selling drugs to our students leaves us with no choice. If he were to do it again and a child was injured, we would both be liable and feel we had let down all the other students at St. John's."

Arthur, who had already decided not to attempt to contest the expulsion for the principal's reasons, nodded. "I guess we need to know two things: First, where do you recommend Murray attend for the time being? We talked this morning, and it seemed that our choice is between a public school near one of our homes or a private school specializing in similar situations. Second, would St. John's consider readmitting him if he sits out for a semester or two in another school?"

"It is premature to talk about the future. I do not think Murray would do well in a military school atmosphere. He might, but I think it is unlikely. There are, however, other schools that have programs specifically designed for situations like this. If you wish to keep him close to the two of you—and I think there are good reasons to believe that would be a good idea—then one of the local public schools might be okay.

"Here is what I would warn you about. This is not the first such situation I have handled. What matters most here is Murray. If he is unwilling to change and remains determined to be dysfunctional, then no school is the right school. If Murray is willing to change, then any school will be right. The key is to get Murray to a place where he recognizes that his situation is not his parents' fault or his school's fault but his fault. He needs to change."

Gwynn, who had been silent up to now, taking in everything, spoke up for the first time.

"What about the charges for dealing drugs?"

"Unfortunately, we at the school have no control over what happens there. From my limited experience, as a fourteen-year-old first-time offender, he is unlikely to go to jail. He will probably be sentenced to counseling, some community service, and be monitored."

He looked at both Arthur and Gwynn.

"I am sure the two of you will see that he has the best counsel possible."

Returning to the possibility of readmittance, Arthur asked his second question again.

"Can he ever return to St. John's?"

"I don't want to foreclose that possibility right now. On the other hand, generally, once one has a reputation at a school, it is not wise to return. Murray has a lot to deal with right now. Winks, teasing, and an occasional prejudiced teacher are probably not what he needs or will need. I can say that Murray is not the first St. John's student to be expelled for misbehavior. I know many who are now quite happy and successful in life. This is not the end for Murray. It is a new beginning, at least if his parents and he see it that way. Even after you leave today, I am happy to help in any way, especially in choosing his next school."

Arthur and Gwynn thanked the principal. In the parking lot, they agreed to meet for lunch in a few minutes. Arthur noted that Gwynn was crying as she pulled out of the parking place.

LUNCH FOR TWO
HOUSTON, TEXAS
NOVEMBER 15, 2001

When they arrived at Arthur's office, it was after 12:45. Roger, who knew about the meeting, met them in the hallway and walked with them to Arthur's office. When they arrived, he turned and, with compassion, said, "I think everything is ready for the two of you. We will see you are not interrupted. My prayers are with you."

One of the oddities of Roger Romny was the dramatic change in his personality when he recovered from the injuries he received in a car bombing that resulted in the death of Stephen Winchester. It did not happen suddenly, but Romny went from a high-risk carouser to a complete gentleman. Within the firm, he was unusually sensitive to the needs of the lawyers, partners, and staff.

Everyone at the firm thought his third wife, who everyone initially thought married him for money, would leave him. Instead, she began attending Second Baptist Church, joined something called "Bible Study Fellowship," and underwent a transformation. Roger started attending services and physical therapy shortly after he was released from the hospital. Over time, he, too, changed. It was there, and as a result of his marriage, that the old Roger Romny slowly became a different person.

Eventually, he and Arthur became friends. When Patrick retired and Arthur refused to become managing partner, Roger became managing partner. Arthur became chairperson of the executive committee. Over the years, they had worked together very well.

The small conference table in Arthur's office was just large enough for lunch for two. They sat down and began eating quietly. It was as if neither knew precisely where to start. Both feared the conversation would turn into a blame-filled shouting match, which both wanted to avoid for Murray's sake. It was Gwynn who broke the silence.

"Arthur, before I say anything else, this is my fault. I have seen it coming for a long time."

Gwynn looked down as if gathering the courage to say what was on her heart.

"Murray blames you for the divorce. I know that. We both know it was 90% my fault. I betrayed you, our children, and our marriage. I have tried to help him understand the situation while not destroying his respect for his mother. But I have failed."

With that, Gwynn broke down. Arthur reached across the table as he would have in earlier years and took her hand as gently as he knew how. He looked out the window, seeing that the cold rain had stopped, the clouds were parting, and the sky was turning clear and blue.

"D . . . (He caught himself before saying 'Dear') Gwynn, thank you for saying it, but we both know it is not that simple. I was full of myself and my career. I was also clueless about what you were going through, moving from being a lawyer with a career to being the mother of three children while still attempting to have some kind of legal practice. I did not appreciate your sacrifices to be a wife and mother. Most importantly, while I loved you, I did not attempt to understand and meet your needs. I knew your background and family but never really tried to understand. In my naive way, I just thought everything would work out as it did for my parents without my taking any steps to change. I was wrong."

All the anger, tension, and blame between them was dissipated in two short paragraphs spoken without rehearsal. Gwynn looked up and smiled for the first time in a long time. Arthur smiled back. Outside, a bright Houston early winter sun filled the office with a new brightness.

Gwynn looked at Arthur and made her proposal.

"Arthur, this is going to seem silly to you. But I have an idea. It won't be easy, but I think it can work if we try. I talked with Alicia (Alicia Mallory), and she agreed to continue the practice without me for the next few weeks. I can work at home until after the new year. Our kind of practice is usually not very busy at Christmas anyway. This will give you time to work out the details of Murray living with you if he agrees, which I think he will do."

Arthur interrupted.

"Gwynn, I don't know. I am a bachelor. There is no one in the house most of the time. I would have to hire a nanny or someone to be with him. He is difficult right now. I do not know if I could find someone who can handle the situation."

It was Gwynn's turn to speak.

"If he stays with me until January, you will have six weeks to find someone. It does not have to be a woman. It could be a man. The important thing is to find someone who can handle him. It might even be best if it were a man. Murray is challenging right now. The person could live in the garage apartment, which no one uses these days. I know it is asking a lot, but we can make it work."

Arthur noted the "we." It could be a woman, but Arthur did not like the idea of a young woman in the house alone. Of course, an older woman was possible. This gave Arthur yet another idea. He made a mental note to follow up on it.

"OK. I am not saying 'Yes,' but I will work on it. What about schools? Are you happy with him ultimately attending Lamar?"

"One reason I want him to live with you is that he would attend Lamar in High School, which I think is the best choice for him. We can tell him we love him and send him away, but I am not sure he will believe us in his heart of hearts. As a mother, I think it is best if we can keep him close to us."

Arthur then brought up the criminal charges.

"I have a friend who used to be with the Harris County District Attorney's Office. He was an outstanding criminal lawyer in the day and is now one of the best trial lawyers in the city, even the state. I will call him. He may have a recommendation. He might even take the case himself. With your approval, I will take responsibility for finding a lawyer for Murray."

Gwynn nodded. She delayed her answer as if the worst was yet to come. It was.

"Arthur, I have one last favor to ask. I have no right to ask it. But I think we should do it. Lance and I are going skiing for Christmas in Jackson Hole, Wyoming. We have rented a huge condominium in Teton Lodge, right on the slopes. It is ski in and ski out."

Arthur did not wait for her to finish, indicating that she was entering dangerous territory.

"Gwynn, there is no way I could stay in Jackson Hole in a house or condo with Lance for a week. We hate each other. We are also adversaries in not one but two different litigations. It would be a total disaster for you and the children."

Gwynn nodded. She expected this response.

"Yes. I know you and Lance cannot spend time together. However, there is a very quaint hotel in Jackson Hole called the Alpenhof Lodge. It is located right at the bottom of the lifts. At the "Big One." It has a nice bar and pretty good food. It is not part of a chain. I think you would like it. I spoke to them this morning. They are booked. However, I offered to rent another room for anyone they could move at any price. They are looking into it. The owners are quite nice. The wife is especially nice. She is trying to help me. If that does not work out, we will find you a place. The goal is for you to spend Christmas with your children."

Arthur reluctantly agreed to the idea, which he thought would make Christmas vacation a disaster. *This is going to make Chevy Chase's Christmas Vacation look tame.*

"If you can work out the details, I agree."

As it turned out, perhaps he should have paid attention to his instincts.

DETAILS AND DECISIONS
HOUSTON, TEXAS
NOVEMBER 2001

AFTER ARTHUR SHOWED GWYNN OUT and returned to his office, he called his friend who had worked with the DA. They knew each other well both from church and other community activities.

"Fred, I have a problem and need your advice. My son has gotten himself in trouble. It is kind of serious. He was pushing drugs, mostly marijuana, at St. John's. He was not discovered by the school but by an undercover operation. They arrested him, and he will face charges of some kind. He needs legal counsel. Can you recommend someone?"

They discussed the case details and Murray's status as a minor. Arthur tried not to ask for too great a favor from someone he admired greatly. After listening carefully, Fred made a suggestion.

"Let me look into this. I will find out where the case is at this point. We may be able to do something without much time and work being involved. Murray will have to plead guilty to some kind of charge and do some remedial work. Is he in counseling?"

"Yes."

"Good. I will mention that to the prosecutor. We may even be able to keep his record clean of a felony. But, Arthur, you understand, there are consequences. He may have issues. If he is clean for some years, we can expunge the record, but until we do, he may find some schools will not accept him, some scholarships will not be available, and some employers will simply not look at an application."

"I understand."

Out of law school, Arthur clerked for a federal judge and worked for the Texas Attorney General. He understood only too well.

After the conversation, Arthur decided to call Ahn Winchester to see if he could come by for a chat. He was too upset to work on anything complicated. He needed a drink with a friend and advice from someone he trusted. Ahn was a friend he trusted. Before he could make the call, Roger and Thomas Mallory knocked on the door.

"Can we come in?"

"Sure. Does it have to do with Battle Mountain?"

"Indirectly, yes."

The two came in and sat at the same conference table he and Gwynn used at lunch.

"How can I help?"

Thomas began.

"Arthur, I know this comes at a terrible time, but I must leave the firm for a while."

"What? You are my top guy. You can't leave."

"It is the army. You remember I was in the 101st Airborne. Because of the attack on 9-11, we are just about to invade Afghanistan. The army needs me. They have asked that I come back into active duty. I don't think I can refuse. As a lawyer, I have skills in helping the army comply with the laws of war. Perhaps more importantly, I have special combat skills that are useful in the type of warfare our soldiers will experience there. I would not feel right about refusing."

"I see."

Arthur slumped in his chair, thinking. Unfortunately, the answer he had to give was abundantly evident.

"Thomas, I know you have to do this. We will put you on a leave of absence. Given the nature of your duties, your absence will not set you back at the firm in any way. We just pray for your safe return."

The conversation turned to replacing Thomas with people with the same experience and capacity. In many cases, that was not too difficult. The litigation involving E-Titan was different. The case was very complex. Thomas had been the central intermediary between Eddie Morales, the lead trial lawyer in San Antonio, and Winchester & Wells. Eddie and Arthur Stone went back a long way. Thomas made the obvious suggestion.

"Eddie Morales can handle almost anything. Most of our work is related to legal research, document review, and taking a few of the depositions. The significant depositions remaining are those of Lance and the new CFO of E-Titan, Adrianna Wong. However, we have received mounds of documents in discovery. Some of the younger people here review and index them for trial.

"I think you must become a bit more involved in the case. Because we are close to a trial, you would have become more involved in any case. Roger may have to become more involved. The biggest thing is to get through the final discovery. I do not know if the case will ever go to trial. Frankly, I think the settlement time is near. In reviewing the documents, we found a few things that I believe you will find interesting."

At that point, Thomas pushed two documents across the table. One was a spreadsheet, and the other was a memorandum marked "Personal and Confidential." The spreadsheet was dated two months before the closure of the Battle Mountain Pipeline sale. Scribbled in a margin was the final purchase price number and the words, "At this price, Buddy will surely buy the company and close before year-end."

Arthur looked up.

"This is dated before Buddy was approached to buy Battle Mountain."

"Correct."

"The handwriting looks like Lance's."

"We have handwriting experts who will testify that it is Lance DuFort's handwriting."

Arthur nodded and turned to the memorandum.

The memorandum was from Brad Gilliland to Lance DuFort. It was dated just a few days before Lance's interview with the *Wall Street Journal*, in which he had indicated that Buddy had defrauded the Dawson Corporation concerning the purchase of Battle Mountain. The copy Arthur was reading contained the following paragraph:

In speaking to the press about this matter, it is essential to remember that you set the price at a meeting with me several days before we approached Buddy about purchasing the company. When we finished the meeting, several employees were briefed about the sale. At least three are no longer with the company and would undoubtedly testify that you set the price.

Arthur turned to look out the window, then turned to look at Roger.

"I think we have them. No San Antonio jury will believe E-Titan's case after this is read to them. Aren't we taking the deposition of the new CFO next week?"

"Yes. The other side has delayed her deposition for a long time, but the judge is antsy. The last time we were in court, she indicated she was out of patience. This judge is good. She worked for Cox & Smith as a litigator before the governor put her on the bench. She has won a couple of elections since. I can't be sure, but I think she sees through Lance and understands the case as well as we do. She had been suggesting a settlement. When she does, she looks at E-Titan's lawyers, not us."

The conversation about the case went on for a few more minutes. As Roger and Thomas were about to leave, Thomas brought up one last problem.

"Boss, there is one last thing we need to discuss. If you would rather, we can discuss it without Roger because it concerns you and Gwynn."

Arthur thought for a moment, then motioned for Roger to leave. He left. When he was gone, he looked over at Thomas.

"So, what's up?"

"My wife, Alicia, and Gwynn have been talking. You may not know this, but Alicia has agreed to cover for Gwynn while she takes care of some family business. You might already know this."

"I do know."

"My being in uniform and gone from Winchester & Wells may not be the worst thing about my being on active duty. We have talked about it, and she thinks she and the kids should stay here and not follow me to Kentucky, where I am going in the next few days. It does not make sense for so short a time. However, I could be gone a long time. Six months at least, maybe more—a lot more. And, well, there is always the chance that I won't come home. Alicia will need to visit me several times before I go overseas. That might interfere with her being available to Gwynn."

Arthur nodded. He was already a step ahead.

"I will find a trial lawyer to help if we need to. I can think of several people around town and even in the firm whom we might approach. I will hire someone to care for the children when they are with me. Murray is going to live with me full-time. I think Gwynn will be able to cope. She had an excellent assistant and paralegal. She may find she can do just fine without Alicia if necessary."

The conversation was winding down, but Arthur was reluctant to let Thomas go. He needed to say something.

"Thomas, you have been like a son to me. I remember as if it were yesterday the first time I saw you on a basketball court in Memphis, sitting on the ball at midcourt while everyone else engaged in a brawl. Since joining the firm, you have also been my chief associate. You are the person I rely on most. You have done an excellent job. I could not expect more. If anything happened to you, I would not know what to do. Take care of yourself.

"Also, if there is anything, and I mean anything, I can do for you to help smooth the transition for Alicia, the children, or you, please let me know. I never served in the military, but I appreciate what you are doing. Godspeed."

It was now getting dark. It was time for Thomas to go home to his family. They hugged each other, and Thomas left.

Arthur sat thoughtfully considering the news for some time.

Gee, I hope nothing happens to him.

13

Pretrial Maneuvers

GETTING READY FOR COURT
HOUSTON, TEXAS
NOVEMBER 2001

NO ONE LIKES PREPARING FOR trial during the holidays. Usually, trial practice slows down during the seasons. From Thanksgiving to New Year's Day, the wheels of justice turn with more than typical slowness. The fall of 2001 was an exception at Winchester & Wells. The judge in the Marshland litigation had set a firm deadline for the trial in mid-January. There was to be a pretrial hearing in early December before the holidays. The pressure was on.

The news that Thomas Mallory was headed for Afghanistan hit everyone hard. Arthur was usually calm, well-organized, and patient when preparing for trial. This time, he was a driving force of nervous and intellectual energy, with endless questions for everyone involved in the case. Without Mallory's presence, Arthur requested numerous memoranda on legal and factual points related to the case. Arthur Stone was getting ready for trial.

Most people unfamiliar with large corporate litigations cannot imagine how much paper is involved. Today, a good bit of that paper is put into digital form and can be searched electronically. In 2001, Winchester & Wells had not yet entered that era. Every document had to be reviewed by hand. If there was any question about its relevancy, someone had to review the reviewer's work. In a significant litigation, not everything can be put into evidence. Decisions have to be made. In the end, Eddie Morales and Arthur Stone had to make the decision.

Cynthia Maynard was one of the younger associates drawn into the vortex of trial preparation. Her status at the firm was somewhat unusual. Roger and Thomas had kept her off the Marshland case because she dated a young man at the firm representing E-Titan. They didn't want any information getting out, not even accidentally. Arthur was inclined to give the girl a chance. Roger, who was not as trusting as Arthur, watched Cynthia like a hawk watching a rabbit in a cotton field in West Texas. Even Roger had to admit he did not see a problem.

Maynard was an unusual hire for the firm. She graduated from the University of Oklahoma Law School, not a law school Winchester & Wells normally interviewed with. After law school she clerked with a judge in Oklahoma. She wanted to live in Houston near her fiancé; Arthur had heard of her family and wanted to give her a chance. Eventually, she joined the firm.

Arthur saw in Cynthia pragmatic common sense. He had always enjoyed discussing the facts of cases with Gwynn. Now that Gwynn was gone, it was natural for Arthur to seek out others to discuss issues before trial. In some ways, Cynthia reminded Arthur of Gwynn. She had a practical mind and was easy to talk to. One evening, in a conversation reminiscent of many that Arthur had had with Pat Armbruster, Arthur explained to her what he was about.

"Getting ready for trial is like laying bricks. Each little piece of evidence is a brick. The first thing you have to do is look at the brick. Does it have any imperfections? Is it somehow not the right brick for the place on the wall where you want to put a brick?

"To build a wall, you use bricks. So, you must ask, 'Is the brick somehow inappropriate?' To build a sound wall, you have to find the right bricks. Once you have picked the right bricks, you must lay them in the right place. A case needs to unfold so that the jury follows the logic of your case. Putting the right brick in the right place means giving the proper evidence to the jury at the right time.

"Patrick Armbruster used to talk to me about the case's narrative, which is very important. When you tell the jury the story of your client's problem, you have to tell it in exactly the right way so that the jury gets the point. If evidence is introduced too early, the jury won't understand or remember it at the right time. A good trial lawyer wants the jury to remember specific evidence at the right time during their deliberations.

"It may seem that we are wasting a lot of time reviewing all these documents and the testimony we already have. We are not. We are trying to present the best case to the judge and jury."

Maynard understood. As the conversation continued, she felt free to share her thoughts with Arthur.

"I was a bit surprised when I was put on this case. My fiancé is working for opposing counsel. He's not on this particular case, but everyone in the city knows about this case. Roger watches me like a hawk. I think he's fearful that I'll share something with Will. I won't. But everyone makes mistakes."

Arthur was quick to answer.

"Frankly, we watch everyone on a case like this. You can be sure that we seek to understand if there has been a leak of information. There are a lot of lawyers working on this. Some of them have a reputation for occasionally talking in restaurants and bars. We watch for that.

"Only Eddie Morales, Roger and I know everything about our strategy and tactics. That is what makes our position so lonely. Someday, you may be in the same situation."

Cynthia nodded and paused as if there was more she wanted to say. Arthur had the sort of personality that both attracted people and put them at ease. In depositions, he was often able to bring out information that few other attorneys could elicit from an unwilling witness. Arthur exuded a genuine interest in people, like his late mentor, Stephen Winchester. Cynthia sensed that despite Arthur's interest in this case, he was also interested in her happiness.

"Will and I often talk about our lives and Big Firm Litigation. I am not sure it is for me. I can see the hours you and the team members put into this kind of practice. I can also see that it will be a long time before I can try a case like this on my own. It will be a long time before I try any case at all. I compare this to what lawyers do in smaller firms. They try a lot more cases a lot faster. I thought about working in another area, perhaps marriage and family law. Will and I won't need the money. He's a good tax lawyer. There's no question but that he can make a living."

Arthur thought for a minute before answering.

"I might be able to give you a chance to see if you'd like to try something else. As you know, Alicia Mallory is now responsible for their children and has a faraway husband. Gwynn and I have an issue with one of our children, and Gwynn is stepping back from her practice for now. I think she might need some help. You wouldn't have to leave Winchester & Wells. You would just be available to help. Taking this opportunity will not hurt you at the firm. You would be doing the firm and me a favor."

"I think I would like to do that, even if it meant that I would have to pull back on some other things."

"I will talk with Gwynn about it."

With that, they returned to the case and the documents she was briefing him on.

THE DEPOSITION
SAN ANTONIO, TEXAS
NOVEMBER 2001

WHILE ADRIANNA WONG'S DEPOSITION WAS not considered as crucial as Brad Gilliland's would have been, Eddie Morales spent a good deal of time getting ready. It was one of those depositions that might not help Battle Mountain's case; however, it was essential that her testimony at trial not hurt the case. Battle Mountain needed to know what she would say.

Arthur made a special trip to San Antonio to be present for the deposition. As Houston's most eligible bachelor, he had a history with Adrianna Wong and wanted her to know he was present and involved. He even sat second-chair to Eddie during the deposition, something he rarely did. Arthur was a nice guy but wasn't above some psychological maneuvering if the case demanded it.

It took a long time to schedule this deposition. E-Titan delayed it as long as possible because Adrianna didn't know anything, was new to the job, and needed to spend time on other matters. Eddie pointed out that she had worked in the accounting department at E-Titan for some time and might know something. In addition, he needed someone in authority to validate certain documents. The judge agreed with Eddie.

The weather in San Antonio is often clear, calm, and cloudless in early November. This particular day was as warm and clear as far as one could see into the Texas Hill Country beyond. It was a day to play golf, not a day for taking a deposition. The night before, Eddie and Arthur met for dinner in the dark paneled dining room at the Argyle Club in Olmos Park to determine their strategy for the next day. One specific part of this deposition was going to be interesting.

All depositions begin in much the same way. Adrianna was sworn in. Eddie asked her name, title at the company, background, education, experience, and many other questions, all designed to establish her credentials as an expert witness on finance matters and her experience with the company. They began going through the documents. About an hour into the deposition, after going through documents of questionable relevance and arguing about innumerable objections by counsel, he asked the first question about which Arthur cared.

"Ms. Wong, I'm showing you a document marked exhibit N in this deposition. Can you tell me what this document is?"

"Well, it appears to be a calculation of the value of Battle Mountain."

"What is the date of this document?"

"The document is dated in early October 1997."

"If I told you that this document was dated almost three months before the closing of the sale of Battle Mountain to Buddy Bennett and at least a few weeks before negotiations began, would that surprise you?"

The counsel for the company interjected.

"We object. Ms. Wong was not involved in the negotiations between Buddy Bennett and E-Titan. She was not the CFO at the time. Any answer she gave would be speculative."

The objection was noted for the record. Ms. Wong took the hint and expressed that she did not know about the dating at the beginning of the transaction. Eddie Morales went on to get to the point.

"Ms. Wong, you have worked at E-Titan for some time and are familiar with many of its top executives. You will note that a comment in the margin reads, 'Buddy will surely buy the company and close at year-end for this price.' Can you verify whose handwriting it is for me? In other words, is this in Lance DuFort's handwriting?"

"I'm not sure."

"I'm sure you've seen Mr. DuFort's handwriting on many occasions. Can you recognize this handwriting?"

Counsel for E-Titan jumped in.

"Objection. She's already stated that she's unfamiliar with Lance DuFort's handwriting."

Eddie did not care about the objection. He had other ways of getting the document into evidence. He wanted E-Titan and their attorneys to know that the time had come to settle.

"Would it surprise you to know that we have handwriting experts who will testify that the handwriting is Lance DuFort's?"

Again, the disclosure was deliberate. Eddie wanted opposing counsel to know that Battle Mountain could prove Lance had written that comment at trial. Arthur had watched opposing counsel closely. It was obvious that they were concerned.

A bit later, the deposition got to the second point of interest.

"Ms. Wong, I want to show you what has been marked as plaintiff Exhibit O. It is a memorandum from you to Mr. Gilliland dated the month before the sale of Battle Mountain occurred. Can you verify that this is your memorandum?"

Wong looked long and hard at the memorandum, and her eye looked like she recognized it but wished she did not.

"I believe I wrote this memorandum."

"Can you explain its contents to us?"

"It's a discussion about the appropriate accounting treatment for the Battle Mountain transaction. It deals with whether or not it's appropriate to use profits on the sale of an ongoing business to offset operating losses during a fiscal year."

"And was it your opinion that it was appropriate to do so?"

"Not originally."

A series of objections to the testimony followed, to which Eddie replied that it was relevant because it established E-Titan's intentions in entering the transaction. Arthur was 100% certain that the judge would admit this evidence at trial.

"Can you tell me what changed your mind?"

"Our accounting firm ultimately agreed that we could account for the transaction in the way we did. We followed the advice of our outside accountants."

The deposition went on for some time longer. Reviewing all the evidence took the better part of two days. One interesting aspect of taking depositions in large corporate litigation is the sheer amount of tedium involved in going through endless documents and the importance of sewing little seeds of doubt in the minds of opposing counsel and their client about their case, and many such moments occurred in the three days of depositions involving Adrianna Wong.

At the end of the deposition, Arthur was satisfied that the conditions for a settlement were in place. He expected a call from opposing counsel.

THE FOLLOWING DAY, WHEN LANCE called, Arthur was still in San Antonio, having breakfast in his room at the Palacio del Rio on the San Antonio River.

"Arthur, your office told me you were in San Antonio. They gave me this number. I'm sorry if there's a problem with my calling. We need to talk."

Arthur thought for a moment. He knew what was coming.

"What would you like to talk about?"

"About this case involving Battle Mountain."

Arthur was correct. The deposition had indeed provoked a response.

"Lance, don't you think this should come from your lawyers?"

"I am a lawyer, remember?"

"Yes. But in this case, you are the client, and the rules against ex parte communications bind me. I will be here in San Antonio for a couple of days. If you and your counsel want to meet with Buddy, Eddie, and me about the case, that would seem more appropriate. Remember, I am not the lead trial counsel on this case; Eddie Morales is. He will handle any settlement negotiations."

Arthur could almost hear Lance snort in disbelief. It was beyond Lance to believe for a moment that anyone but Arthur Stone was calling the shots on the case. Lance's problem was that his ego got in his way when it came to understanding other people. Eddie was calling the shots on the case, and he would have a big say in any settlement.

"Why don't you talk it over with your lawyers? If you want to meet, you can fly over here tomorrow. We can meet in Eddie's offices or at my hotel. I am at the Palacio del Rio on the river. I have some family business today and will not be around. I am going to visit my parents near Kerrville."

Lance was obviously upset by the call and its necessity. He knew he was holding the weaker hand.

"All right, I will be back with you. If we can get together, I suggest somewhere around noon tomorrow."

Arthur was not in the mood to waste time on fruitless negotiations. Therefore, he ended the call with one last shot across Lance's bow.

"Lance, I do not want to suggest for a moment that Buddy and Eddie are not more or less in charge of this case. However, I am reasonably certain that they would not be willing to pay anything to get out of the case. They believe they have a winning case, as do I. Any settlement will probably involve E-Titan paying at least some Battle Mountain legal fees. Don't come if all we are going to do is trade unrealistic offers."

Lance hung up with a curt, "I understand your position."

It was about an hour and a half drive from San Antonio to Kerrville and further west to Hunt and the North Fork of the Guadalupe, where his parents' ranch and his own were located. Arthur was glad for the drive and time to think. Those times when the facts were confusing, and he needed someone to run ideas by were the times he missed Gwynn the most. They could always talk over any problem and reach a reasonable conclusion and wise course of action. Gwynn's hard-nosed realism about people and situations was an excellent counterbalance to Arthur's tendency to make people happy and think the best of them. Dealing with Lance DuFort in business was not a situation that favored idealism.

I wish I could talk to Gwynn. I don't want to be involved in the negotiations for fear that I will either go easy on Lance or be accused of taking my anger as a cuckolded husband out on him.

Arthur had enough of the competitive high school athlete in him to hate being beaten at anything, including love.

Eddie is going to have to take the lead in any negotiations. Buddy intensely dislikes Lance and distrusts him. He might not be able to make a deal. No, that is unfair. Buddy knows how to control his emotions in business. He is paying substantial legal fees. Cutting off those fees alone will be a strong inducement to settle.

When Lance hinted at a settlement, Arthur figured the ultimate deal would involve dropping the lawsuit, acknowledging that neither Buddy nor Battle Mountain had done anything wrong, and E-Titan paying some legal fees. Otherwise, Battle Mountain would roll the dice, seek damages and punitive damages on some of its claims, and hope for a considerable judgment.

By the time Arthur reached the town of Comfort, he was thinking about the family, Christmas, and the future.

Gwynn is right. I have to spend more time with the children, and especially Murray. Gwynn probably wants the children out of the house because she is trying to figure out how to leave Lance. But it isn't straightforward. Just as our divorce has injured Murray, Stephen, and Margaret, inevitably, Claire will be hurt if Gwynn leaves Lance. She has handled many divorces and knows what she might get into if she leaves Lance. Lance has a mean streak; if his ego is damaged, he will make life as difficult as possible for Gwynn.

Arthur tried to reconstruct the last conversation he and Ahn had about Gwynn and the children. Arthur had shared Gwynn's Christmas plans, Murray's plans to live with him, and Arthur's sense that there was something deeply wrong with Lance. After 7:00, Arthur had gotten free and had seen Ahn at her home in a high rise on San Felipe in Houston.

❄

After Stephen's death, Ahn continued to wear black for a long time. Even after she returned to a more normal wardrobe, she favored dark colors and subdued patterns. It seemed as if she was in a state of mourning. At the same time, she devoted time to her various investments and the many charities she supported. She spent an hour each day in complete silence. Frequently, she went on silent retreats. Her spiritual life resulted in a strange inner luminosity. Most of the time, she seemed at least a step ahead of Arthur in any conversation. Ahn was the most worldly, other-worldly person Arthur could imagine. When Arthur entered the apartment, it was apparent she had been meditating. There was a silence before they began their conversation.

Ahn began with a simple question.

"Why did you need to see me? Is it business or personal?"

Arthur and Ahn had several common investment interests, including the hotel in San Miguel de Allende. Arthur was also her lawyer on many matters and a trustee of a foundation she created and managed. The foundation contained most of the assets she inherited through Jackson Winchester, her husband's brother.

"Tonight is personal. I saw Gwynn today. Murray is in a lot of trouble in school. St. John's is going to have to expel him. Gwynn wants him to come and live with me for a while. I think she is right about that, but she is worried about something else. She has lost weight. There are circles under her eyes. Underneath the face she puts on, she is unhappy."

Ahn looked at Arthur with her disturbingly penetrating, nearly coal-black eyes.

"Wouldn't you be if you had a child in trouble and a husband who didn't seem to care? Lance has never taken any interest in your children. You know that."

"Yes. But there is something more."

Ahn looked at Arthur quietly. She had already decided to point out the elephant in the room.

"Arthur, have you done any investigation of the Los Cabos trip in which that young Mexican heiress was killed?"

"I have seen the same information you probably saw from Bardero."

"If you have read that report, you know that the facts don't add up. Lance is hiding something. Do you believe the story that Lance and his employees are telling about the night that she died?"

"No."

"I have made inquiries. Juan Bardero does not believe that Lance's story is 'the whole truth and nothing but the truth.' He does not think the authorities in Mexico believe the story of Lance and the others. Worst of all, El Halcón does not believe the story. He has been leaning on the authorities in Mexico and his friends in the United States to investigate the matter. If Dobie Dawson and Lance were not significant contributors to both parties in Washington, El Halcón would be getting his way by now. In the end, he will get his way. He is a powerful man.

"Gwynn can see Lance is worried about something. Lance's friends in Washington have probably told him about El Halcón's attempts to find the truth. If they have warned him of the pressure they are under, they have also warned him that El Halcón has many contacts with violent people. He also has contacts with various intelligence agencies worldwide, including our own in the United States."

She paused to let her words sink into Arthur's consciousness.

"You are saying that Lance, Gwynn, and the children could also be in danger."

"Yes."

After Arthur left Ahn's apartment, he called Ben Stone, who confirmed her story. The police in Mexico did not buy the story of E-Titan's management. Javier "El Halcón" Velasco did not, and Juan de la Cruz Bardero did not. Finally, Ben Stone did not buy the story.

"Arthur, I cannot tell you the exact source of my information, but I believe the police now have a pretty good idea who ordered the death of Brad Gilliland. I also think that the police in Mexico know more than they are saying about the circumstances of Javiera Velasco's death. I would not want to point the finger at Lance for both these murders, but others might be about to do so."

Arthur agreed.

Somehow, I need to get the children away from Lance. Gwynn is no longer my responsibility, but El Halcón is a scary person with even more dangerous friends. I must at least warn Gwynn of the danger.

He was now near the family ranch and his soon-to-be retreat. In his musings, he did not realize that a car had been following him since leaving San Antonio. A few miles beyond Hunt, Texas, he turned off FM 1340 at Bear Creek Road and drove up a mile-long hill until he reached the gate with the family brand on it.

nothing before it was completely worn out. It was a habit that John, his brother, had maintained. Arthur was not so frugal. There was a moment of awkward silence. His father broke it.

"Arthur, you know that I have been suffering from a bit of dementia. I am eighty years old this October. Your mother and I have been married for more than fifty years. We have had a great life. The doctors tell me they cannot possibly estimate how long I have or how quickly the disease will progress. However, we have been considering moving to Houston, where we would be near our children. Johnny recommends the Hallmark, founded by a group of Presbyterians, many from his church. It is quite nice. As a pastor in Brenham, I visited a few people who retired, grew old, and went there to be near their grown children. It is a nice place."

Arthur knew the Hallmark well. Stephen Winchester's mother had lived there—and had been in the Alzheimer's ward. It was excellent.

"The Hallmark is a tremendous choice. You can keep the farm for the weekends or when you want to get out of town."

His mother now broke in.

"Johnny has offered to buy it from us. The purchase will be enough for us to buy into the Hallmark. Because I am a Presbyterian pastor, we feel certain they will let us in."

Arthur knew the management well.

"We can work it out. I don't think there is a thing to worry about."

Turning to his brother, Arthur asked the obvious question.

"Do you think you can swing the financing for the ranch?"

"Yes."

He did not elaborate. John did not like to be seen as reliant upon his successful brother. He would make arrangements for the loan, and Arthur was sure he had the financial statement to support the loan. He also inherited his father's frugality.

Uncle Ben chimed in.

"Your aunt and I are not interested in the family farm. We are beach people. We have a place in Galveston, Jamaica Beach, and we don't need any more property to look after at our age. We think this plan is just fine."

Arthur was not upset that his earlier plans for his parents' estate would have to be changed. Things would be fine. It was a good idea for them to move to Houston so their children could be nearer. He did have one request.

"Even though we are not going to be waiting for your estate to transfer the property, I still think it's a good idea for me to have an option to buy the property if Johnny ever sells it. I think we all want to keep it in the family."

Everyone agreed.

The conversation went on for a bit longer. Arthur agreed to call the Hallmark when he returned home and get copies of the documents his parents would be asked to sign. John decided to work on the financing. Arthur suggested that his firm would be happy to look at the documentation for the purchase on behalf of his brother. Ben looked on, glad that his brother would be so well taken care of by his children.

His mother concluded the conversation with a happy smile and a word of thanks.

"We are grateful for you all being here today. I think I will fix some dinner. Why don't you boys take Bill for a little walk around the property?"

They agreed, though it was getting a bit cool outside.

A WALK ON THE RANCH
HUNT, TEXAS
NOVEMBER 2001

THE STONE FAMILY RANCH WAS about 500 acres. It was mainly on a long slope down towards the North Fork of the Guadalupe River. It had been in the Stone family since the 19th century when Arthur's great-great-grandfather settled there after the Civil War. The family lost everything in the American Civil War, and reconstruction was bitter in South Carolina, so the family made the long trek on foot, train, and by covered wagon to Texas and settled in the Hill Country. At the time, raising goats was the primary way to make a living in Kerr County, Texas.

The land in the Texas Hill Country was poor and filled with limestone. It was almost impossible to raise crops except near a river. Fortunately, the farm had a large field in the Guadalupe floodplain. In former days, the family raised hay there to get the livestock through the winter and vegetables to eat every season in a plot near the house. The remainder had been used to raise goats and a few cattle. It was a hard life.

When Bill and Ben's parents died, the farm sat empty for a few years. Juniper cedar began its inevitable invasion. By the time Arthur bought his land, the juniper cedar, which takes much of the water other plants need, had taken over much of the property. When Arthur cleared Avalon Ranch, he cleared the family farm as well. It was now possible to see for a reasonable distance, and grass and other plants were returning to the pasture.

The family place was on the northern end of a long road, about a mile off a Texas highway. The main gate sat at the southern end, where the property lines of the two ranches met. Arthur's larger property ranged off to the east, while the "Stone

Ranch" began straight at the gate, with its main road to the house winding its way across the 500 acres.

Late in the afternoon, the four men wore their jackets against the November wind and silently walked south along the drive towards the road.

Ben broke the silence.

"How long will it take for your ranch house to be ready?"

Arthur had asked himself and the builder the very same question many times.

"It is hard to say. It is sometimes difficult to get craftsmen, especially finishing craftsmen, out in the country. We are having to import carpenters from Bandera and some of the stone masons from Fredericksburg. I think perhaps another six months. We cannot begin the pool until spring. I will feel lucky to celebrate Labor Day next year with the family at the new house."

"When do you think that the Battle Mountain litigation will end?"

"I am not sure. Recently, there have been feelers about a settlement. The judge has made it plain that she thinks it should settle before trial. When I return to San Antonio, there will be a meeting about a potential settlement."

Ben thought a moment before his next question.

"I understand that Murray may be coming to live with you this spring."

"I think so."

Bill broke in. His dementia had not dimmed his opinions, though his legendary capacity for diplomacy was suffering a bit.

"A boy needs his father at this age. Puberty is a difficult time in a man's life. Today, many young people make terrible decisions due to a lack of parental supervision. With boys, it can be extremely anti-social and unwise behavior."

He looked directly at Arthur.

"A lot of young men from broken homes get involved in drugs."

Arthur tried to change the subject. He was not in the mood for a lecture, even a well-meaning lecture.

Ben wanted to say something but was unsure if he should speak.

"Have you heard anything more about who might have shot Brad Gilliland?"

Arthur replied, "Our interest in the killing has to do with Gilliland's potential testimony in the Battle Mountain case. As we understand matters, there is no evidence that Lance DuFort or anyone else at E-Titan was involved. The police have looked. They found nothing. You might know more than I do."

"I might," Ben replied. "We can talk about it later in private."

"Would anything you know impact our settlement?"

"I don't think so."

"Would anything impact Gwynn or the children?"

"Not directly."

Bill pointed out a small flock of exotic goats in the pasture below.

"Those are Catalina goats. They came from Spain a long time ago. One of our neighbors had an exotic game ranch. When he died, his children argued over the business and failed to maintain the fences. Some of them escaped. Now, we have exotic goats. We also have a few other species."

Arthur looked at the goats carefully.

"I will buy some from you to breed on my property. For history's sake, I plan on getting a few Longhorns. I might as well have a flock of Catalina goats."

At this point, Ben broke into the conversation.

"Do you see those two cars parked near the gate?"

The men looked down a draw to where the front gate was visible in the distance. They saw the two cars.

"I believe one of them, the Nissan, followed me from Houston. Do you recognize the other, Arthur?"

"I am afraid I was thinking about family matters and lawsuits all the way from San Antonio. I don't know if I ever looked in the rearview mirror after I got on I-10."

At that moment, a rifle shot was fired. The bullet went through the fleshy part of Ben Stone's shoulder and grazed Arthur's arm as well. All three men fell to the ground. Ben pulled a nine-millimeter Browning 1911 service automatic concealed in his waist, removed the safety, and inched his way forward. He did not get far.

From behind a rocky ledge nearly thirty yards from where they were lying, a hand grenade was thrown. It landed between them. Bill Stone took one look at his sons and jumped on the grenade. He died immediately from the blast.

Ben rolled over and took a shot at a figure running in the twilight. He was not sure, but he thought he grazed the running figure. Drawing on his years of FBI training, he worked his way toward the road. He was too late. Three figures ran out of the tree line, got into the two cars, and sped away. Ben worked his way back to where Arthur was sitting in disbelief. John Stone was holding his father's head in his arms, covered with blood.

They left the body where it lay, knowing the police would want the scene to remain as undisturbed as possible. Arthur's mother had heard the shots and explosion. She was waiting at the door with a worried look when they arrived. The fact that Arthur, John, and Ben were alone at the mesquite door of the ranch house told her all she needed to know. It was Bill.

"What happened?"

They told her.

She made her way to the couch, collapsing in grief.

Ben excused himself to call the county sheriff's office. Hunt, where the ranch was located, had no police. It had a volunteer fire department. The only business to speak of was the Hunt store, where locals ate on occasion and shopped for minor groceries in an emergency. Beer and barbeque were its main claim to fame. The campers from the surrounding camps loved the Hunt store, as did their parents when they visited.

It took a while for the police to arrive. In the meantime, the three sat in silent and grief-filled shock. Betty cleaned the superficial wounds of the two men and called a local doctor, who agreed to come out to the house. They sat and talked.

After a while, Betty looked up in tears.

"Strangely enough, I think Bill was fine with what happened. You know he fought at Iwo Jima and other places in the war. He told me two stories of men who jumped on Japanese grenades. In one case, he blamed himself for surviving. He was closest to the grenade but froze in shock. Another soldier jumped on the grenade and died. Today, he gave himself for the two of you. It does not make it any easier, but it does explain what he did. If he had not done what he did, all of you might be dead. He died a hero."

She paused and grimly looked at Ben and Arthur sitting on the couch before her.

"Now, you two, find out who did this and bring them to justice."

FUNERAL FOR A SOLDIER
INGRAM, TEXAS
NOVEMBER 2001

THE FUNERAL WAS HELD AT the Ingram Presbyterian Church a week later. The Stones attended the little church after his retirement. It was struggling and smaller than the more prominent and wealthier First Presbyterian Church of Kerrville. They felt their calling was to support and help the little church survive. The members rallied around Betty and the family in the days before the funeral. The refrigerator and freezer were filled with leftover casseroles from kindly friends.

The body was not present at the memorial service. The police were holding the body so that any forensic evidence it contained might be discovered. Once the body was released, Betty made arrangements for it to be cremated and buried at nearby Mo Ranch, a Presbyterian camp just down the road off FM 1340. It was a lovely place where Arthur, his brother, and his parents made many beautiful memories during their childhood. Gwynn and the children came to the funeral. Lance did not attend. Arthur and Lance had a brief conversation when Arthur called him to cancel his participation in the settlement negotiations.

"Obviously, I can't be present for any settlement negotiations. I'm not sure that matters, Lance. Eddie and Buddy are well-equipped to conduct the negotiations."

Lance agreed. In a rare display of humanity, he expressed his condolences. He asked whether or not he should attend the funeral.

"If you don't mind, I think it's best if it's just family. Gwynn will have to come to bring the children. I doubt she'll stay long. She and my mother have what might be called a strained relationship. I'll have a limousine pick her and the children up at the San Antonio airport and bring them to the funeral. They'll be back home the next day."

There was a pause.

"Arthur, I hope you don't think I had anything to do with this. I promise you I know nothing. Like you, I can see it's a little bit too coincidental that there have been three deaths surrounding E-Titan. However, I had nothing to do with the death of Brad Gilliland or your father."

Arthur thanked him for his consideration. After they hung up, he sat long, pondering the conversation. It was some time before he remembered that Lance never mentioned Javiera.

Even a narcissist has his moments of human feeling. Even a sociopath can be kind to children and cry at funerals. We are all human, even Lance.

For some reason, that realization made Arthur feel better. He was not convinced that Lance was innocent of Brad Gilliland's or his father's deaths. But, at least on the surface, there was something human that might be saved—or his father would have thought so.

Still, Lance is a con man. It would be best if you remembered that.

Gwynn and the children came the night before the funeral. They stayed at a motel in Kerrville and drove to the funeral the following day. Gwynn was dressed in black. It was obvious that she had been crying. Murray was unusually grim. Stephen tried to look manly until he broke down. Margaret cried throughout the service. Claire was well-behaved, lying quietly in Gwynn's arms for the entire funeral. Arthur sat in the front row, alone with his mother and Ben.

The funeral itself was exactly the kind of funeral that Bill Stone would have wanted. There was a call to worship, followed by a hymn, his father's favorite, "Amazing Grace." Then, there were two readings of passages from the Old and New Testaments, a short homily by his son, which contained memories of his father, and a brief memory from Arthur. This was followed by a solo of "The Lord's Prayer," another prayer, and a responsive reading from the Heidelberg Catechism. The reader began with the question, "What is your only comfort in life and death?" To which the congregation responded:

That I am not my own but belong— body and soul, in life and in death— to my faithful Savior, Jesus Christ. He has fully paid for all my sins with his precious blood and has delivered me from the tyranny of the devil. He also watches over me so that not a hair can fall from my head without the will of my Father in heaven; in fact, all things must work together for my salvation. Because I belong to him, Christ, by his Holy Spirit, also assures me of eternal life and makes me wholeheartedly willing and ready from now on to live for him.

The service continued with another hymn, "Be Thou My Vision." John Stone then got up and said the words of committal:

"In Ecclesiastes, Solomon tells us that for everything, there is a season and a time to every purpose on earth, a time to be born and a time to die. For my father, last week was his time to die. But we do not believe that his death was the end. In Christ's life, death, and resurrection, we learn and believe that death is not the end. My father has heard, "Well done, thou good and faithful servant. Enter my rest.

"In sorrow but without fear, in love and appreciation, we commit our dear friend, father, and grandfather to the grave in faith that we shall meet again in Eternity. We lovingly and reverently return your body to the elements from which it came, ashes to ashes, dust to dust. We leave you now to rest, grateful you were in our lives. Let us now depart in peace.”

The part of the service that was the most emotional for Arthur involved his brother's comments.

"As many of you know, my father fought in the Pacific during the Second World War. Some people faced with that kind of tragedy completely lost their faith. In my father's case, it had the opposite effect. Sitting in the heat of a tropical island, surrounded by the stench of dead and decaying bodies, contemplating the unimaginable horror of war, my father decided to embrace love. He thought love was the most essential thing in the universe.

"My father didn't blame God for what he did and saw in the Pacific. He blamed human beings and himself. Once, he told me that the reason he liked the theologian Dietrich Bonhoeffer so much had to do with the fact that Bonhoeffer understood that he was making questionable choices in an impossible situation in Nazi Germany during the war. He once told me all of the war was like that. It was full of morally ambiguous daily decisions in combat in a morally impossible situation.

"When he returned from the war, he married my mother and went to seminary. He never pastored a large church. He never wanted to. He wanted to love people. After he retired, he told me that no one from his churches ever commented on any sermon he preached or any building project he led in a church. He told me, 'When people talk to me, they talk about some minor incident where I shared love with another human being.' My father knew that love matters. I try to remember his example in my pastoral career, though never as successfully as Dad."

It was then that Arthur Stone began to silently cry.

There was a reception after the service in the small congregational dining room near the sanctuary. Arthur was surprised at how many people had come from all over Texas. Most of the people in his father's congregations were now quite elderly, but many who could come did come. In the reception line, many of them told of his love for their congregation, his sacrifice for their well-being, and his constant presence in times of trouble and loss. "It was the least I could do to come," said one of them.

My funeral will probably be at the First Presbyterian Church in Houston. Partners in law firms and the business elite of the community will be in attendance. I doubt that any of them will feel about me the way these people felt about my father.

After the reception, Arthur rode with the family to the San Antonio airport. They sat quietly, each with their memories, and shared memories of their father, father-in-law, and grandfather. He put them on the plane. By the time he finished, Uncle Ben was in San Antonio and picked him up for the two-and-a-half-hour drive to Houston. John Stone stayed with his mother for another few days.

Ben and Arthur had things to do in Houston.

Just as Arthur was about to leave the limousine, Gwynn reached across the seat and took his hand. It was the first time she had reached out to touch him in all the years since their divorce. He felt the warm softness of her touch precisely as he had felt when they first held hands many years ago. He looked up into her eyes and could see her concern.

"Do what you must, but be careful, and do not do anything foolish. Please. For the children—and me."

Arthur leaned over to whisper so the children could not hear, as he often did when they were younger. "Believe me, my dear, I will."

As Arthur exited the car, all the anger, pain, and agony of betrayal disappeared. The awful spiritual and emotional separation between them was gone forever. He and Gwynn might never be together again in this world, but Arthur Stone was free of the iron chains of the past, with its shame, anger, and rage.

(**15**)

Plans and Possibilities

RETURN TO BATTLE

I-10 EAST OF SAN ANTONIO, TEXAS

NOVEMBER 2001

FOR THE RETURN, AHN DECIDED to ride back to Houston with Ben and Arthur rather than fly on Southwest Airlines with Gwynn and the children. She knew Ben and Arthur would make plans to find out who killed Arthur's father. She shared Gwynn's concern that the two might be rash, given the murder. More importantly, she wanted to help.

Ben was driving just as he had on the trip to the farm with John. Ahn sat in the back seat. Arthur sat next to Ben in the front passenger seat. Initially, there was complete silence as the trio pulled out of the parking lot and drove down the McAllister Freeway to where Highway 281 picks up IH-10 to Houston. As soon as they were out of city traffic, the council of war began. Arthur broke the silence.

"What have the police discovered thus far?"

Ben responded.

"A car matching the description of the black Nissan we saw near the front gate was picked up by Border Patrol cameras crossing the Hidalgo Bridge into Mexico about six hours after your father died. I've seen the tape. It is too blurry to make out details, but three men were in the car. That was not a lot of help to us because we never saw the faces of the men. The second car has not been found. I would bet it ended up in a chop shop in San Antonio.

"The bullet that hit the two of us was found lodged in a mesquite tree on the property. It was from an AK-47 used by the Mexican army and many drug cartels, among many other armies and groups around the world. Not much help there. The grenade fragments were from a type of grenade used by the Mexican marines. The Zeta's come to mind as a cartel familiar with Mexican military weaponry and tactics. If you take all this evidence together, it gives support to the view that the hit was ordered by someone using Mexican nationals."

Arthur considered the evidence.

"None of this points to any specific person, particularly Lance DuFort. Lance denied to me that he had anything to do with the death. Of course, that is precisely what he would say, but I don't see a provable connection unless we turn up more evidence. Lance had nothing to gain by your death. It would be my death that might benefit Lance."

Arthur paused, then continued. "So Ben, what I want to know is, who do you think they were trying to kill? You or me or both of us."

Ben understood Arthur's point.

"I think it was me. Arthur, there are things about the investigation into the killing of Brad Gilliland that I have kept from you. Some days ago, I came into possession of some evidence. It was not conclusive as to who contracted the death of

Brad Gilliland, but it opened up a new line of inquiry concerning Gilliland's death."

He paused, not wanting to continue.

"The problem with the evidence is that I gathered it illegally. The police cannot use it, nor can you."

"You gathered evidence illegally?"

"I am afraid so. Through Heather Gilliland, I learned that Marjorie Melton might have kept a safety deposit box in Las Vegas. We watched Melton carefully and even bugged her telephone. Eventually, she arranged to go to Las Vegas to empty her safety deposit box there. As she left the bank, an associate grabbed her bag. In the bag were letters and memoranda, some of which concern the death of Javiera Velasco, the girl in Los Cabos, and some of which concern Brad Gilliland and Marjorie.

"The story the three told the Mexican police is not entirely true. The letters and memoranda I have seen relate that the three of them (Brad, M&M, and Lance) went to Lance's room for a drink. After a while, Brad and Marjorie went to his room. Several hours later, Brad got a call, left the room, and only returned after dawn. He was shaken and announced that the group was leaving Los Cabos. They left out that piece of the puzzle when they gave their statements.

"The events deeply shook Brad. When he returned home, he broke off his relationship with Marjorie. One of the letters indicates that he decided he owed his family an attempt to reconstruct his marriage. In addition, in a tape of a phone call, Brad told Marjorie, 'I am through lying for Lance.' It does not say what he is through lying about. It could be Los Cabos or his testimony in the deposition you had scheduled when he was killed."

Arthur was stunned by the information, how it was acquired, and how far Ben had gone. His voice was angry when he replied.

"I cannot believe you did this. If discovered, it might implicate Winchester & Wells in a crime to gain evidence for trial. It could hurt our case."

Ben looked across at Arthur.

"I would not have done it if it had only been the Battle Mountain case. I did it because Gwynn and your children may be living with a murderer. Not someone who ordered a murder but a murderer."

Arthur stared at the road in silence. Ahn broke in.

"Arthur, we have all been trying to protect Gwynn and the children. I know you have. We sent Bardero to investigate after the death of Gilliland. Since then, I have sent one of his associates to Los Cabos on more than one occasion. The police in Los Cabos do not believe the story Lance, Brad Gilliland, and Marjorie told them. Javiera Velasco's body was in terrible condition when it was recovered. However, the police believe she was strangled before she was put in the water. There was evidence of bruises around her neck shortly before she died. There was no water in what was left of her lungs. The police do not believe she drowned. They believe she was dead when she was put in the water."

The conversation continued for a while as Ben and Arthur began discussing details. Usually, Ahn would have listened with rapt attention to be sure she understood what would happen. Uncharacteristically, she felt tired, bone tired. Leaning against the door beside her, she fell asleep. In her sleep, she dreamed.

In her dream, Ahn was at Avalon Ranch with Arthur and the children. Gwynn was on the porch with Arthur. Suddenly, Stephen Winchester appeared, walking towards her out of nowhere. She ran to his embrace.

"Have you come for me?"

Stephen looked down at her in adoration.

"No, my love. Not now. Arthur still needs you. You and I, however, are lucky, for our vows and love were not for this life only but for eternity."

Ahn pondered in wonder.

"I cannot leave to be with you?"

"No, your labors are not over. Arthur and Gwynn need you. Arthur's battle is not over, and neither is Gwynn's healing. One day, we will be reunited. For now, Arthur and Gwynn must not be left alone."

"Will he ever be wise?"

"You cannot see it, but he is already wise. In some ways, he is already wiser than I was in this life. His talent is greater and different from mine, however. I was the better lawyer, but he is the better leader. He has the greater destiny. He was born for a battle yet to come. You have watched him mature, so you cannot see his greatness. I could move the law, but Arthur can move human hearts."

Ahn looked at her Stephen with her dark eyes flashing.

"No one could be better than you in any possible way. You were the perfect husband, the perfect lawyer, and the perfect partner."

Stephen looked down with loving indulgence.

"It is good to hear you say this for my benefit. Where I am now, I can see that what I was doing mattered, but it mattered little. Our love was more important to the universe than any accomplishments of mine, personal, military, or legal. You remember the verse 'Faith, Hope, and Love, but the greatest of these is love.' Arthur does not yet know the passing of those things done by human striving. But he will—as will you, my dear. When the time comes, I shall be waiting. For now, part of Arthur's greatness is in his sheer ordinariness.

"Those of us who are not ordinary often mistake the greatness of ordinary men and women who simply do their worldly tasks with devotion. The father of our nation was such a man, and there have been others. The world is often made better by ordinary people in extraordinary times."

Ahn could see the wisdom in Stephen's words, but still, she could not bear to be parted.

"I have missed you every moment of these past fourteen years. Most people cannot see it, but there is a great emptiness in me. Your love filled my heart. Now, you are gone."

"Then do not let it be so. My love has never left your heart, nor has that Divine Love that is greater than my or any human love. Our love cannot pass away because love is the ultimate reality. It cannot and does not pass away. Love endures forever. Our love will endure beyond the end of time."

Stephen Winchester turned to walk away into the cloud from which he came.

When Ahn awoke from the dream, Ben and Arthur had finished reviewing the facts and evidence. Ben drove in silence while Arthur thought. Arthur broke his meditation as the three passed by Columbus, Texas.

"Ben, here is what I would like you to do. Pack up everything you took from Melton in Las Vegas. Have one of your people send it back to her. Just send everything back. Be sure you are careful in how you do this. We do not want it to be traceable.

"Then, I would like you to see Heather Gilliland and ask if you can search her house and their lake house one more time. If Gilliland sent letters to Melton, he might have kept copies or other documents we would like to see. Don't just look in obvious places. He may have buried it somewhere in the yard. Don't leave a stone unturned.

"Ahn, I need you to visit San Miguel de Allende. We need Bardero to shake the trees in Mexico. We also need him to have his people talk to the folks in Los Cabos. If I need to pay for additional forensics on Javiera's body, I will pay. Whoever ordered the death of Javiera is afraid of something—scared enough to try to kill Ben. Let's find out why."

TRIP TO THE LAKE
NEAR CANYON LAKE, NEW BRAUNFELS, TEXAS
NOVEMBER 2001

BEN STONE'S FIRST CALL UPON arrival in his office the next day was to Rico Diaz.

"Rico, I need your assistance—and I think you will profit from mine."

"What is it?"

"I want to ask Heather Gilliland to let us search her house and the lake house one last time. I think she will consent to the search."

"What are we looking for?"

"It is possible that Brad Gilliland hid private correspondence between himself and Marjorie Melton. We have reason to believe that she had some kind of correspondence with Gilliland after the death of Javiera Velasco. If we can find any such correspondence, it may shed light on the crime you are investigating. It might also shed light on more recent events. By the way, I think it is more likely that we will find something at the lake house than the home. Brad would have been carefully hiding his relationship and correspondence from Heather."

"When would you like to do this?"

"As soon as possible. If we find anything, we share the information. We will keep anything confidential you need to keep confidential. I am going to see Heather this afternoon."

"Let me know what I can do."

With that, the conversation ended.

Heather Gilliland trusted Ben Stone. There was something solid and old-fashioned about him. She immediately consented to the visit when he asked to see her again. He came alone. They sat in the family room overlooking the small lake in Sandlewood. Heather Gilliland was an attractive woman who seemed to have aged yet become more attractive during (or perhaps because of) her recent suffering and loss.

Ben began by asking her how she was doing.

"I think I am doing as well as can be expected. Losing Brad was a tragedy, but it would appear that I lost him a long time before he died."

Ben looked at her.

"I am not sure that is true. I cannot tell you exactly how I know this, but I have every reason to believe that Brad told his mistress that he was returning to you and recommitting himself to your marriage shortly before he died."

Heather stared at him.

"Is this true?"

"I think so. Once again, I cannot tell you exactly why I believe this, but it is part of why I came to see you today. I would like you to agree to allow the police and my firm to search this house and the lake house one last time. It is possible we overlooked something in our first searches. I hope there might be something here or there that will lead us to the killer.

"I don't think anything we discover will reflect poorly on Brad, at least regarding his relationship with you. You already know he was having an affair. Your children already know. We already know that the accounting for some transactions concerning E-Titan may have been one of the reasons Brad was killed. What we don't know is who ordered the killing. That is what we are trying to discover. Any clue, any piece of evidence, however small, we can uncover will help."

Heather considered the request. She was resigned to what had happened and the facts. Her children were another matter. They were still angry. They needed closure. Whatever was to be disclosed, the family needed closure.

"All right. You can go to the lake house any time. I will supply you with a key today. As to a search here, give me some notice so that I can be ready for my home to be invaded."

With that, she smiled and changed the subject.

A few days later, armed with shovels, a metal detector, and other equipment, a group from the Stone Detective Agency traveled to Canyon Lake with the police. The investigators had been there once before, but they did not stay long. A cursory search did not disclose any relevant evidence. This time was to be different.

The Canyon Lake house presented itself as a seldom-used second home. It was sparsely and inexpensively furnished. There were three bedrooms, three baths, a kitchen, a living area, and an office off the master bedroom. There was a large deck overlooking the lake. A huge garage included a small boat house where the family-owned ski boat could be stored when not in the water. The entire complex was on a one-acre site. The previous search had focused on the office. This time, everything was carefully searched.

The search of the main house disclosed nothing not uncovered in the first search. Paydirt was discovered in the garage. The walls of the boat house contained a previously undiscovered hidden safe carefully and secretly installed at the bottom of a storage bin. When the safe was opened, it was filled with papers, some personal and some related to E-Titan. Sure enough, Gilliland had hidden copies of his letters to Marjorie Melton and a long memorandum pertaining to the formation of the Cheetahs and the assets it was holding.

The contents of the safe were delivered to the police. Ben Stone kept a copy for his files. Arthur and the Securities and Exchange Commission received copies of the Cheetah memorandum. It made for fascinating reading.

UNHAPPY DAYS AND NIGHTS
HOUSTON, TEXAS
DECEMBER 2001

MARJORIE MELTON STARED AT HERSELF in her bedroom mirror. She was not happy with what she saw. It had been days since she had last slept. She had been bingeing on drugs, alcohol, and food. Once, her figure had been young and athletic—the body of a voluptuous and highly athletic chorus girl; now, there were signs of weight gain and wrinkles. The kind of figure that she possessed was challenging to keep slender in middle age. The stress she was under did not help.

To an outside observer, she was still a lovely woman, but in her mind, she was past her prime. All of her life, she had relied on her beauty. She could now see time passing away. She did not like what she saw coming. The sleeping pills and alcohol she relied on to sleep did not help matters at all.

I have to get control of myself.

She met her first husband while a young show-girl in Las Vegas, where her mother had landed after her first divorce. She lived with her mother when she could, but she had been in and out of Las Vegas for most of her childhood, living with relatives here and there. She had always attracted the attention of men— and some of that attraction was emotionally damaging. When her first husband, Harry, was in Vietnam, she divorced him after a series of affairs and the promise of marriage from someone with connections in Hollywood. It did not work out.

I wonder what happened to Harry? She had heard that he disappeared some years ago during a mission.

Whatever Harry was doing, it was not straight. Harry was never straight.

After one of her breakups, Marjorie spent time in a psychiatric clinic. M&M had always suffered from depression, but the breakup with a lover from Tinsel Town left her in a dark place. The clinic had not helped. She became increasingly dependent on various drugs, even to sleep.

Then, she met Dobie Dawson. At first, he seemed her ticket to security. (She was beyond loving a man by that time, but security and possessions did not require the reality of love, just an illusion of love.) There was something almost childlike about Dobie, and she thought she could manage him. It was not long before his peculiarities and drug use convinced her to keep the relationship on the level of "friendship with privileges."

Eventually, it was just a friendship. After Dobie, there had been no one until Brad Gilliland. Brad might have been "the one," but the death of Javiera Velasco created a deep sense of guilt and shame in him. He told her it was over. Something inside her snapped.

The police have already interrogated me three times over Brad's death. Now, they want me to testify under oath before a grand jury.

She mixed herself another drink.

In addition, there is the Securities and Exchange Commission.

The SEC had announced an investigation of the finances of E-Titan, alleging that the Cheetah transactions did not appear to meet the requirements for off-balance sheet financing. E-Titan's accounting firm was pressing the company to bring the assets and liabilities of the Cheetah transactions back on the company's books. Marjorie knew better than almost anyone else that such a restatement would wipe out most of E-Titan's earnings and a good bit of its net worth. Wall Street would be very unhappy— and the bank loans that financed Cheetah would be in default. M&M was about to spend a long time as a defendant in state, federal, and local lawsuits. Dobie was going to be furious.

Dobie is going to be furious. Can I trust him to protect me? Could he even if he wanted to? I could end up the fall guy in this thing.

In every prior situation, Dobie Dawson had stepped in to make things right. This time, although Dawson Companies could work out the loans and losses, the cost would put a considerable dent in DD's net worth. He might not be as inclined to be her savior.

Dobie is not answering my calls. He knows something, or he thinks he knows something.

M&M was worried.

I wish I had never told him about Brad, the trip to Mexico, or the safety deposit box.

She took another sleeping pill.

I need to rest.

Ever since her bag was stolen, she had been worried. When it was returned, she became even more worried. A thief would have kept the jewelry and ditched the rest. The fact that the contents of the files had been sent back to her meant the thief, whoever it was, had decided to return everything for a purpose.

Sooner or later, blackmail will probably come. I need to get Dobie prepared for that to happen.

Her mind was beginning to become hazy. She poured herself another drink and took another sleeping pill. It was time to go back to bed.

When the maids found her the following day, she lay naked and alone in her bed.

The coroner initially ruled the death an accidental suicide. M&M had ingested a quantity of alcohol and various sleeping and anti-anxiety drugs before her death.

The police found the contents of her Las Vegas safety deposit box, the letter returning them, and a rambling memorandum Marjorie had written for her use in a safe in her home. They also found her checkbook and canceled checks.

Ben Stone and Rico Diaz sat in Stone's office in suburban Houston near the Galleria. Ben was drinking a soft drink, and Rico had coffee. They exchanged Christmas greetings, and Rico thanked Stone for his help on the case.

Ben was the first to get down to business.

"So, she had him killed."

Rico nodded

"Yeh, apparently, she was furious when Gilliland told her he was returning to his wife. She knew how to get a hold of a hitman from her days in Las Vegas. She arranged the hit through a friend in Las Vegas. She had the common sense to pay for it with a foreign bank account, but we found a canceled check in her apartment when we cleaned out the safe. We also discovered a rambling memorandum that covered a lot of things, including some of the inside details about E-Titan. The FBI has the file. I think some things will be hitting the news after Christmas.

"You know, I feel sorry for her. From the beginning, I thought it was probably Lance DuFort who ordered the hit. Most of the time, I was just trying to find evidence to force her to testify against Lance. I couldn't see the facts for what they were. It appears now it was a case of a spurned lover."

Rico shook his head before he continued.

"You were in the FBI. I've been a policeman ever since I got out of the army. Both of us know that human beings are capable of anything. Wrapping up this murder does not wrap up everything, however. We still don't know for sure who murdered Javiera Velasco in Mexico, nor do we know who murdered Bill Stone. Somehow, I believe they're related. The most mysterious to me is the death of your brother. I can understand why someone might want to kill you. But to take such a risk doesn't seem rational. On the other hand, it must have been a professional job. Why would anyone do that where they did it? It would've made more sense to wait until you were alone."

Stone nodded.

"Yes, that murder seems to be the work of someone not very sophisticated and, perhaps, accustomed to using violence without repercussions. That points to a gang in Mexico."

Rico was in an uncommonly philosophical mood.

"She was a stunner. I saw the body. She was also rich. Dobie Dawson had made her a wealthy woman. I saw her checkbooks and bank statements. She was able to do anything she wanted—and even at her age, she was going to be able to get nearly any man she wanted. Some people don't know what they have."

Ben, who had been around longer, was less philosophical.

"Sometimes, it does not matter what you have. You grow up a certain way. You do things to get ahead. You don't know that you are gradually warping yourself beyond recognition, but you are. At least, that is what my brother would have said. He would have felt sorry for Marjorie."

He paused and went on.

"How long before you wind up the investigation?"

"Reviewing all the documents in her safe will take a long time. She had a will. She had a sister. Everything goes to her. It's a suspicious death, and so there will have to be an autopsy. We won't know for sure it was not a murder until after the coroner's report. We still have your brother's murder to consider and the death of Javiera Velasco. It might take weeks, even months."

"Well, if you find anything that sheds light on my brother's death, I hope you will whisper in my ear. One last thing: I am not sure I would put this down to a jilted lover quite yet. Wait for the autopsy. From what I know of Marjorie Melton, she is not the kind to commit suicide. She was a survivor. Of course, it could have been an accident."

"I will consider your advice. Say, it is almost Christmas Eve. I need to buy a present for my wife. I better go."

With that, the conversation ended.

16

White Christmas

ARRIVAL AT JACKSON HOLE

JACKSON HOLE, WYOMING

DECEMBER 22-24, 2001

CHRISTMAS IN JACKSON HOLE STARTED better than Arthur had anticipated. Gwynn and the children arrived in Wyoming on December 22. Arthur arrived the following day. Lance arrived on Christmas Eve. On December 23rd, Arthur hosted a dinner for the family at Alpenhof Lodge. In his room, Arthur read over the final details of the settlement documents Eddie Morales sent him from San Antonio. Lance had already signed the primary documents, which was one reason he was the last to arrive at Jackson Hole. Lance had also sent an apology to Buddy. The case was nearly over. All that was left was to file the dismissal papers with the court.

On Christmas Eve, Ben called.

"Marjorie Melton is dead. The doctors believe she overdosed on sleeping pills and booze."

Arthur paused to take in the news.

"I am sorry to hear this. Was there a suicide note?"

"No, but the police found the documents taken in Las Vegas in a safe in her office. There was also a long memorandum she wrote to herself. It is rambling. She might have been on booze, drugs, or both when she wrote it. The police would not show it to me, but apparently, the police believe Marjorie had Brad Gilliland killed."

"Evidence can be planted, as we both know."

"I don't think that Rico would do that. He is straight."

"I did not mean Rico."

Ben thought a moment.

"Believe me, I am keeping an open mind about the police department's conclusions.

"There is another reason I called. The memorandum also contained information that indicates Lance knows more about Javiera's death than he has admitted. She recounts that Lance awakened her and Gilliland after midnight. Gilliland left the room and did not return until after dawn. He announced that they were leaving Los Cabos."

"We already knew this."

"Yes, but it was immediately after their return that Gilliland broke off his relationship with Melton. As we know, Brad felt guilty about something. We also know that Brad told her, 'I am never going to lie for Lance DuFort again.' We know enough to know that the lies might refer to Javiera's death, E-Titan's finances, or both."

Arthur thought a moment.

"Gilliland's death might not have been a crime of passion. The lies she was talking about could have involved the financial trickery perpetrated by Lance and E-Titan. She was involved in the Cheetah partnerships up to her neck and profited from them. We know she made millions in salaries, bonuses, and profit-sharing arrangements. She was one of Dobie Dawson's chief lieutenants. It might be that she had Brad killed because she did not want her financial transactions with the Cheetah partnerships disclosed."

The two of them continued to talk for several minutes. The conversation got Arthur thinking. He wanted to wait for the autopsy report before making up his mind about M&M.

✳

Late in the afternoon, Roger and Ben called on Roger's conference phone to wish Arthur a Merry Christmas. Roger began.

"I have all the settlement papers in the Battle Mountain case on my desk. Eddie did a great job getting this done with Thomas off in Afghanistan. We can be proud of the team. Buddy called. He is happy to have this over. 'The greatest Christmas present I could get' was how he put it.

"Ever since Enron declared bankruptcy three weeks ago, the shares of E-Titan and other energy traders have been falling like rocks off a cliff. We've been getting phone calls. Everyone knows our firm has been on the other side of the Battle Mountain case. We're getting a lot of solicitations to represent people who are concerned about E-Titan.

"I also had a call from Ahn today. She says that your friend in Mexico heard that the police in Mexico are getting ready to act on information that leads them to believe Lance was involved in the disappearance of Javiera Velasco. Dobie Dawson has decided to leave his hotel in Acapulco. He is now located in Ambergris Caye, off the coast of Belize. A buddy from the oil business built the resort some years ago. Dobie doesn't want to be around if a case is brought against Lance."

At this point, Ben Stone entered the conversation.

"There is more. I hear from the grapevine that Lance has been disappearing. He spends a lot of time alone. When he is at work, he has difficulty focusing. He is easily distracted. His staff thinks he is depressed. People say he is extremely paranoid about the investigations, you, Gwynn, Dobie, and his entire staff. He is disheveled a good bit of the time. There is a bar near his office. He spends a lot of time there drinking bourbon alone. Ahn is worried. She thinks Lance could crack."

Ben concluded, "I wouldn't want to be Lance DuFort right now."

"No," replied Arthur before Ben went on with the real purpose of the call.

"In any case, Arthur, we think you need to be careful. It would be best to ensure that Gwynn and the children are safe. If the reports from Mexico are accurate, and if Lance DuFort was involved in the death of Javiera Velasco, we are dealing with someone who is potentially violent. He could be a physical danger to you, Gwynn, and the children.

"Whatever the future holds, we know the Securities and Exchange Commission will investigate him. We understand that the stock price has been falling in recent weeks. We know there will be shareholder litigation. We know he has loan covenants that require a level of security and a certain level of performance. E-Titan is in trouble. Big trouble. Lance is going to have significant liquidity problems. Finally, we know there is a chance he will have to appear before Congress. The fallout is going to be very big. Very big."

Arthur shuddered.

"I know. I've been trying to figure out how to protect the family. I could demand that our children live with me. I'm already hiring someone to care for Murray when I cannot be around, and it wouldn't take much to ensure that the other two children are cared for as well. However, if he snaps, that solution still leaves Gwynn and Claire with Lance. She might get hurt, and Claire might get hurt."

Ben did not want to say more but felt he had to.

"Arthur, we have dealt with people like Lance before. I try not to classify people, but Lance could be described as a sociopath. He breaks the rules. His repeated affairs are a symptom of deep character flaws. So are the convoluted financial transactions he has created at E-Titan.

"We know from discovery that there are transactions intended to hide the company's actual financial situation. Lance manipulated Brad Gilliland and others to do things that violated their consciences. I have heard that the annual review policy he instituted at E-Titan is used to manipulate people into extreme risk-taking in the search for profits and bonuses. Finally, he seems not to feel any guilt about his behavior. Such people can be impulsively violent. If he harmed Javiera, it was probably in a moment of impulsive aggression."

Arthur had done his own reflecting on Lance's personality.

"Lance deliberately broke up Gwynn and myself to satisfy his ego needs. He deliberately broke up his own family when he divorced his first wife. I don't think that he really cared for Gwynn. He just wanted her. Once he got her, he didn't care for her. Despite his charm, Lance doesn't seem to have a conscience or care about anyone. I'm not sure he even cares about himself. I am worried."

Arthur went on.

"Let me ask you this: What causes a person like Lance to snap? How much danger is there to Gwynn and the children?"

Ben had thought about what he would say to this question.

"Frankly, any kind of pressure or rejection can be a trigger. Lance likes to be at the center of attention. When you're around, he's not. That is a considerable risk during this holiday season, which tends to bring out the best and worst in people. It would be best if you were careful not to make yourself the center of the family.

"Second, a person like Lance creates chaos everywhere he goes; when that chaos begins to backfire, people like him can become violent. Most murders that I've investigated involve intense emotional reactions flowing out of rejection. If Lance hurt Javiera, it may have been caused by a rejection of his advances. My understanding is that she was a big tease. Being a big tease can be dangerous with some people. Neither you nor Gwynn must confront Lance during this holiday.

"Finally, and I think this may be the most significant risk of all, Lance's entire feeling of self-worth is built upon being a success. Right now, Lance is looking at an abyss. He's going to lose a lot of money. Maybe everything. He's probably going to lose his position. You and I both know he's going to lose his wife sooner or later. I'm not sure Lance won't suffer a complete breakdown when he finally realizes the deep, dark hole he has dug for himself."

Arthur sighed. He knew that Ben and Roger were right. He needed to think and meditate on the problem. More importantly, he needed to be careful.

"I see. I'll be careful. Call me after Christmas."

The family attended a Christmas Eve service in town and ate at a local steak house. Arthur noted that Lance seemed to be distracted. He carefully let Lance be the center of attention at the meal. Arthur left first to allow their family to be together. As he was about to leave the restaurant to return to his hotel, Lance came up behind him.

"I suppose you've seen the settlement documents?"

"I have. I understand the case is settled. Do you know anything different?"

"No."

"Lance, it's Christmas. When we get back home, we can talk business. This weekend, we should forget our problems, get along, and help the children have a good time."

Arthur stared into Lance's eyes, trying to figure out what was happening behind the fake smile and overt affability. Lance was under a lot of pressure. The lawsuit had not turned out as he hoped. The SEC was investigating E-Titan's financial reports. Marjorie was dead, and questions would be asked about everyone who knew her. Lance probably knew that the Mexican authorities had not cleared him of involvement in Javiera's death. If pressure could cause Lance to break, he was in a position to break.

Arthur smiled as encouragingly with as much friendliness as he could muster.

"It's Christmas Eve. You need to be with your family. I need to call my mother and wish her a Merry Christmas. She's with my brother in Houston. They are arranging an apartment for her. She doesn't want to live alone near Kerrville anymore. With my father gone, that stage of her life is over. I'll see you at Christmas lunch tomorrow. I probably won't stay long after the dinner. We can go skiing the day after tomorrow."

With that, Arthur left.

A QUIET CHRISTMAS
JACKSON HOLE, WYOMING
DECEMBER 25, 2001

CHRISTMAS DAY DAWNED DARK, COLD, and snowy. The weather forecast was for light snow early on Christmas Day, clearing just after noon. December 26th was to be a beautiful skiing day. Arthur woke up early, went to the condominium the DuForts rented to watch the children open presents, and then returned to his hotel room. He was careful to sit in a chair behind the family, where he would not become the center of attention. His secretary had sent his presents along early, so they were waiting for Gwynn and the children to arrive.

It is almost impossible not to have fun on Christmas, he thought to himself. *No matter the situation, children brighten every family on Christmas Day.*

The whole world seems to brighten up on Christmas Day. It is as if love has won a small, temporary victory, and the world wants to be at peace. It would be nice if Christmas Day characterized every day—but it doesn't.

After the children opened their presents, there was a long breakfast. After lunch, the DuFort family was going to go skiing on the children's slopes despite the weather. Arthur returned to the Alpenhaus. However, he spent some time in the early afternoon with the younger children at the ski school. Murray was already an accomplished skier. He went up a bit higher on the mountain with his mother. The smaller children were in the ski school and on the green slopes. Lance, it turned out, stayed at the condominium.

Jackson Hole is a difficult mountain on which to learn to ski. Most slopes are pretty tricky, and even the green slopes can be challenging for beginners. Arthur had learned to ski after he married Gwynn. Although he was athletic, Arthur was never an enthusiastic skier. At about 4 p.m., everyone went home to continue the celebrations, get the smaller children fed, and put them to bed. Arthur went to be alone at the Alpenhof.

Before he left Houston, Arthur's brother gave him a transcript of what was to be his Christmas sermon. It was entitled "When Love Comes Down." He read the sermon with interest. It began with a memory Arthur shared with his brother:

The Christmas story is familiar to all of us—perhaps too familiar. If you are like me, if you close your eyes as you listen to the words, your mind and emotions drift back to a simpler time. In my case, my mind drifts back to a small rural church in a small city in Texas. I see a candlelit sanctuary and a stocky Presbyterian minister with a quiet bass voice preaching a midnight Christmas Eve candlelight communion service after a festive dinner and a long evening waiting to go to church.

It is long past the bedtime of a small boy. Sitting in a hard wooden pew, on the edge of consciousness in a dark church, sitting by my mother, listening to my father speak the familiar words, "In those days a decree went out from Caesar Augustus, that all the world should be taxed." The sermon that year and every year was on that single chapter from the gospel of St. Luke.

Christmas is pregnant with memories of presents, bicycles, electric trains, food, turkey and dressing, hot chocolate, school plays, shopping in department stores, Christmas cards, school Christmas plays, and the like. These are rich memories of a brief interlude when the normal rules of our society: push, pull, study, work, and get ahead, are, for most of us, put aside.

Eventually, my father would tell the story of the birth, the stable, the shepherds in the fields, the angels, and Mary pondering the meaning of it all in her heart. So tonight, like my father, I ask you to come back with me now two millennia ago to Bethlehem, a small town just south of Jerusalem, to a crowded inn and a manger. Come with me to a stable in Bethlehem where we find Joseph and Mary. . . ."

From there, the sermon was just a straightforward telling of the Christmas story. The sermon ended simply.

You know the story, but what about the <u>meaning</u> of it all, not the theological meaning, but the real human meaning? The best sermon on the birth of Christ was written by the apostle John in his gospel, which reads in part, "For God so loved the world that he gave his One and Only Son, that whosoever believes in him, should not perish, but have everlasting life" (John 3:16). This is another all too familiar verse. We say it so frequently that we forget its meaning—or its meaning is hidden in warm childhood memories and the mindlessness of endless repetition. We need to hear again the truth: "For God so loved the world that he gave..." He gave himself. He gave the Word. He gave with an unfathomable self-giving love. These words are easy to say but so hard to comprehend and put to work in our lives.

Arthur read the entire sermon two or three times. It was too long for a Christmas Eve meditation to his lawyer's mind.

Knowing his father and brother, however, he knew that John was trying to say something more profound than the words he spoke. Bill Stone had not been known as an orator. He was known as a pastor who loved his congregation. Inside, he was deep. Very deep. His son John was very much the same. He made fun of his preaching abilities. Ordinarily, he might not have been chosen to be the pastor of the First Presbyterian Church of Houston, known for its preaching. But, after past trouble and division, the leadership decided it needed someone who would love the congregation and lead it wisely. They did not regret the decision. For all his success in law, Arthur envied his father and brother.

I have not been much of a giver. Oh, I give a little money to the church, but it's not much of a sacrifice. I have a lot of money. I give my children a little bit of time. But I never give any more time than I can afford. I gave my wife a little time, but I never gave any more time than was prudent. Maybe that is why I ended up alone in the Alpenhof while the woman I love is in another man's house on the side of a mountain.

Typically, Arthur Stone was not introspective. However, that Christmas evening was a quiet evening of introspection as the snow fell quietly outside his window, and the world was at peace. Before drifting to sleep, his final thoughts were simply this:

I have to find a way to help Gwynn and the children and make up as much as I can for the past.

The following day, he was awakened by a call from the front desk.

"There is a woman who claims to be your ex-wife, who wants to see you in the restaurant by the lobby. She sounds pretty upset."

Arthur jumped out of bed, dressed in jeans, a wool shirt, heavy socks, and Christmas slippers his children had given him the day before. He ran down the stairs, skipping the aging elevator, which he thought was too slow. Gwynn was waiting in the lobby.

"Can you talk?"

"Of course, I can talk. I am here to be with you and the children."

They walked into the restaurant. Arthur ordered coffee and the kind of breakfast he usually ate before skiing. Gwynn had already eaten something at the house. Besides, she didn't feel like eating. She did have a cup of coffee.

"Arthur, I need you to meet me at the top of the mountain today. Lance and I are going to have lunch there. I know you don't like skiing down the slopes from the top of the mountain here in Jackson Hole. You can take the ski lift back down the mountain if you want to. I don't want to be alone with Lance today. He's acting strange."

Arthur could see concern, even fear, in her eyes.

"What happened? You don't have to tell me anything private. Just tell me what you can."

Gwynn looked down, reserved and embarrassed.

"After Lance and I married, he seemed to lose interest in me. We had a child, and after Claire was born, he was even more disinterested. It has been months since we've slept in the same room. Unfortunately, the children are aware of the tension between us.

"Last night, after you left for the hotel and Claire was in bed, I went to my room. In the middle of the night, Lance started banging on my door. He demanded to be let in. He was screaming at the top of his lungs. I was afraid. He was not in control of himself. I did not open the door. Eventually, the children came out to see what was going on. He put on a good face and went back to his room. This morning, however, he was surly. I don't know how to say it, but I feel worried and concerned.

"When he left, he told me to meet him at the top of the mountain at noon. I agreed. Then, I came here to get you after taking the children to the ski school. Murray is waiting for me at home. We're going to ski together this morning."

Arthur remembered the conversation with Roger and Ben the day before.

"Gwynn, this is not the time to have a detailed conversation. I am not surprised that Lance is upset. He's just had to settle the case against Battle Mountain. The terms of the settlement are favorable to my client. On top of that, Enron's recent bankruptcy is washing over all the companies engaged in the industry. You can imagine he doesn't like to look at the financial news. I understand that the SEC has demanded a restatement of E-Titan's financial statements. In addition, I am aware that the SEC is considering an enforcement action against E-Titan. I don't know if he told you, but Marjorie Melton died the day before yesterday. It seems to have been an accidental death or suicide. However, there will be an inquiry into her death. The authorities will be interviewing Lance."

He decided not to tell her about Javiera just then.

"You can see from all this that your husband is under great pressure. I'm not sure he's the kind of person that reacts well to this kind of pressure. You need to be careful what you say and do right now."

Gwynn trembled. Under the circumstances, Arthur could only sit at a distance and watch until she could speak.

"I did not know about Marjorie's death. I can make it through the holiday, but I can't continue this any longer. Ahn already knows that I'm at my wit's end. This is not good for any of the children. It's especially damaging to Murray. That is why I want him to come to live with you."

Arthur agreed.

"I've been giving all this a lot of thought. It might be best if our children came to live with me—all of them. I can't take Claire. Perhaps your mother or Lance's mother could come for a visit. You and Lance need time to work things out or decide what comes next. I can't be involved in that directly. However, you know I will support you in any way I can.

"I know now that I have not been fair to you. I was not a good husband. On the surface, I was being a good guy. But underneath, I was trying to prove that I was the best lawyer in Texas, making the most money and winning the most cases. I should've seen what was coming. I was too blind to see. I regret that. I hope you will forgive me. In the meantime, if there's anything I can do, I will do it."

Arthur could tell Gwynn was holding back tears. Her face got stern, and her green eyes flashed as they nearly always did when she hid her feelings.

"I appreciate that. I guess I better be going. I don't want Lance to get suspicious. I'll see you at the top of the mountain at noon."

They said goodbye. Arthur went to his room, changed into his ski clothes, had a brief, tense phone conversation with Gwynn about the location for lunch, went to the ski school to be with the children, and waited for noon. There was a lot to consider.

The goal was to meet at Rendezvous Lodge at noon. During their earlier phone conversation, Lance had wanted to meet at Corbett's Cabin for waffles at lunch, but Arthur had declined.

"I am not a good enough skier to navigate some of those runs. Let's just meet at Rendezvous Lodge. You can go up the mountain later to ski the harder runs."

After some not-so-friendly teasing—and Gwynn's intervention—Lance agreed.

As it turned out, Arthur was a few minutes late arriving for lunch. He had been with the younger children, and the lifts were busy. The lift he was on stopped when a skier missed the turn and had to be helped off. When Arthur finally arrived, he removed his skis and walked to the restaurant from the lift. As he entered the room, he could see that Lance and Gwynn had been quarreling. He decided to try the cheerful and clueless approach.

"So, how was the morning? The kids seem to be having a good time at the ski school below. I thought Murray was here with you."

Gwynn looked up.

"He is here having lunch, but he made some friends his age yesterday and is skiing with them."

"Maybe I can ski with him when we leave."

Lance was looking angry and upset. It is usual for a skier to look a bit disheveled after a morning on the slopes, but Arthur noted that Lance had not shaved, which was unusual. They talked pleasantly, got their food, and returned to the table. The conversation was strained. Arthur felt that the couple had been arguing. Lance seemed abnormally uneasy. He was physically shaking. Arthur decided he had to inquire.

"Lance, are you OK? Did you fall this morning? You look shaky."

Lance looked up with a suspicious look.

"Why do you ask? I am just fine."

Arthur decided it would be best to place the blame on himself, if any.

"It is probably just me. I have taken a few falls on this mountain. This morning, I took a pretty bad one on a green slope near the ski school. I was shaky for fifteen minutes or more."

Lance was having difficulty focusing.

"I am just fine. It is too loud in here. I don't see why people have to talk so loudly."

Arthur looked at Gwynn, hoping for some help.

"I was just telling Lance that you had offered to keep our children for a few weeks to give us time to work on our marriage. This is not a good time with the problems at E-Titan, the various investigations, and the fact that Murray has been so difficult."

Arthur caught the point. He looked at Lance with as disarming a smile as he could muster.

"Murray's teachers think he belongs in a different school, and they have suggested he live with me so that he can attend a school near my home on Avalon."

Lance was suspicious. All of a sudden, there was a dead look in his eyes.

"Don't you try to trick me! I know you are after Gwynn—you have always been since I took her from you. It will not work. There is no way that I would give up the children. What would we do with Claire?"

Gwynn tried to make peace.

"I thought your parents or my mother might take Claire for a week or two. Lance, you know that things are not good between us. We need time."

Arthur never could exactly recall what happened next. In the beginning, Lance began speaking rapidly. There was a kind of wild light in his eyes. He accused Gwynn of sleeping with Arthur. He started to yell. Gwynn tried to calm him down. It did not work. People around them began to stare. Finally, Gwynn got up and left. Lance looked down, then up at Arthur. Arthur was scared at the look in his eyes.

Lance got up from his chair. He struggled with his ski parka and began to walk towards the slopes through the door from which Gwynn had exited. He turned towards where Arthur was getting out of his chair.

"I will show her. She cannot do this to me."

With that, he was gone.

Arthur stared at Lance silently for a moment, then got up and ran after him. In his haste, he slipped on a wet spot on the floor and hit another skier. He picked himself up, apologized, and hurried to catch Lance. He was too late. Lance and Gwynn were both already on the slopes.

DOWN THE SLOPE
JACKSON HOLE, WYOMING
DECEMBER 26, 2001

WHEN GWYNN LEFT THE LODGE, she had no plan beyond getting to the bottom of the mountain, collecting her children, and finding a place to spend the night. Her Irish temper was in full-anger mode. Of the three, she was technically the best skier. Lance was good and more athletic but not as coordinated and accomplished on his skis as Gwynn. Arthur was never comfortable on black slopes and hesitant a lot of the time, though he had the athletic muscle memory from his youth.

When she left, Gwynn quickly clicked on her skis and began descending the mountain, taking the Upper Sundance trail, the most direct route down the Sundance trails. She was skiing fast, and her attention was on the mountain.

Behind her, Lance struggled with his skis and started down the mountain, skiing like the madman he had become. He was determined to catch up with Gwynn. As he passed other skiers, they were astonished at his apparent fearlessness and speed.

That guy is crazy! One of them thought to himself.

Arthur was not far behind Lance, though as Lance picked up speed, Arthur fell behind. In the distance, where the trail was straight, he could see Gwynn traversing the mountain with nearly perfect form. She was skiing for form, not speed, while Lance was strictly skiing for speed. Arthur was skiing for survival—just trying not to fall while desperately trying to see what was happening ahead and catch up with Lance and Gwynn.

Halfway down the mountain, Gwynn traversed onto another run and began her descent again. Later, she could not remember why she left the most direct route. Perhaps because it was more challenging, and this would be her last run of the trip. Maybe it was just instinct from the past. Perhaps it was because she was upset.

My mind is made up. I am leaving Lance with the children. All the children.

She never saw Lance approaching.

Arthur, from behind, saw Lance take the traverse. He considered meeting them at the bottom of the mountain.

What if he catches up with her? I had better stay with them.

The day was bright, and the conditions were good. Arthur was skiing well—better than ever before. He was closing in on Lance as he caught up with Gwynn. The skiers were in a slow zone, which Gwynn obeyed, and Lance disregarded. To his horror, as Lance passed Gwynn, he came close enough to shove her towards the slope's edge, where a few small trees bordered a steep, sharp fall. Gwynn tumbled over the edge, catching a small tree as she fell.

Arthur's heart froze.

Arthur reached where Gwynn had fallen, clicked off his skis, and stumbled clumsily in his ski boots towards the edge. He dropped to his knees, stretched out on the snow, and grabbed Gwynn's arm. A couple from Brenham, Texas, who had seen Lance push her, were already there. Miraculously, Murray, who had followed Gwynn from the traverse, thinking he would surprise her before they reached Teton Village and the lifts also arrived. All three skiers got behind Arthur's legs, holding him on the mountain while he attempted to lift Gwynn back onto the slopes. The husband from Brenham was already on his Blackberry, trying to call for help. There was no coverage.

Arthur looked over the edge. Gwynn was holding onto the limbs of a small tree for dear life. Arthur did not wait for her to speak.

"Gwynn, whatever you do, do not let go of that tree. I am going to try to lift you. Don't worry; your weight cannot drag me off this slope. Murray and another couple who stopped when you fell are here. They are holding my legs. It is going to be OK."

With that, he pulled her up and into his arms.

They sat there holding each other for what seemed an eternity. Arthur tried to calm her down. Murray held her as well. She shook uncontrollably for a long time before she looked up at Arthur.

"I am so sorry for this. I did not know."

Arthur did not let her finish.

"No, I should have protected you when I could. I failed you. I will never fail you or the children again, I promise."

Gwynn was too shaken to ski. Eventually, the ski patrol arrived with a sled to take her down the mountain. They needed to check her to be sure she was OK. After the ski patrol left with Gwynn, Arthur, Murray, and the couple from Texas made their way down the mountain.

Beyond where Gwynn had been pushed off the slope's edge, a cluster of skiers and even more ski patrol were gathered, staring at the trees. A skier had lost control and hit a tree. He wasn't dead. But he was severely injured. The injured skier was Lance DuFort.

One of the bystanders who had seen what happened said to Arthur, "I was skiing behind him. He was skiing like a madman. Then, this guy in a black ski suit came out of nowhere. I don't know whether he pushed him or not. I do know he lost control and hit the tree. The skier in black appeared not to notice. He just went on to the bottom of the mountain."

Lance was so severely injured that he had to be life-flighted to the hospital. When they returned to the lodge, Gwynn already knew about the injury. The ski patrol had told her about the accident.

"Arthur, I need to go to the hospital. After all, I'm his wife. If he needs surgery, I need to be there to give instructions. I'm pretty sure we will want to transfer Lance to Houston as soon as possible. If you can take the children, I'll return before they go to bed. I'm not sure exactly where I'm going to spend the night. I will probably return here to rest and be ready in the morning."

Arthur quickly agreed to take the children to dinner. The DuForts had brought their *au pair*, Melena Babiarez. She would care for Claire, and Arthur would check in when he brought Murray, Margaret, and Stephen home. They parted ways with a brief hug and a word of encouragement from Arthur.

"This is going to work out. I don't know how, but it will."

I hope, he silently thought to himself.

17

Titan's Fall

AFTERMATH

JACKSON HOLE, WYOMING

DECEMBER 26-27, 2001

IT WAS AFTER 11:00 WHEN Gwynn finally got back to Teton Village. Arthur was waiting. Everyone else, including Melena, had gone to bed. The two shared a glass of wine and discussed the day's events. Gwynn and Arthur were physically, mentally, and emotionally exhausted but needed time to unwind. No one was going to find it easy to sleep tonight.

Arthur wanted to know about Lance and what would need to happen next.

"What did the doctor say?"

Gwynn dreaded the question and its answer.

"Lance is out of surgery. The doctors have told me that they do not think he will ever walk or be able to use his arms again fully. The injury is somewhere around his seventh vertebra. We won't know for weeks because the swelling needs to come down before the doctors can tell how much progress he will be able to make.

He's not in a good place right now. He's awake, but he's not lucid. He keeps screaming and yelling in a kind of delirium. He screams about me. He screams about you. He screams about E-Titan."

Arthur could only say, "I am sorry."

Gwynn looked at him.

"There is more. He talks about Javiera Velasco. When he does, he says, 'I didn't mean to do it. It just happened. The b***h was teasing me and making fun of me. I did not mean to do it.' Arthur, I think he killed her."

"So do the police in Mexico."

Arthur went on.

"Uncle Ben and Roger called me yesterday. The authorities in Mexico have evidence tying Lance to Javiera's murder. There is more. Some of the mismanagement at E-Titan is also about to come out. If Lance survives this, he will have a lot to answer for. This is going to be very hard on you and the children. There will be a lot of publicity—a lot of publicity. There is also going to be a lot of litigation. You need to be prepared for a long, long suffering.

"By the way, have you called his parents?"

"Yes, they know. They will try to get here from Paris as soon as possible. The big question is, 'Where should they come?' I think Lance needs to be in Houston. The Texas Medical Center provides some of the best medical care in the world. But he may not be able to travel for a time. The doctors say he needs to be stabilized here."

"Have you notified the company?"

"Yes. I called his assistant, who called Dobie Dawson. Dobie called me from the hospital. He's in Belize, where he intends to stay for a considerable time. They are arranging a press release about the accident. I can tell that Dobie is concerned. He's afraid the stock price, which is already falling, will drop even further. He also voiced concern about who is going to run E-Titan. Its board of directors will need to meet this week to decide. It is amazing. Although E-Titan is a public company, it has no continuity plan concerning a tragedy like this."

Arthur nodded.

"I need to let you sleep. I'm going to the Alpenhof to sleep. It would be best if you get as much sleep as possible. If you don't mind, I will stay at the hotel in the morning and make a few calls. Roger needs to know about this, as does Ahn. Ahn is going to want to come up here and help you. You might like to decide if you need her.

"I am not sure this is the best time to take the children back to Houston. They need to see you and know you are OK. We have the rooms booked until after the New Year's Day. If you cannot leave by then, I can take the children to Houston and return them to school. Before I go, I want to take Murray to breakfast at the Alpenhof."

Gwynn was utterly exhausted. They hugged each other again, and Arthur left. Gwynn took one last sip from her glass, turned off the lights, and went to her room. It took a long time for Gwynn to get to sleep. She had a lot to think about.

A HEALING BREAKFAST
JACKSON HOLE, WYOMING
JANUARY 1, 2002

NEW YEAR'S DAY DAWNED BRIGHT and clear in Jackson Hole. Under ordinary circumstances, it would have been an excellent time to ski and spend time with the family. Amid the unfolding tragedy of Lance's injuries, the end of a long time of cold and darkness was slowly unfolding. Lance was now stable and scheduled to be transferred to Houston soon. For the last week, Gwynn had been almost constantly by his bedside, listening to his ramblings, trying to make sense of them, and sharing whatever she might learn with Arthur. Arthur spent most of his daytime with the children. The family skied, played games, shopped in Jackson Hole, and shared their griefs and fears. Arthur slept at the Alpenhof, which he was coming to love. Melena cared for Claire and the other children until Gwynn returned home.

During that long week, Arthur made it a point to spend time alone with each of the children. He saved Murray for last. New Year's Day, after a family New Year's Eve party the night before, which was heavy on pizza, soft drinks, and a little champagne for the adults, Murray came to the Alpenhof for breakfast. In previous months, it would have been an uncomfortable event. It began awkwardly, but the awkwardness soon disappeared. As the two ate breakfast, the subject of Arthur and Gwynn came up.

"Dad, why did you ever let Mom leave with Lance?"

"The simple answer is I should never have let your mother go. But with adults, it's not that easy. My feelings were hurt; I felt helpless and angry. My anger got the best of my love. My anger got the best of my love for a long time."

Murray seemed to think that was a good explanation.

"I think that's what happened to me. I was so mad at you because of the divorce and angry at Mom for what she had done that I got scrambled in my thinking. I forgot who I loved or that I loved my family. I am sorry for the drugs and bad behavior. It was stupid.

"As often as Aunt Ahn would tell me, 'Sometimes you just have to forgive and understand that adults are human and make mistakes,' I couldn't let go of my anger. Maybe that's why I started acting the way I acted. I also think maybe I blamed myself for what happened. You know I've never been an easy child."

Arthur and Murray both smiled at the admission. As quickly as the moment passed, Murray moved on to another matter.

"What happens now?"

"I can't answer that question. Lance is still alive. Even though he acted dreadfully towards your mother, she's married to him. The reason she's been spending so much time at the hospital is to fulfill her duty. She has to take care of him 'for better or worse.' This may not seem logical after all that has happened, but sometimes, the right thing doesn't seem logical at first.

"In a way, Murray, what happens next doesn't matter. Our family is together. We have made it through a difficult time. Your mother knows that I love her and always will. I know your mother loves me and always will. I would do anything for your mother. I know she would do anything for me. We would do anything for you, your brother, and your sisters. Our family is not the family we started to create; it's not the family God intended, but it is the family we created between us."

"What about Lance?"

"Lance is very sick. He may never recover, although he may linger on for a long time. Right now, our family will have to endure some challenges. There will be repercussions because of what happened on the mountain—and before. All we can do is take care of one another through difficult times. I don't like Lance. But I will learn to take care of him for the sake of your mother and your little sister. I think you will have to do that, too."

Breakfast was almost over, but one last matter needed to be discussed. Arthur broached the subject.

"I've been talking to your lawyer and the prosecutor. Because you're a first offender, I think you'll get off a bit easier than perhaps is best for you. Right now, the prosecutor is offering to sentence you to attend a drug awareness seminar and weekly public service until you graduate from high school. You must attend an 'Outward Bound' type program in the summer. The summer requirement was my suggestion. Naturally, if you were to break any of the conditions of the sentence, you're going to go to jail. We don't want that to happen."

Murray had known that this was coming.

"It's not as bad as I feared. Going to an educational program instead of jail is easy to agree to. I'm sure the community service will get old, but I can do it. As for the Outward Bound program, it sounds like fun. If I go for a year or two and don't like it, or if there's something else just as wholesome to do during the summer, do you think it can be changed?"

"I am sure that the judge would change the terms of that requirement if everyone agreed that it was for the best. Frankly, we don't want to make the rest of your time at home with us as a family more stressful than we need to. It won't be long before you are gone to college."

Murray nodded.

"It would be nice if we could stay up here and ski all winter, but I guess we've got to go home and face real life."

Arthur felt like there was just a little more to be said.

"I know many families that are alienated from one another. I've met many adults who carry baggage into adulthood because of the problems they had growing up. I don't want that to happen to you. I also don't want you and me to be estranged. You know that I'm busy. The next few months are going to be very busy. But no matter how busy, I have time for you whenever you need me."

Murray got up from the table, walked around, and hugged Arthur. Together, they left the hotel and went to find the girls. It was New Year's Day; they needed to celebrate. Tomorrow, they would leave for Houston. Christmas was over, and it was time to return to "real life," whatever that meant.

COLLAPSE OF A TITAN
HOUSTON, TEXAS
JANUARY 4, 2002

JACKSON HOLE IS A WATERING hole for the rich and famous, so the wire services immediately picked up the story of Lance DuFort's accident. It is difficult to describe the chaos that ensued. Dobie Dawson was in Belize in a hotel. All he could do was watch the stock ticker. By noon, he realized the game was up. He made a call to Buddy Bennett.

"Buddy, it's DD. If you have been keeping up with the news, you know that E-Titan is in trouble. Ever since Enron collapsed, our stock has been under pressure. With Marjorie committing suicide and Lance having a ski accident, the market is focused on us. You know the business better than anyone on the outside. I can't think of anyone on the inside who can take over. I wonder if you would be interested in coming back to the Dawson Corporation or some kind of a merger between Battle Mountain and E-Titan?"

It didn't take Buddy long to respond.

"I'm not sure that's possible. I don't know what Lance has been doing since I left the company. Battle Mountain is a pipeline company. That's what we do. Our trading operation is just a hedging operation for the pipelines. There's no way we could 'merge with' E-Titan. Frankly, at this point, it would hurt our stock. I wish I could help but can't think of a way. Honestly, DD, I am sorry things turned out this way for you."

DD had expected this response. He knew Buddy never liked the energy trading business. He had a counterproposal.

"Henry Zhao, the chief trader, might take over the position of President of E-Titan. Can you think of anyone better?"

"No, but I don't know the company anymore. E-Titan is a long way from the trading operation of the old Battle Mountain Pipeline Company.

"DD, I want to be honest. I don't see how E-Titan can avoid bankruptcy. the *Wall Street Journal* had a lead article about the Cheetah limited partnerships this morning. It more than insinuated that the debt must come back onto your balance sheet. It also revealed that E-Titan must issue additional shares to prop up the balance sheets for the limited partnerships. You can see the results in the market today: E-Titan is in a death spiral. I don't think a merger can be arranged quickly enough to save it."

DD had been considering the bankruptcy option.

"What if we put E-Titan into bankruptcy? The bankruptcy filings are already drawn up, just in case. Would Battle Mountain consider acquiring the company if we put E-Titan into bankruptcy? Buddy, I don't think anybody but you can straighten this mess out. I certainly can't. Besides, I don't want to return to the United States from Belize just now."

Buddy was non-committal.

"I don't know. I can't talk to Arthur Stone right now. He is just back from Jackson Hole and is caring for his children. Everyone is pretty devastated by the news and Lance's injuries. If you don't already know, it seems there is more to what happened than just Lance hitting a tree skiing. At lunch, Lance had some kind of mental breakdown at the top of the mountain. He pushed Gwynn on the mountain coming down. He's been babbling incoherently ever since."

Buddy paused to think for a moment.

"What if you did this: appoint Henry Zhao to be the president of E-Titan? Get that done today if possible. There needs to be an emergency board meeting. Have the board approve the bankruptcy filing if that's the course of action you think is wise. Battle Mountain will become a minor E-Titan creditor because we've done some hedging trades through your operation. Winchester & Wells will unquestionably be our lawyers. We will work to get an experienced energy lawyer appointed as a trustee in the bankruptcy. If it's someone that Arthur can work with, we can see what we can do to help with the reorganization. There might be assets that Battle Mountain would be willing to buy. That is the best I can do."

DD understood this was the end of E-Titan. He hadn't bothered to mention the assets that the Dawson companies had managed to place in the Cheetah partnerships, the compensation Marjorie Melton had taken out of those partnerships, making her a wealthy woman, or the liability that Dawson Companies might have in any bankruptcy. He did not want to disclose too much. The conversation was over.

"Look, I don't know exactly what I will do. I understand that the board of directors of E-Titan has to have a meeting. We've already called it for this afternoon. I won't be able to attend. However, I will be on the telephone, listening in and giving whatever input I can. You'll know what we decide when you read the *Wall Street Journal* in a few days.

Buddy, always wanting to let anyone down easy, gave Dobie one last word of encouragement.

"DD, I know this seems impossibly bad. It isn't good. But you'll work your way out of it. You have lots of assets. This will set the Dawson Corporation and you back, but it won't be the end.

At least, I don't think it will. Just move forward as calmly as you can. If there's anything we can do at Battle Mountain, I'm sure it'll come to my mind."

He did not say all he knew. Privately, he was not sure DD or the Dawson Corporation would survive.

By the end of the day, the shares of E-Titan had fallen to less than a dollar. The share price had been at $100 only six months earlier. The company filed for bankruptcy the following Monday morning in Houston. The following day, the *Wall Street Journal* printed another exposé on the company. It was devastating. In part, it read:

Yesterday, in a federal courtroom in Houston, Texas, one of America's hottest companies hit the wall like a race car out of control on a Texas speedway. E-Titan Energy was the darling of Wall Street. The stock price reached over $100 a share before it began to fall in the wake of the Enron collapse. Behind the collapse are some of the common elements of modern financial fraud. Accounting principles were used in ways that were never intended to create an illusion of profitability.

Mark-to-market accounting is designed to picture a company's financial situation accurately. At E-Titan, mark-to-market accounting was used to estimate future profits that never materialized. Special Purpose Entities, intended to allow companies with assets that would produce an income stream to transfer them off their balance sheet, were apparently used to hide massive losses. It's a sad story. And the story is not over.

The article was correct. The story was not over.

(**18**)

TRIALS AND TRIBULATIONS

NEW DEVELOPMENTS
HOUSTON, TEXAS
JANUARY 2002

IN HOUSTON, WINTER WAS NOT yet over. It's like that in Houston. Sometimes, February can be the coldest month of the year. Then March comes, and spring is in the air. In January, even on the nicest days, tomorrow, it could turn cold. It was that way when Arthur and the family returned from Christmas. Freezing one day, warm the next.

Under the circumstances, Arthur had considerable responsibility for the children. Murray was enrolled in a public school and living in the house on Avalon. Gwynn and the children were living in Lance's home. Lance was at St. Luke's Hospital in the Texas Medical Center.

One morning, just two weeks after the family's return, Arthur received a call from home. It was from Gwynn.

"Has Roger called you?"

"Not this morning."

"Thomas Mallory has been injured in Afghanistan. His unit was near Kabul. A roadside bomb exploded. He is being sent to Walter Reed in Maryland. Alicia is flying there this weekend to be with him."

Arthur and Gwynn talked about Thomas and Alicia and the problems this event created for Gwynn. In the end, Arthur asked the obvious question.

"What can I do?"

"Do you remember indicating that one of your associates might agree to work with Alicia and me for a while if my situation demanded it?"

"Yes. Her name was Cynthia Maynard. She seems nice but is a little bored by corporate practice. Like you, she would like to try her hand at something else just to see if she likes it. We can't provide her with that opportunity. You can. In this situation, she is not risking anything. If and when she returns, her work for you will not interfere with her career here."

"Can you find out if she is still willing?"

"I will do that today. What about you? Do I need to take all the children? I have hired someone to look after Murray when I am gone. I can make things work for a few days."

"If it is all right with you, I want to keep the children close to me just now. I can't say what the next week will bring. Let's play things by ear. Frankly, Arthur, I don't know what I will do. Ahn is trying to be helpful. Your brother has called and visited Lance. He is a wonderful guy. I am trying to decide what the next course should be with Lance, his hospitalization, the children, and me. Lance's parents are here and trying to be helpful, but they really can't help. Being around his family, I understand Lance better.

"One reason I might take you up on the offer is that the press has started camping outside the house. They've heard the rumors about what happened in Wyoming. Of course, there are daily developments in E-Titan's bankruptcy. They just want a story. Unfortunately, the children are caught up in all this. We can't get out of the driveway without someone trying to stop us. I'm not sure it's healthy for the children to see this."

Arthur agreed.

"I don't want to be seen as forcing anything on you. However, I agree with you. It isn't healthy for children to live in the middle of a media storm. I've read the papers. Many bad things are coming out, but some stories describe bad things that never happened. Younger children cannot understand, sort through, and discern between truth and falsehood. Why don't we consider you keeping Claire and me keeping our children? Another possibility is that you and the children move in here, and I live somewhere else for now."

There was a pause. Then Gwynn went on with her train of thought.

"So, Arthur, how much of the reporting on E-Titan is accurate?"

"I can only tell you what I believe I know from our discovery concerning the lawsuit. From the beginning, Lance used mark-to-market accounting in a way that, intentionally or unintentionally, inflated E-Titan's profits. I don't want to suggest there was anything criminal, although there could have been. Marking-to-market speculative assets involves an element of judgment. It is our view that E-Titan was consistently judging on the high side. As that continued, there was pressure to create more profits each quarter. I think it got out of hand.

"The second thing has to do with these Cheetah partnerships. If we understand correctly, E-Titan took assets and liabilities off its balance sheet and placed them in one of the Cheetahs with associated debt. Unfortunately, they would typically take them off the balance sheet at somewhat more than they were worth, so the related debt was more significant than it appeared to be. Once again, was this intentional or just bad judgment? I can't say. I can say it wasn't very wise.

"Finally, the banks are all lining up to sue E-Titan, the auditors, the law firms, Lance, DD, and others. Frankly, I don't believe the banks were totally deceived, though they will claim to be. Everyone was making a lot of money. The investment bankers were making fees, the banks were receiving interest and fees, and E-Titan reported profits. Everyone was having fun at the circus as long as the merry-go-round kept turning.

"Unfortunately, the difference between the assets' value and the debt amount became unsustainable over time. In the midst of that, Enron failed. There was a lot of industry lousy press, two senior officers died, and the stock market collapsed.

"All I can tell you is that I wouldn't run my business the way Lance runs E-Titan."

There was another long pause. Gwynn had been a corporate attorney before turning to family and estate law. She was also a quick study, generally seeing problems faster than Arthur.

"I see. Now, what do you know about Javiera Velasco? You don't need to sugarcoat your answer. I have known that Lance was cheating on me for a long time. Javiera was just one in a long line if he slept with her. In his delirium, he has been confessing to her murder over and over again."

Gwynn and Arthur were now in tricky territory.

"We became interested in Javiera's death because of its proximity to Brad Gilliland's death. We thought there might be a link. I didn't want to presume to tell you that your husband was cheating on you. You had already read the *Texas Quarterly* article.

"After Brad Gilliland died, we hired someone you might remember from Mexico to investigate. He confirmed that on the night Javiera was killed, she was with Lance. When they left the party downstairs, Lance, Brad Gilliland, and Marjorie Melton testified that she did not come to Lance's hotel room. If that were true, Lance had an alibi. Our friend in Mexico and the authorities there did not think the group was being entirely truthful. Now, two of the little group are dead, and one is seriously injured. Ben has been doing some looking around, and we believe that my father's death was an attempt to kill Ben because he was looking into the connection between Brad Gilliland, Marjorie, Lance, and Javiera. It is possible someone wanted to get rid of me."

"Just before Christmas, we became aware that the now-dead Marjorie had written memoranda casting doubt on Lance's story. In addition, we learned Brad Gilliland had stated that he 'would not lie for Lance again.' We don't know whether the issue concerned Javiera or E-Titan.

"I believe that if Marjorie were not dead, she would already have been indicted for the murder of Brad Gilliland. The police found canceled checks and other information indicating she was the person who hired the hitman. They also found evidence that Brad was so traumatized by whatever happened in Mexico that he rededicated himself to his marriage and broke off things with Marjorie.

"We don't know if she ordered the killing as a 'woman scorned' or to cover up her participation in the Cheetahs' financial dealings. We may never know.

"Finally, whatever the truth is about Javiera's death, Lance does not have an alibi, and the police know that. Worse, Javier

Velasco knows. El Halcón has lost a granddaughter, the apple of his eye, and his namesake. If he thinks that Lance had anything to do with the death of his granddaughter, he could strike out at you or Claire. We need a security service at your house 24-7. That is one of the reasons I am anxious to take the children."

Gwynn was quiet for a long, long while.

"Do you think Lance ordered your father's death?"

"Honestly, I don't think so. First, we don't think anyone ordered Dad's death. We believe someone ordered Uncle Ben's death or perhaps mine. Second, Ben was not investigating the death of Javiera. He was investigating the death of Brad Gilliland. That was always the focus of his investigation. He did find out things about the death of Javiera, but that was not what he was primarily looking for. Whoever ordered the hit ordered it on Ben or me. Dad just got in the line of fire.

"When I sent an investigator to Los Cabos, I was trying to see if there could be a link between what happened in Los Cabos and Brad Gilliland's killing. We felt Brad would have honestly testified about Titan and the Battle Mountain sale. It seemed to me and the rest of the team that the timing of the murder, the day before his deposition, was a bit too convenient. It might have been a deliberate attempt to prevent him from testifying.

"We were also looking for evidence that Lance acted in bad faith when E-Titan sued Battle Mountain. As you might remember, to win our case on one of the counts, we had to prove that the press releases issued by E-Titan were intended to harm Battle Mountain and made in full awareness that they weren't true. That's a heavy burden of proof. We were looking for support for our position.

"Finally, I was concerned about you and the children. I didn't want you or the children dragged into some 'sexcapade' in

Mexico that ended in the death of El Halcón's granddaughter. We both know he is bad news."

"Yes."

Gwynn remembered his involvement in a death years earlier with a shudder.

Arthur could tell Gwynn was getting upset. He had seen those green eyes go hard and the full lips go thin in the past, so he could imagine what she was thinking. She seemed about to say something, but then she changed her mind and returned to the children.

"Knowing this, I think it might be best if the children came to live with you, and we hired a bodyguard to be at the house with Claire and me."

Arthur agreed. There didn't seem to be any more point in continuing the conversation. She needed to take care of her business, and he needed to take care of his. In particular, he needed to check on Thomas Mallory and talk to Ben about protecting the children.

BATTLE SCARS
HOUSTON, TEXAS
JANUARY 15, 2002

AS ARTHUR EXPECTED, ROGER IMMEDIATELY came to see him when he entered the office.

"I suppose you already know about TL?"

"Yes. Gwynn called me this morning. She is directly affected by this development, and it could not come at a worse time, with Lance in the hospital. I was shocked. With Alicia gone to be with Thomas and Lance in the hospital, Gwynn needs help. I talked to Cynthia Maynard a few weeks ago about helping in a crisis. I think we're in a crisis.

"I'd appreciate it if you see if she is still willing to help with Gwynn's clientele. We should agree with Gwynn that her net billings would be paid to us, and we will pay her salary. She will not be leaving the firm, and Cynthia will know she has a place here and remains part of our operation. If she bills any hours for Winchester & Wells during this time, that would be great.

"If she agrees, the Executive Committee needs to approve. Also, we need to be sure that the partner mentoring her agrees." (Every associate at Winchester & Wells had a partner in charge of mentoring them.)

The conversation came back to Thomas Mallory.

"Gwynn said there was some kind of a roadside bomb incident. Do you know more?"

"Not really. His unit had been sent into a Taliban-dominated area. A roadside bomb exploded near the vehicle in which Thomas was riding at the time. A couple of soldiers were killed. Others were injured, some seriously. TL was pretty badly injured but will recover. He's going to lose a part of his leg below the knee. He will be at Walter Reed Hospital for his initial recovery. Obviously, he is not going to return to Afghanistan."

Arthur nodded and went on.

"We need to convey the firm's wishes for a speedy recovery to Alicia. We also need to assure Thomas that he has a place at the firm whenever he is ready to return to work. Can we do that? I could use him today!"

Arthur smiled his most disarming smile. As was often the case, there was truth in what he said. Roger smiled in return and went on.

"I will see that the firm sends something to the hospital. Flowers, some kind of remembrance, or a card are always appropriate. I'll be sure that everyone on his team signs the card. The Executive Committee will want to assure Thomas about his future."

Arthur changed the subject.

"When I was in Jackson Hole, you sent word that we were getting a lot of inquiries about representing companies in connection with the bankruptcy and other litigation deriving from the collapse of E-Titan. Whatever we do, we need to check with Buddy and Battle Mountain about representations. I feel that Battle Mountain will end up owning some of the assets of E-Titan and perhaps the Dawson Corporation. I don't think anyone other than Buddy understands the history and can profitably unravel some business relations. We don't want to get into a position where we can't represent the person who will end up being the winner."

Roger smiled. Over the years, it had always amazed him that Arthur, for all his apparent naivete about some things, usually managed to see the bottom line and the best strategic course of action. Arthur was thinking beyond the bankruptcy filing to how that filing would end. It was a kind of instinct.

Arthur went on.

"How do we stand with the settlement? I'm concerned that, because of the bankruptcy, we might not be able to fully consummate our deal with E-Titan."

"Don't worry. The settlement is complete. Before Christmas, we signed all the papers approved by the E-Titan board. We were paid some of our legal fees for representing Battle Mountain as part of the settlement. Naturally, someone can object to the settlement, but I don't think Battle Mountain will have to give back any money. I also don't see how anyone would want to unwind the settlement. It would add to E-Titan's liabilities. Recent developments make it even more likely that we would prevail on the merits and might even receive a judgment greater than the settlement. Last but not least, there was not a lot of money involved."

Arthur nodded. Roger was his sounding board, best advisor, and the person who always saw that things were done correctly. It was a friendship and partnership Arthur treasured.

"The last thing we need to talk about is Gwynn and me. You already know that Gwynn and I agreed before Christmas that Murray would come and live with me. Now, we think that Margaret and Stephen may also need to live with me. As soon as we finish, I'm going to call Ben. I'm concerned that Gwynn and Claire need protection. Lance is still alive, and anyone with animosity towards Lance might try to hurt Gwynn and the baby.

"There are plenty of people who think Lance was behind the murder of my father. I don't think I agree. Lance did know that I was going to stay in San Antonio. But he only learned this a few hours before I left for the ranch. You can't arrange a hit in that short a time—not even if you have regular contacts with the kind of people who hire themselves as assassins. Lance, for all his failures, didn't have those contacts. I don't think he could have arranged the murder that quickly. It probably had been in the planning much earlier.

"One last thing bothers me. When we arrived at the scene of Lance's injury, one of the bystanders was convinced he had seen someone ski up beside Lance just before he fell. If someone pushed Lance deliberately, that might mean someone else was behind the assassination attempt.

"Lance may have been involved in something darker than he knew. In that case, Gwynn or the children might be targets. I might be a target. I need to arrange some security for both sides of the family."

Roger agreed.

"I think that might be a good idea."

Arthur continued.

"Roger. I'm going to need help. Please let me know if I need to pay attention to specific details at the firm. This won't last forever, but I think it will last a few months."

Roger nodded. Then he remembered something.

"Oh yes. There is one more thing I forgot to mention. The governor called. He would like to speak with you. I hate to speculate, but it might concern the need for a new attorney general. Rumor has it that there is going to be an opening. Either he wants to talk about you becoming attorney general, or he wants to talk about who you recommend. Probably the latter."

"I will eventually return the call. Be sure I have the information. Right now, I am focused on the family and bringing the fallout of the Battle Mountain case to a conclusion."

With that, the conversation ended, and the future began.

VINDICATION OF BEN STONE
HOUSTON, TEXAS
JANUARY 2002

WHEN THE DOOR CLOSED BEHIND Romny, Arthur turned and called his uncle. He needed help, and there was unfinished business between them. Because his son ran the agency these days, and Ben was retired, he could not immediately reach him.

Ben was on the golf course. Later that afternoon, they were able to talk.

"Arthur, this is Ben. I understand you have been trying to reach me."

Arthur explained his need for security both at his house and Gwynn's. Ben agreed to look into the matter.

"I don't think it will be too difficult to arrange. It might take a day or two, however."

"Just make it as quick as possible. The second reason for my call is for you to update me on your various Battle Mountain investigations."

"That will take a bit more time. Let's deal with Lance first. My sources tell me that, despite his injuries, Lance is going to be indicted for the attempted murder of your ex-wife. The Wyoming authorities know Lance will probably never be able to stand trial. Nevertheless, they think an indictment is warranted.

"More worrying for us is that Javier Velasco unquestionably knows about the incident in Jackson Hole. It's been in newspapers across America and beyond. I'm sure the Mexican police are also aware of the incident. If he suspected Lance before, you can be sure he is going to suspect that he's behind Javiera's death now."

Arthur agreed. "I mentioned to Roger a few minutes ago that at least one person in Jackson Hole who saw Lance fall thought they saw another skier ski towards him and push him before he entered the trees. If that is true, someone out there was trying to get at Lance. Javier Velasco ranks high on my list of suspects. He certainly has the connections to make something like that happen."

Ben agreed. "It is possible that El Halcón is behind Lance's injury. However, I don't see why Velasco would be tempted to have me killed. I was investigating matters that pertained to the murder of his granddaughter. Any information I turned up might help the Mexican authorities find the person who killed Javiera. It wouldn't make any sense for El Halcón to try to have me killed."

What Ben was saying was correct. There had to be more.

Ben went on.

"The second piece of information I have for you concerns Marjorie Melton. The results of her autopsy were surprising. The barbiturates in her body were greater than the possible contents of containers the authorities recovered. Usually, when someone takes barbiturates and drinks, you find the containers beside the body or nearby. Somewhere, there's a container the authorities haven't found.

"In addition, the condition of the body leaves open the possibility that someone was with Marjorie on the night of her death. The police are not talking about what they know. But there is something unusual about the death. They haven't ruled out suicide, but they can't rule out the involvement of another person."

Arthur tried to make sense of the new information.

Could there be a connection between Brad Gilliland's murder, Marjorie's death, and my father's death? If there is, who could it be? Lance could not have murdered Marjorie, or could he? He arrived in Jackson Hole the day after her death.

"We had better investigate where Lance was the night Marjorie died. He arrived in Jackson Hole the next day. Of course, he flew in a private plane. He explained that a business meeting caused the delay. I think I'd like to know the nature of that meeting. If there was a business meeting, Lance probably has an alibi. He lied to cover up something if there was no business meeting."

Arthur went on.

"In evaluating this new information, we can't forget that we don't think it's possible that Lance ordered the killing that ended with my father's death. He just didn't have enough time to order a killing in Kerrville, Texas. I spoke to him the morning of the day of the murder. If it is true that you were followed from Houston, and if someone followed me from San Antonio, as we suspect, the murder was already ordered before Lance knew anything.

"This leads us back to Javier. Once again, I can't imagine Javier Velasco ordering the murder. Not unless he had something to gain. I can't see that he had anything to gain.

"We are certain that M&M paid for the hit on Brad. There must be two different persons at work here."

Ben thought for a moment.

"We have forgotten Dobie Dawson. Dobie lived in Las Vegas for a long time. He had contacts with the underworld. He likes being seen as a 'tough guy.' Dobie also has long-standing relations with various intelligence agencies through his business. Dobie has the contacts to order a hit."

Arthur picked up the train of thought. Things were becoming clearer.

"Yes. Dobie has the means. He might also have a motive. What if he was trying to cover his tracks because of Dawson Corporation's involvement in the Cheetah partnership deals? What if Dobie ordered the death of Gilliland to keep him from talking, your death for getting too close, an attempt on Lance to cover up his involvement with Lance's misdeeds, and finally, the death of Marjorie to cover up her involvement?"

Ben nodded.

"If Dobie was concerned that he might get dragged into investigations of the Cheetah partnerships and Lance might cop a plea and leave him holding the bag, he might have ordered the deaths. Once Gilliland was killed, there would be a danger to DD if he were involved. It is possible that Dobie got Marjorie to front the hit on Gilliland, which began this entire series of murders.

"Finally, there is his move to Belize. While Belize has an extradition treaty with the United States, people with means can avoid extradition for a long time."

Arthur brought the speculation down to reality.

"All these are fine theories, but we have to have evidence. There must be some way to test our hypothesis. Dawson is a weakling, but very few people would consider him a murderer. Let's give ourselves time to ponder the facts and how we might get additional evidence. In a few days, we will get back together.

"One thing is certain: Gwynn and the children need additional security. Let's make that our priority."

Ben left the conversation convinced Dobie Dawson held the key to at least some of the murders and attempts, though he was not sure how many. They needed a way to test the theory.

(**19**)

Love and Fate

GWYNN'S DREAM

EPIPHANY 2002

JACKSON HOLE, WYOMING

ONCE ARTHUR AND THE CHILDREN returned to Houston, Gwynn was left with Claire, Melena, who cared for Claire when Gwynn was in the hospital, Lance, and her thoughts. Her days developed a similar routine. She got up and made breakfast for Claire. She talked to Melena about her schedule and then left for the hospital. Around noon, she returned for lunch, at least when she was not needed at the hospital. She spent the afternoon in Lance's hospital room or consulting with doctors. She went home for dinner. After dinner, she would either return to the hospital for one last time or spend time with her daughter and watch television to unwind. She talked with the other children nightly.

More than once, she asked herself, "Why am I dealing with this?" There was nothing left of her love for Lance. There was no desire. There was no friendship. There was no admiration. There was no attraction. There was nothing.

I must be a fool.

Yet, there was an inner compulsion to fulfill her duty to Lance.

In the past, I haven't fulfilled my responsibilities to my husband, children, or anyone else. I might as well start now.

❄

Before Ahn left Jackson Hole to return to Houston, Ahn and Gwynn had a conversation. As was often the case, Ahn seemed to know what she was thinking before she knew. Her friendship was of an unusual kind. Ahn knew what was in Gwynn, yet unconditionally loved her.

On the day in question, Lance had been raging in his madness, accusing Gwynn of infidelity. It was all she could bear just to listen. Finally, she walked out of the room. After a moment, Ahn followed. They went to the little coffee shop in the hospital, purchased two cups of not-very-good coffee, and sat at a small metal table. Gwynn began.

"The funny thing is, although I have not done any of what Lance accuses me of doing, I would. It is like condemnation in advance of the crime."

Ahn smiled with a look of understanding.

"Yes, I know."

After looking silently into Gwynn's green eyes and thinking, *What deep and watery eyes. There is a kind of compelling sadness in them. No man could resist those eyes—least of all Arthur.* Ahn went on.

"You are at a complex, challenging, and dangerous point. I know that, after what happened on the mountain, there is no chance that you can remain with Lance. But, for now, you are all he has. His parents have proved they are incapable. Over the years, you have become very accomplished at causing men to love you. You're not as good at loving them. Maybe this is a chance to love without hope of ever receiving anything in return."

Gwynn could feel the anger rising within her and just as quickly realized Ahn was correct. Ahn went on.

"Take this time to think and heal. What happened between you and Lance has happened to many women. You are no worse than any of them. What is essential is not the past—you can't change it. What is important is the future and your choices now. Arthur is there—I think he will always be there. But it may not be that Arthur and you are to be together again.

"It took me a long time in my own life to realize that you do not have to possess a man to love him. Men need to learn the same lesson: you don't have to possess a woman to love a woman. A long time ago, in Vietnam, I read a book that changed my life. The author defined love:

To love a person is to desire the best for that person and to make any reasonable and moral sacrifice for that person to achieve happiness and fulfillment.

"When I first read that quote, I memorized it. I was young and beautiful. In Vietnam, my father was an important person. I had many suitors. But I didn't love any of them, and they didn't love me. We were living in a world of pleasure-seeking and self-satisfaction. We thought we were ever so sophisticated. We thought of ourselves as the elite of South Vietnam. We were full of ourselves—and we were very wrong.

"To love, you have to live outside yourself. To love a person, you must do things that benefit them. For example, if you want to make Arthur happy, you must ask yourself whether you can. You must ask yourself if you are willing to make reasonable and moral sacrifices to accomplish his happiness. If Arthur is to love you, he must ask himself the very same questions.

"Before the two of you married, you never stopped to ask these questions. You were filled with desire and the emotion of romantic love. You never asked yourselves the question, 'What will I do if the day comes when I don't feel like this?'

"Unfortunately, that day comes in every marriage, in every relationship.

"In America, we think of falling in love as a feeling. In part, it is. What is masked by the phrase 'falling in love' is the truth that love is an action, not a feeling. It's holding your tongue when you'd rather speak. It's getting up in the middle of the night to feed a child when you'd rather rest. It's watching a football game when you don't like football. It's going to the ballet when you don't like ballet. Making those sacrifices for the other person makes life worth living for both parties in a relationship.

"Our human loves are finite. None of us is capable of loving another person without limitations or selfishness. Stephen and I had a wonderful marriage. However, we were two strong people who learned to accommodate ourselves to each other's needs and desires. Our love was built on sacrificing for the other. It was not automatic, nor was it easy."

The task of loving Lance seemed beyond anything Gwynn desired to do and beyond her capacity. It was impossible.

"With Lance, I cannot do that."

"I think you are right. But this phase of your life will not last forever. For now, Lance has no one else. The thing to do is to start. I don't want you to feel hopeless. The Eternal knows your limits and never asks of us what we cannot bear to give."

Gwynn was unconvinced and unwilling.

That night, after she returned to her room, Gwynn DuFort dreamed. It was such a dream that she had never had before. In her dream, Lance was lying in his bed, first, a young man in his prime, then an old man, withered and dying. Arthur was in the dream, young and handsome, just as he had been the day they first met, and then an old man sitting in a rocking chair on a porch, barely able to speak. Gwynn was in the dream. She was young and beautiful, surrounded by lovers, all the lovers of her past, and then a very old woman. Once smooth and warm, her skin was wrinkled and cold.

In her dream, she cried out in despair.

"What sense can be made of a life that begins with beauty, strength, ability, and pleasure and ends like this?"

None of the men in her dream could give her an answer. Lance could not answer, Arthur could not answer, her high school boyfriend could not answer, her college sweetheart could not answer, and the men she had known in law school could not answer. They were old and silent, asking the same questions of themselves.

Suddenly, there was a change. She was no longer old. She was young again. Lance was no longer a cripple. Arthur was no longer a silent and dying man. They were all young again. She looked up. An angel of light appeared. This angel wore a coat of many colors, a satin robe turning from white into the deepest red and then back to white again and again. The angel looked at her with shining eyes of love surrounded by light.

"Remember, I make all things new."

Gwynn looked up into those eyes, filled with love.

"Will you do this now?

"It is not for you to know the future. The times and the seasons are in my hands. The spring you knew is not the spring you can know again. The summer you are in is not a summer you will know again. Fall is coming, and there will be a winter. No season, once gone, returns. When I say I make things new, I mean new."

With that, Gwynn DuFort woke up. She went downstairs and made a pot of coffee. Then she turned on the gas fireplace and stared for a long time into the flames. Finally, she heard Claire upstairs crying for her mother. She put down the coffee cup on the stone hearth and went to comfort her child.

OLD ENEMIES VISIT
HOUSTON, TEXAS AND MEXICO CITY, MEXICO
FEBRUARY 2002

IT CAME AS A SURPRISE to Arthur and Ben when John Stone asked to meet. His brother wanted an update on the investigation of his father's death. The local authorities in Kerrville did not have the resources to conduct a potentially transnational investigation. The FBI in San Antonio looked into the case, but there were few leads, and everyone expected that whatever leads they came up with would lead to a dead end in Mexico. They met late in the evening in Arthur's office.

Ben began by giving the actual update.

"The authorities do not believe your father was the intended target. I was the target. We are confident that the attempt was on my life.

"Unfortunately, your father was killed instead. The attempt involved at least two persons, maybe three. There were two cars, which we saw, parked near the gate. Both of them were dark, mid-priced sedans. It is possible that one of those cars was seen crossing the border several hours later. There were three people inside that car. There is, however, no direct evidence that the vehicle contained the actual assassins.

"Recently, Arthur and I had a conversation about the case. We believe the murder of Javiera Velasco is unrelated to the other murders. There is plenty of evidence that Lance, intentionally or unintentionally, was responsible for her death. If Lance is ever in a condition to stand trial, we feel sure he will stand trial for that crime. The Mexican authorities are already trying to work out a deal for his extradition.

"That leaves the murders of Brad Gilliland and your father, the death of Marjorie Melton, and the possible attempted assassination of Lance DuFort. The police have enough evidence to conclude that Marjorie Melton was somehow involved in arranging the death of Brad Gilliland. However, it is unclear whether it was a crime of passion or if Marjorie acted on behalf of a third party. We will get back to that in a moment.

"If she was acting alone, then the murder of your father and the attempted murder of Lance, if there was an attempted murder, are unrelated.

"However, if she acted on behalf of a third party, that third party must have a motive, the means, and the opportunity to commit the crime. This leads us to Dobie Dawson.

"When the authorities examined the documentation in Marjorie Melton's house, it became apparent that she had long been sharing information with Dawson about various aspects of the businesses of E-Titan. We believe that DD was aware that Gilliland was not going to lie in his deposition scheduled for the day after his murder. We also believe Dawson was aware that any investigation of E-Titan would eventually bring to light the transactions between Dawson Corporation and the Cheetahs in which various assets were purchased by one of the Cheetah partnerships. Cash went back to the Dawson companies. If it could be proved that those transactions were fraudulent, that would entail a significant liability to the Dawson Corporation and Dobie Dawson personally.

"This indicates that Dobie Dawson had a motive to silence Brad Gilliland and, perhaps, Lance DuFort. It also means he had a motive to remove Marjorie from the scene."

Ben paused long enough to glance at Arthur. Thus far, Arthur understood what was being said, but what was about to come was new information.

"In preparing for a meeting today, I touched base with the local police about the investigation of Marjorie Melton's murder. There have been developments.

"The police were already suspicious that this was not entirely a suicide. The quantity of barbiturates in her system was greater than that contained in bottles they found in the apartment. In addition, they had other evidence, which, until today, they were unwilling to disclose to me. Here's what I found out today.

"One reason the authorities are unwilling to declare Marjorie's death a suicide had to do with evidence that she had relations with a man on the evening she died. There were bruises on her body consistent with what we might call 'rough sex.' The authorities somehow knew that Marjorie was capable of engaging in such activities. The DNA the authorities were able to retrieve from her body matched the DNA of a mid-level organized crime figure in Las Vegas. This person served time for a violent crime some years ago, and the authorities already had his DNA. In addition, while Marjorie was a showgirl in Las Vegas, she dated this individual. Interestingly, this individual is no longer in the United States. He has gone to Sicily to visit his family."

Arthur visibly reacted to this news.

Ben continued. "All of this information supports a hypothesis Arthur and I developed when he returned from Jackson Hole. Suppose Dobie Dawson used Marjorie to contact his friends in the underworld in Las Vegas to contract the death of Brad Gilliland through Marjorie.

"I began investigating Brad Gilliland's death because Arthur thought it suspicious that Gilliland was killed the night before his deposition. He was also concerned about Gwynn and the family and wondered if Lance was somehow involved in the death. We were eventually led to look at Marjorie in connection with that investigation. For reasons I would rather not talk about, we know that the evidence Marjorie possessed fell into the hands of a third party. She told that to Dobie Dawson.

"At that point, Dawson would have known two things: First, Marjorie might be arrested for her involvement in Brad Gilliland's murder and turn state's evidence. Second, I was getting close to finding the truth. This would be a motive to overreact and try to have me killed. Finally, once he wanted to have me killed, he would have known that Marjorie would be able to put two and two together and know who ordered the hit.

"The problem is that we have no proof of any of this.

"For the past few weeks, I have been trying to develop some proof, but it is difficult. Marjorie is dead, and she is a crucial link. The police know that Dobie called Las Vegas several times and visited with people with underworld connections. He even talked to the suspect. However, he has hotel and other business interests in Las Vegas. He will claim there was nothing sinister about the calls. They will back him up. We are at a dead end unless we can develop some new evidence."

John interjected a question. "What do you think should be our next course of action?"

"What do you think should be our next course of action?

"I have a suggestion. I have visited with a friend with the FBI in Washington. He has intelligence contacts. He thinks he can get me an interview with Javier Velasco."

Arthur grimaced. "I don't like that idea. We have friends in Mexico whom we would not want Javier El Halcón to investigate."

Ben was not convinced. "I am not sure that matters. A man like Velasco already knows that you have an investment in a hotel in Mexico. He knows that I am a retired FBI agent and your uncle. If he agrees to an interview off the record, it will be because he knows something that points away from him and his associates."

The conversation continued for some time. In the end, Arthur agreed to Ben's making a trip to see El Halcón.

A FINAL CONNECTION
MEXICO CITY, MEXICO
FEBRUARY 2002

THE FLIGHT FROM HOUSTON TO Mexico City is not long. After his injuries, Velasco settled in a mansion in Polanco, the wealthiest neighborhood in the city, filled with cultural institutions and luxury shopping areas. His home was secluded and well-protected. Ben Stone was searched from head to toe when admitted to the house. Then, he was led to the study of El Halcón. The study was large and decorated in the style of late 19th-century Mexico. There were bookshelves filled with leather-bound books, expensive paintings from the history of Spain and Mexico, portraits of his distinguished family, and a giant stuffed falcon that surveyed the room with black and piercing eyes. El Halcón himself was brought into the room in his wheelchair. He had been paralyzed since an attempt on his life many years before. Once, he had been a tall, elegant, imperious man. Now, he was a skeletal shell of his former self.

An essential talent of an effective detective is developing rapport with those being interviewed. Ben Stone had that talent in spades. Over many years, he developed an instinct for treating persons of interest and responding to their suspicions. Javier Velasco was not a man without his suspicions or fears. But, in this case, he seemed to be a man who had nothing to hide—at least nothing to do with Ben's brother's death.

Velasco welcomed Stone to his home, as any gentleman would. Then, he brought things to a point.

"You are here about the death of your brother?"

"Yes."

"I had nothing to do with it, nor do I think any Mexican national had anything to do with it. I do not speak of hired hands."

"Can you give me a reason why I should believe you?"

"I certainly can. I had nothing to gain by your death or by the death of your brother. I have known for some time that you have been investigating the death of my granddaughter. I have been investigating her death as well. Anything you might learn, I would eventually learn. Anything you learned would benefit me. Far from wanting you dead, I wanted you alive and working."

"You spoke of hired hands. Do you know who it was that killed my brother?"

"That is a difficult question to answer. I have no reason to discover the answer. Of course, I may have the ability to find out the answer. You would not be here if you did not suspect that the hired killers came from Mexico and returned to Mexico. As you know, your press speaks of the drug cartels and the organized crime of our country as if it were one thing. It is not. There are several cartels. They compete with one another. They have different friends in the United States. They rarely cooperate. In addition, many people who are not citizens live in Mexico. Some of them have, shall we say, unsavory connections."

He took time to stop and look directly into Ben's eyes. He was signaling that the person who ordered the murder might have been a foreigner living in Mexico.

"These foreigners have their own contacts. If, for example, one of them had contacts with the American mafia, they might be able to arrange an assassination that simply looked like it came from Mexico. Anyone can cross the border, and, as we all know, anyone can come back across that border without being seen. It's just a walk across a river at some unpoliced spot."

Velasco stopped again, allowing the meaning of his words to sink in. Then, he went on with a question of his own.

"Before recent events, I had no reason to be interested in this American company, E-Titan. Even after these events, my interest in that company only concerns its president, whom I thought then and think now either killed my granddaughter or knows more than he has said about the circumstances of her death. I lean towards the first possibility. It is with interest that I follow his tragedy. Is it your opinion that he will recover?"

"He will not recover if you mean, 'Will he recover his ability to walk and use his arms?' My understanding is that his mental state is not good. It is not known whether he will regain his mind."

Velasco made the point he intended to make.

"I have been a cripple for many years. Nearly fifteen years ago, I was the victim of a bombing. It left me with injuries, which you cannot see, and paralysis, which you can see. For whatever it might be to you, I am not inclined to kill Lance DuFort just now. The punishment he is receiving is worse than death. Believe me, I know. However, if he ever gains the ability to stand trial, I would like to see him be tried for murder.

"My granddaughter was born before I was paralyzed. She was born before my family disintegrated. I rarely saw Javiera in recent years, but she was my namesake and the only member of my family who paid any attention to me. I do not want her murderer to go free. If you uncover any information that I do not know about her death, I would assume you would inform me?"

Ben responded.

"Any information I gather, you will receive by reading the newspaper. The police and our FBI are aware of everything we have uncovered. They will be informed of anything we subsequently uncover. There is nothing about the death of your granddaughter that you will not know."

Ben Stone, however, had his own request to make.

"You have lost a granddaughter, and I have lost a brother. The person who employs me has lost a father. I hope you will see I receive any information you might uncover."

He looked at Velasco, his pale blue eyes as direct as he could make them. Velasco replied.

"I believe our interests coincide in this matter. If I learn anything, you will know if it is possible for me to disclose it. I know a great deal about Mexico and a considerable amount about your country. I do not think our interests will be divergent regarding this matter."

El Halcón paused. Stone was an old man, and the man before him was even older. He was getting tired, and it was easy to see he was not in good health. Velasco went on.

"As you can see, I am a dying man. I'm afraid a lifelong habit of smoking cigarettes has finally caught up with me. My doctors tell me that my cancer is both inoperable and terminal. My family, however, will always want to know that justice has been given to Javiera. Her father and mother will do precisely as I would if I were here."

The conversation continued for a few moments longer. El Halcón asked Ben about his experiences in World War II and the FBI. It was evident he had done his research. He knew all about Bill Stone, his two sons, and Ben Stone and his son.

"If I ever have the opportunity or necessity to hire a private investigator in Houston, I hope your firm will be willing to work with me. Is your son as dogged in his investigations as you are?"

"He is. His background is in special forces and military police, while mine is in the FBI. He is accustomed to dealing with difficult people. He's been doing a good job. Like you, I am getting old. My doctors tell me to stop going to the office and slow down. I am a widower. My children are grown. I simply enjoyed doing a little bit of work now and then."

Velasco smiled.

"I can understand. I have been officially retired for many years. My sons run the family business. However, I interfere all the time. It keeps me active and prevents me from being lonely. After my injuries, my wife left me. I'm afraid I was not easy to live with in those days. At the end of my life, I wish things had been different.

Stone felt compassion for the old and dying man.

We are as different as night and day. I am an ordinary man. He is wealthy and powerful. I've spent all of my life investigating people exactly like Javier Velasco. He spent his life avoiding being investigated by people like me. Here we are at the end of life—and instead of being adversaries and hating one another, we could be friends.

He looked at the dying man across from him.

"We have all made mistakes in life. I think we are both at this time in life to understand this: Family becomes the most important thing at the end of life. I can see you are at that point. I wish you luck and hope that the person who killed your granddaughter is brought to justice. If I can help, you can be sure that I will."

With that, the conversation was over. Bill Stone returned to the airport, caught his plane, and flew to Houston. He never saw Velasco again.

20

Spring Thaw

ABNORMAL NORMALCY

HOUSTON, TEXAS

FEBRUARY 2002

WHEN GWYNN RETURNED TO HOUSTON with Lance, an "Abnormal Normalcy" developed: Gwynn continued looking over Lance and managing his care. The doctors did not believe he would walk again or have the use of his arms, but as to his mind, they were not so sure. One of the doctors put it this way:

"He had a psychotic break. The pressure of E-Titan and its collapse, which he must have known was coming, the unraveling of his marriage, and the reality of failure were more than he could handle. Will he completely recover? We can't say. Maybe. In any case, we can say he is gradually improving."

Gwynn, who faced litigation involving Lance, a family in crisis, and a law practice with one of two partners gone to be with an injured husband, grew even thinner. She and Ahn met regularly. Ahn often covered for her at the hospital. She and Arthur maintained the relationship divorced parents must maintain. Every day, there were decisions about the children, schools, who would go to which recital or sports activity, and the like. To the casual observer, nothing had changed.

For Ahn and Roger, who knew both of them well, everything had changed. The anger, distance, shame, and regret were gone. They did not just talk about matters; they communicated. Arthur felt the change. His closest friend and advisor was back in his life.

One afternoon, after two especially trying days, Arthur suggested dinner out. Gwynn was not sure.

"People will talk."

"I am not sure I care. Let them talk."

"I think you may care one day. For now, the children should not be exposed to the risk of rumors and innuendo. Why don't I just come over with Claire for dinner? We can eat together as a family. It has been a long, long time."

The family ate together at the Avalon house in River Oaks for the first time in years. Murray seemed especially happy. He sensed that his parents had reconciled. The family was not together. It might never be as together as it might have been. But emotionally, it was together. Stephen and Margaret felt the unity as well. There was a comfortable, caring love in the atmosphere of the house—an atmosphere missing for years.

After dinner, the children played. Melena watched the children while Gwynn and Arthur sat in his study and talked among the memories of easier and more innocent times. Arthur was in a reflective mood. It was as if the future was coming, while both of them were still trapped in the past—but that past was gradually evolving into a new present they could not yet see.

"We messed up. Both of us."

"Yes. We messed up. Now, we must live with the consequences."

"Yes, we do, and we are. Whatever happens, we will deal with it."

"Tell me about Lance."

"He is improving slowly. He has not recovered from the psychic break he experienced in Jackson Hole but now seems to have some lucid moments. He is not as agitated. He does not know about the collapse of E-Titan, nor does he know about the various lawsuits pending against E-Titan and its officers and directors. The doctors think it would be premature to let him know about things he cannot handle right now.

"He also does not remember anything he has told us about Javiera and his trip to Mexico. Frankly, if Lance recovers, he may claim that his admissions were a fantasy of his broken psyche. If he does, there is little possibility of a conviction based on statements made during a psychotic break. I am not sure a judge would admit his statements into evidence."

Arthur nodded.

"And, what about you? What are you going to do?"

Gwynn's eyes, which of late spoke eloquently of hidden suffering and emotional pain, looked directly into Arthur's.

"He is my husband. Claire is his daughter. It will be many years before Claire can understand the events of these past few weeks and years. Our children are ashamed of me. I don't want Claire to have the same experience.

"Arthur, I do not like my situation. However, it is my bed, and I made it. For now, I must continue to support Lance. He is helpless, and he cannot hurt me any more than he already has. Can you understand?"

"Yes, I do understand—more than understanding, I will support you with the children and personally, no matter how long it takes. You are doing the most noble thing possible in an impossible situation. I am not sure the children can understand what you are doing, but they will. Eventually, children realize it is harder to be an adult than they imagine. They also have not made mistakes from which they cannot recover the past. We have."

COURTSHIP IN SAN MIGUEL
SAN MIGUEL DE ALLENDE, MEXICO
SPRING 2002

JUAN DE LA CRUZ BARDERO never called his United States partners except in unusual circumstances, always involving the hotel. In this case, the unusual circumstance was a woman— Maria Mendoza. The phone rang in Ahn's apartment early one Monday morning in May. Ahn was surprised to hear Bardero's voice asking for an unusual favor, though there was a business side to the favor. Bardero got right to the point.

"Ahn, this is Juan. I was wondering if you might send Maria Mendoza to San Miguel again to finish the audit she began for the investors. I do not want to put you or her out at all. I would also like for her to bring her son with her. You can assure Maria that I will handle all the travel arrangements and pay for the trip's costs, including any special arrangements necessary for Manny. I thought it would be nice if she could combine a trip to San Miguel for Manuel's spring break in the United States with a visit here."

"I see. There is more to this trip than just finishing some business?"

"I cannot be sure, but I think yes."

Ahn pondered the request for a moment, then agreed to the visit. When Maria was contacted, she responded with enthusiasm.

"I had to leave early on the last trip. It would be nice to complete what I had begun on that trip and to see Juan again."

So Maria and Manuel Mendoza made a trip to San Miguel—the first of many—for spring break. They stayed at the hotel, visited the farm, and spent time with Juan de la Cruz Bardero, who was an attentive and diligent host. When Maria was busy with the business side of the trip, Manny spent his days at the farm and vineyard near the monastery. When time permitted, they saw all of San Miguel, much of the surrounding countryside, and charming nearby cities and towns. On the last night of that trip, Juan and Maria had dinner alone at the hotel while the staff ensured that Manny was well-entertained, well-fed, and safe.

The dinner was in a private dining room. Bardero wanted what was said to be confidential. The dinner began as the dinners that week had always started, with chatter about the day, questions about whether Manny was having a good time, and plans for the next day. The working vacation was ending, and the time was coming to decide if there was any future for them, as improbable as it seemed. Bardero began the conversation.

"It has been a good week. I hope you two have had a wonderful time. Perhaps you can even return in the future."

"I hope so."

Looking up, Maria reinforced the point.

"I do. I am not just being polite."

Bardero sensed the connection between them. He trusted her judgment. He went on.

"There are some things I would like you to know. I am not a poor man. As you know, I manage this hotel for the investors and have a substantial interest in it. I own the farm, and there is no mortgage on the property. I also have an interest in a few other businesses in the area.

"You already know that I have never married. There are reasons. In the beginning, I was young and led the life of a soldier. Several years ago, that came to an end. There is a reason. Juan de la Cruz Bardero is not my birth name. I was born in another country. On a mission for my government, I was betrayed. I ended up here at the monastery, making a new life. I cannot return home, nor can I visit the United States. If I were to return home, my life and the life of anyone close to me would be in danger. You need to know this, but never speak of what I tell you."

Maria pondered what Bardero was saying. She knew Bardero was not Mexican by birth. She had asked herself many times, "Who is Juan Bardero?" He had not just a head knowledge of American culture but the ability to make her comfortable in Mexico in a way that only someone who was both Mexican and American could. Back in Houston, she had done her research.

"Since our first meeting, I have often thought of you. As you remember, my father was killed in a plane crash just over the Mexican border with the US. In the end, it is my understanding that a trust was formed by someone to care for the families of the victims and those whose lives were impacted by those sad events. Ahn Winchester is the trustee of that trust, which was funded by the assets of her dead husband's brother's estate, which she refused to treat as her own.

"As one of the company's auditors, I know enough that some of that trust's assets ended up helping families in Mexico. My family, the family of the plane's pilot, and the other passengers have all been helped in small ways, usually with housing or education. I also know that Ahn and Arthur Stone helped you by investing in your businesses. You do not need to say more. I think I understand all I need to understand, John Mirador."

With that last statement, their eyes met. There was a long silence, each lost in their thoughts. The candles on the table flickered their light into the room's darkness. The flowers he had carefully chosen were fragrant, and the light gave them a magical quality. The smell of their after-dinner coffee wafted across the table. It was as if an understanding had been reached. She would return, eventually, for good.

SOLDIER'S FATE
HOUSTON AND SAN ANTONIO, TEXAS
FALL 2003

THOMAS MALLORY SPENT SEVERAL MONTHS, nearly a year, in hospitals. Like many injured soldiers, he was first transported to Bagram Airbase in Afghanistan, put aboard a C-17, and sent to Landstuhl Regional Medical Center in Germany. From there, he traveled to Walter Reed Army Medical Center in Bethesda, Maryland, near Washington, D.C. Because of his injuries, family, and support system in Texas, he was eventually sent to Brook Army Hospital in San Antonio. Although he lost a part of his leg, TL was luckier than many other soldiers in similar circumstances. He had been far enough from the blast that he did not lose his arms, genitals, or other parts of his body. His injuries were located in a relatively narrow area. He was fitted for a prosthesis and almost immediately began to exercise and work out.

Mallory had been on the outside of a group of soldiers, one of whom absorbed the full blast of an IED. He was killed instantly. Other soldiers were very seriously injured, losing arms and legs and having internal damage to various organs. The fireball burned a good many of their faces. TL was at the perimeter of the blast. He might have escaped serious injury if not for a single piece of shrapnel that cut through his lower leg.

Not all of the injuries were physical. There are mental consequences to combat. TL, as strong as he was, was not exempt from the emotional consequences of the blast. Early on, he explained what had happened to Arthur.

"I can't explain it. It's like I have a brain fog. I don't think I'm ready to return to work. I have trouble thinking logically. I forget things. I am easily upset. Alicia tells me that I wake up in the middle of the night wrestling with an unknown enemy and sometimes yelling loud enough that the children can hear me.

"The doctors tell me that my reactions are normal. They call it 'survivor's guilt.' I was in charge of the unit when the blast occurred. I was also the least injured. It is not rational, but I feel I'm somehow responsible for what happened to others. People were killed. Lives were ruined forever. I escaped. Why? It does not make sense.

"Unlike others, I am alive. I've had to learn to walk with the prosthesis, and I can eventually run marathons. I'm not going to be in a wheelchair for the rest of my life. I have both my eyes and both my arms. My mind is pretty much unaffected. Our family life is normal, given the circumstances. I can practice my profession as well or better than before! It's the guilty feeling that I got away easy and others didn't."

Arthur interjected, "We hope you will return soon. But, we want you to take all the time you need to recover."

Mallory went on.

"I have friends who have severe cases of PTSD. They cannot go out in public. They have terrible anxiety. They have constant flashbacks to the event in which they were injured. One guy went on a hunting trip. When the guns began firing, he thought he was in Afghanistan. The group barely stopped him before he shot a bunch of people."

Throughout his recovery, Thomas Mallory maintained a strong interest in the firm despite his injuries. He became especially interested in its newest office. The Battle Mountain litigation and the fact that one of Winchester & Wells' most prominent clients was headquartered in San Antonio led the firm to merge with Eddie Morales' firm in San Antonio. When he could, TL was a part of the group that negotiated the merger. Having something to do at the firm helped give him a sense of purpose and being needed. Eddie visited as often as possible, reported needs to Arthur and Roger in Houston, and Mallory developed a strong bond with Eddie. This bond was essential to the future of the firm.

Alicia and the children supported her husband with unflinching devotion. Once he was in San Antonio, the family spent virtually every weekend together. Arthur and Gwynn ensured they could stay near Fort Sam Houston and Army Hospital. Eventually, Arthur made Avalon Ranch available to the entire family whenever they needed a place to stay.

Alicia had been a military wife before. She had seen the pressures of military life early in her marriage. She had talked to women who were dealing with husbands with PTSD. Although she had this background, it wasn't easy to cope with the changes in her husband.

"When he wakes up at night, screaming, and especially if he grabs me, I'm scared. It's a terrible thing. You don't want to be scared of your husband. People with PTSD have hurt their spouses. It's not like there's no risk at all. I love TL, and I trust him. But, there's always that thought in your mind, 'What if. . . .'

"I also have to deal with anger because of how this is affecting our family. Thomas (Alicia did not like the nickname TL) is sometimes isolated, distant, and emotionally unavailable. Half of him is still in Afghanistan. It's not just me. It involves the children, too. In the beginning, I wondered if he would ever be normal again.

"Fortunately, we've made a lot of progress. His physical injuries have not been hard to get used to, but his emotional, psychological, and spiritual injuries have been much more difficult to accept. Maybe it's because I can't see them. Like many military wives, I feel helpless."

Eventually, Alicia thanked Gwynn for her help, support, and love.

"I appreciate knowing you are always there covering for me. I also appreciate Cynthia (Maynard). I don't worry about work at all.

"It helps to be able to go up into the Hill Country. When the family is in Hunt, we can take walks, swim in the river, play games together, and just sit and watch nature and think. All of this has helped Thomas recover. He has friends that don't have that advantage. They have a more difficult time, and so do their families."

One cool late fall day in late 2002, Alicia and TL sat on the front porch of the Hill Country stone ranch house at Avalon Ranch. The house exuded a feeling of permanence in a world of change, protection in a world of danger, and security in a world of insecurity. The oldest part of the house dated from the 19th century, shortly after settlers reached that part of the Hill Country. It had been initially a goat farm, then a small ranch. Over more than a century, the original family added to the house.

They lost it in the Great Depression. It went through a series of owners who used the property as a hunting camp before Arthur bought it and restored and added to the house.

The children played in the yard, running back and forth along the river bank. It was almost time for dinner.

"The doctors say that I am ready to go home. I think I am ready for work."

"Are you sure?"

"Yeh."

TL reached out for Alicia's hand.

"I am lucky to have you. I have always been lucky to have you. I know the past few months have been hard, but I think we are over the hump."

Alicia bent over to kiss her husband.

"Yes. I think we are."

21

Wheels of Justice

ON THE FLIGHT BACK TO Houston from Mexico City, Ben Stone pondered the case against Dobie Dawson. Evaluating any piece of evidence or testimony involves keeping an open mind. People who appear to be telling the truth may be lying. People who seem to be lying may be telling the truth. It is the job of the investigator to sort out the difference. Ben was under no illusions concerning the character of El Halcón. He had known of Javier Velasco and his alleged ties to the Mexican drug trade for many years. Ben Stone had long suspected Velasco of deep involvement in the Texas savings & loan crisis and the death of Ahn Winchester's husband, Stephen.

These were events with which Stone was familiar—facts that would not change. El Halcón was an old predator, but a predator nonetheless. However, his words in their interview rang true. Velasco had nothing to gain by the death of Brad

Gilliland, Bill Stone, or Marjorie Melton. El Halcón could order a murder; he probably had ordered a few in his long career. Of this, Stone had no doubt. But El Halcón was not a sociopath. He was a criminal and a successful one. He would not order an unnecessary assassination. Furthermore, he was an experienced and sophisticated man. He would not plan or permit a bungled killing like the one that resulted in his brother Bill's death.

Stone often remembered Sherlock Holmes's words during an investigation: "When you have eliminated the impossible, then whatever remains, however improbable, must be the truth." In this situation, it was now pretty certain that El Halcón had not ordered any of the murders. This left the other suspects—of whom Dobie Dawson was by far the most likely.

Brad Gilliland was never a suspect. He was the first to die. Lance is in a hospital bed, paralyzed from the neck down. In his delusions, he admitted the murder of Javiera Velasco. He has never mentioned the other murders. He might have ordered them, but it looked less and less likely. Marjorie might have acted for Lance or Dobie, but it is unlikely that she ordered the attack on Ben or Lance, at which time she was dead herself. That leaves Dobie.

The day after his return, Ben met with Arthur.

"I spent the entire trip home thinking about my interview with Velasco and what we know. In the end, one possibility seems most likely: Dobie Dawson ordered all the killings except for Javiera. He is a person with motive, means, and opportunity. Javier Velasco, who probably knows Dobie or knows of him, did not point fingers. However, the only explanation that holds water is that DD is behind all the killings. Proving it is a different matter."

Arthur leaned back in his chair.

"I agree. Your trip to Mexico was worth it. The question is, 'How do we prove our case in court?' Or perhaps more pertinently, 'How can the state of Texas prove that Dobie ordered these killings beyond a shadow of a doubt?' Right now, I do not think we have the evidence. We are going to have to develop this case further.

"I have been thinking about ways this could be done. One strategy is for my family to file a wrongful death claim against Dobie. We can then do discovery. Anything we discover will be shared with the authorities, which will help them build their case.

"We believe that Marjorie Melton was killed by a mafia-related figure, now located in Sicily. The police also believe this is the case. While you were gone, I did some research on my own. My contacts tell me that they found Nicky Berini's DNA all over Marjorie's house and body. They are in the process of trying to get an extradition order. If we can prove that Nicky was the hitman, we already have phone records that indicate calls were made from Dobie to him. The police are trying to find financial ties between them, but it's difficult. Dobie Dawson owns a couple of hotels in Las Vegas. Money goes to and between the casinos all the time. I'm not sure we will be able to pinpoint exactly how the money reached Nicky. But we can try. Dobie is not the smartest guy in the room, but he is shrewd and has been around a long time."

Ben nodded.

"If you can gather enough evidence to warrant a private action, the discovery process may uncover something."

"I've been thinking about how to do that. Tomorrow, I'm going to fly over to San Antonio. Eddie Morales practices in Bexar County and has friends in Kerr County. I believe we will want to file the lawsuit in Kerr County. That's where my father lived and died. He had a lot of friends. It will not be a friendly county to Dobie Dawson."

Ben nodded.

"Eddie will probably hire a local counsel. He might take the case on a contingent fee, but the family will have to pay all the expenses. I'm OK with that. I'll handle the expenses."

The next day, Arthur flew to San Antonio. He and Eddie had lunch at the Argyle Club on Patterson in Alamo Heights. It is a secluded spot, and they occupied a private table. It was an excellent place to talk about litigation. Arthur always liked the club. He hadn't been there often, but the club dated far back in San Antonio's history. Fort Sam Houston was nearby. Many famous people had dined there, including famous soldiers who served at Fort Sam Houston. Presidents, senators, congressmen, governors, legislators, business people, and many others treasured the club for its food and atmosphere.

Eddie was encouraging.

"Given the information you've given me, I can't imagine a judge dismissing the case. You've got enough circumstantial evidence to file the suit and begin the discovery process."

"I also think it is wise to have me associate with a local counsel in Kerrville. Kerr County police are very interested in this death. They don't like being considered a bunch of hicks. They haven't liked the press constantly implying that they can't solve the case. They have the ability. They just don't have the facts. Kerr County will be favorable to us."

Before the lunch was over, they had agreed to begin the process of investigating and bringing the case against Dobie Dawson, for the murder of Bill Stone. Big things often have small beginnings.

BUILDING BLOCKS
HOUSTON, SAN ANTONIO, AND KERRVILLE, TEXAS
FALL 2005

ARTHUR WAS A CURIOUS COMBINATION of visionary strategist and plodding organizer. The strategy he had already voiced to one of his associates was symbolic of how he conducted litigation. <u>The Stone family versus Dobie Dawson and the Dawson Companies</u> was no different from any other case.

The case was built upon the theory that Dobie Dawson, as president of the Dawson Corporation, used his position to order the assassination of Ben Stone, which resulted in the accidental death of Bill Stone. Many documents were discovered from the Dawson companies and Dobie's records using interrogatories. An army of paralegals and temporary lawyers reviewed all those documents, pulling out anything worth additional investigation. Ultimately, these documents proved a series of phone calls that tied Dobie Dawson and Nicky Berini together.

It turned out that Nicky Berini had been Marjorie Melton's lover while she was also seeing Dobie Dawson. Dobie and Nicky knew each other going way back. They also had a reputation for disliking each other. It was difficult for Dawson or the Dawson Corporation to overcome the impression to the judge and everyone else that Dawson did not call Nicky Berini to have a friendly conversation about Italian food. Eventually, evidence was uncovered proving that Dawson Corporation money was used to order the hit on Ben Stone.

Discovery in a case like this takes a lot of time—years. The criminal justice system takes even more time to work in complicated cases. It took years to bring Dobie Dawson to justice. Eventually, though, the wheels of justice ground to a settlement of the personal injury case.

Along the way, Ben Stone traveled to Sicily to talk to Berini. It was obvious that his lawyers had told him that he would eventually be extradited to the United States to stand trial for murder. He wanted to discuss whether he could cut a deal with the authorities. It took some time, but eventually, Nicky was extradited and pled guilty to murder. His sentencing took into consideration his considerable assistance to the prosecution. He implicated his employers in Las Vegas, Dobie Dawson and Marjorie Melton. It was a coup for the Justice Department's organized crime division.

Turning Nicky Berini was a vital brick in the case against Dobie Dawson and the Dawson companies. Marjorie's diaries and notes were another. Dobie had deliberately placed her at E-Titan to look after Lance, keep a close eye on what was happening, and alert him of opportunities to use E-Titan and the Cheetahs for his benefit.

Initially, she was loyal, but her affair with Gilliland compromised that loyalty, as did the hundreds of thousands and sometimes millions of dollars in compensation from the Cheetahs, E-Titan, and the Dawson Corporation. She was indeed a savvy chick. Her beauty and allure hid a high I.Q. Unfortunately, she was emotionally wounded and incapable of finding happiness. She wasted her beauty, her brains, and much of her money. She died without a will, and her relatives spent a good deal trying to get more than their fair share. There were substantial judgments against the estate, including one that benefited Heather Gilliland.

The iron box Ben Stone found at the Gilliland family retreat on Canyon Lake was a treasure chest of information. Gilliland had kept copies of his reconciliation of various financial statements of E-Titan and the Cheetahs, showing the amount of debt that would have to be placed on E-Titan's balance sheet if the SEC ever demanded a restatement. He had also calculated in a rough way the overstatement of profits created by mark-to-market accounting. He broke out the contribution of Dawson Corporation assets to the total. It was devastating for E-Titan's financial statements and would be devastating at any trial.

Before the Nicky Berini plea bargain was finalized, Dobie Dawson and the Dawson Corporation settled with the Stone family. They wanted the litigation over. With federal, state, and regulatory authorities investigating all of them, claims from former employees of E-Titan for loss of their pensions due to fraud, and other claims, the liabilities of Dawson and his companies were rapidly increasing. The settlement with the Stone family was the least of their worries. The settlement terms were not made public, at least not at the time, but they included sufficient funds for Mrs. Stone to live at the Hallmark in Houston for the rest of her life, which she did.

DOBIE'S DEMISE
BELIZE TO EMIRATE
2006

AS SLOWLY AS THE WHEELS of justice turn, they do turn. In the case of Dobie Dawson, it took several years before he finally met his fate. He was indicted for murder in Texas by a Kerr County grand jury as far back as 2003. In addition, the United States government indicted him for securities fraud in a sealed indictment. The indictment for securities fraud contained several other indictments, including tax evasion.

Throughout the entire period of the investigation, Dawson proclaimed his innocence.

"I am the victim of a gigantic misuse of our legal system. People on Wall Street lost some money. I'm very sorry about the E-Titan situation, but I have nothing to do with the problem. People are just out to get me because they think I have money."

Eventually, Dawson fled his hotel and Belize.

After a search, he was located in West Africa. There was another round of extradition attempts. West Africa, even a luxury hotel in West Africa, was not a good place for an elderly American with a compromised immune system. Dawson put up with the heat and various ailments as long as he could, but eventually, he felt like he had to find a better climate. He chose the mountains of Turkey. Turkey, however, has an extradition treaty with the United States and a complicated political relationship. In the end, the State Department made a deal with the Turkish government that related to the Kurds. Dobie's extradition was a part of the price paid for American cooperation.

Dobie decided his next stop would be an isolated spot in the Himalayas. However, to get to his destination, his plane had to stop somewhere for fuel. Somewhere, a Middle Eastern emirate was trying to develop a better relationship with Washington. The particular emirate has no extradition treaty with the United States (a problem in the war against terror). It is close to certain terror-sponsoring countries that keep large sums of money there. However, the emirate was subject to the influence of the United States. In this case, the emirate was negotiating terms on the United States military presence in the area, and it was to their benefit to arrest Dawson in transit. He was.

Truth is indeed often stranger than fiction. It took a long time for the United States to gain the release of Dawson into their custody. During that time, Dawson decided that his life was in danger. He began to post on social media. He claimed a gigantic conspiracy international in scope to have him killed. One morning, the emirate authorities announced that he had been found dead in his cell. His body was sent back to Texas for burial. That seemed to be the end of the story.

Of course, any time there is a mysterious death, conspiracy theories abound. It wasn't long before Dobie Dawson became a folk hero among conspiracy theorists. It was rumored that he was alive.

When his will was probated, Buddy Bennett, "the only man I ever trusted," was named executor of the will and sole trustee of "The Dawson Family Charitable Trust," to which all his considerable assets were given. The charitable trust was founded to "improve the quality of American law enforcement and its legal system and other charitable activities, as the trustees may determine."

Buddy immediately hired Winchester & Wells as general counsel for the estate and the charitable trust. It took a long time to inventory the estate. During his years of exile, Dobie had spent a lot of time hiding assets all over the world. He knew he might have to leave Belize anytime and had a strategy for hiding his money. When the estate was finally probated, which took many years, Winchester & Wells knew more about hiding money than any other law firm in America.

Buddy was a great businessman, but he didn't like being the trust's sole trustee. Eventually, Ahn Winchester and members of the Stone family joined him as trustees. After paying millions of dollars of claims against the Dawson companies and the estate, there was still quite a bit left over. The foundation still operates today.

Dawson's funeral was a pretty sad affair. Buddy Bennett attended out of loyalty. A few distant relatives came, hoping they would receive money from the estate. (They did not.) Reporters from the *Houston Chronicle* and the *Wall Street Journal* showed up, hoping for a story. That was it. Dobie "DD" Dawson died as he had lived, isolated and alone.

22

ENDINGS AND BEGINNINGS

FATHER AND SON
HOUSTON, TEXAS
MARCH 31, 2002

EASTER ARRIVED EARLY IN 2002, bringing with it a unique charm. The long, frigid winter was gone. In Houston, where Easter can be scorching, this early Easter was cool, clear, and delightful, with hardly a cloud in the sky. To celebrate, Arthur revived a cherished family tradition and decided to treat the entire family to brunch at Brennan's. This was an annual occurrence before Arthur and Gwynn divorced. It was full of memories for the children and held a special place in their hearts. Despite the uncertainties of their future, Arthur was determined to bring back the joy of gathering together for a meal on each holy day.

His brother, as always, gave a fine sermon. The music from the chancel choir was earthshaking in its quality and assurance of Christ's resurrection. At the end of the service, the congregation joined in the Hallelujah Chorus from Handel's Messiah. When the service was over, the family met for brunch. Arthur always had the eggs benedict with his mimosa and coffee. The children talked and joked with one another. At the far end of the table, Gwynn sat with Claire and joined in the festivities.

Ahn and Melena were invited. Uncle Ben joined the family for church and lunch. Arthur's brother, John, did not attend. He and his family had traditions that served the needs (and energy) of a tired pastor who had been doing services for Holy Week since the prior Sunday, preached from sunrise until noon, and would not leave the church until after 1:00 p.m.

After everyone ordered and were served their drinks, Arthur raised a toast.

"To our family and all those we love who could not be here today, either because of duties elsewhere or sickness and injury, may God grant us a year of love for one another."

"Love" had been banished from his vocabulary since he and Gwynn divorced. Now, it was back.

Gwynn smiled at the other end of the table.

"I agree. Whatever the future holds, let us never forget to love one another."

Arthur and Gwynn did talk about the future from time to time. Lance was mentally slowly improving. His body would never recover. The damage to his spine was too severe. Now was not the time for decisions about the future. When Gwynn and Ahn spoke about the future, Gwynn gave her hard-won wisdom on the subject:

"I have spent a lot of time trying to control the future, especially my future. Along the way, I have made many mistakes. I am letting the future unfold this time, taking life one step at a time."

Ahn agreed. "There is a lot of water under the bridge just now. It is best to concentrate on letting the children know that they are loved by both their parents, who still love and respect each other. What the future brings, it will bring."

Arthur realized the healing of their family might not result in the healing he hoped for. As the luncheon went on, he and Murray, sitting beside one another at the end of the long table around which the family was seated, had a brief talk.

"Are you and Mom going to get back together?"

"We are back together. Spiritually and emotionally, we have regained our love and respect for one another. That will never change. Whether we ever live together again is not so important as the best interests of you children. I am sure you have seen the change in the past three months. I don't think that change will be reversed."

"I don't know. It doesn't seem normal."

Arthur laughed a laugh that came from deep within his soul.

"It is not normal, but it is whole and healthy. Our family can never be typical—we aren't ordinary people. Your mother and I have made mistakes and decisions we can never undo or change. We cannot undo the past, but we can love and care for each other and our family.

"Over the past months, I have learned that love is neither an emotion nor an attraction. Love is doing the best for the other person. It is an action. Right now, I am concentrating on acting lovingly towards your mother and all of you."

For a fourteen-year-old, Arthur's words did not all make perfect sense. Yet, he sensed a truth in them. "I guess I will just have to wait and see what happens."

Arthur changed the subject.

"If I can get you back into St. John's, do you want to return there, or would you rather be at Lamar next year?"

"I think I'd better stay where I am. I like school, and I feel at home there now. I am afraid that if I were to return to St. John's, my past would haunt me. But if you and Mom want me to return to St. John's, I will."

Arthur gave him another option.

"There might be another option. I have been offered a chance to become attorney general of Texas. The current attorney general is probably going to resign. The governor thinks I might be the right person to take the job. If I take the position, I will live in Austin much of the time. You might go to school there. I will not do it unless your mother and you three agree. Being attorney general involves politics and being a public figure. The governor wants me to promise that I will run for office in the next election if he appoints me. That means everything you or your family does is fair game in an election year. I am not sure our family would enjoy it."

Murray thought about this completely unexpected turn of events.

"It might be fun. If I can improve my grades and school record, I want to attend the University of Texas."

Arthur remembered his own checkered junior and senior high school career.

"I think you can do it at your age. I was not a very dedicated student when I was your age. I improved enough in high school to get into Plan II at the University of Texas."

Murray took it all in. From across the table, Gwynn smiled. She sensed the quiet healing that had taken place between father and son and between the members of the family as a whole.

We are not a perfect family, and we all have our wounds. But I think everything will be OK.

FROM THE HEART OF DARKNESS
HOUSTON, TEXAS
FALL 2002

LANCE DUFORT LIVED MANY MONTHS in a murky, irrational twilight zone between madness and sanity. He raved for a long, long time. Hatred, fear, and a desire for revenge spewed from his mouth day and night. His injuries were such that he could not move by himself. He could not eat. He could not bathe. He could not shave. He could not even go to the bathroom without help. Every human need had to be supplied by the effort of someone else. He was helpless. An endless train of doctors, nurses, aides, and caregivers kept him alive.

In his raving, he spoke of women, the women he had betrayed, and those who had betrayed him. He spoke of men, the men he had outsmarted, and those who had outsmarted him. He spoke of Arthur, whose fundamental goodness Lance thought was a kind of lunacy. He spoke of Gwynn, who was weak in betraying Arthur. He despised them both. (There is something about evil that fears and loathes the good.) He spoke of his parents, who sent him to private school while they followed their dreams and sought their pleasures. He spoke of Dobie Dawson, whom he thought a fool. He spoke of Marjorie Melton, whom he considered a bimbo. He spoke of their *au pair*, whom he secretly was trying to seduce. In his madness and his lack of human love, he emptied his soul of its dark hatred of goodness and even of life until there was nothing left but darkness and despair.

Gwynn was present for part of each day, participating in care routines. Occasionally, Ahn was there as well. Nearly every person who ministered to him was someone he would have looked down upon in the years of his success.

After several months, Gwynn noticed a change. The raving stopped. There was nothing but silence. Not a single word. Ahn noticed it as well. His empty eyes reflected a wasteland and great emptiness as if all his self-centeredness and brokenness had been spent and nothing was left. He could not or would not communicate except for an occasional whispered groan. He knew there was an outside world, but it was a world in which he was no longer a participant. Lance DuFort had descended into his private purgatory, alone, unloving, and unloved.

For what seemed to be an eternity of weeks, Gwynn spent a part of each day sitting, reading to him aloud, and increasingly silently praying for his soul. Ahn would sometimes spell Gwynn when she had to be at the office, with the children, or in court. Ahn, too, read to him and prayed. Claire was too young to come to the hospital to see such a tragedy. Nevertheless, Gwynn brought pictures of their child to show him. She even told him when Claire's birthday passed, and he had sent Claire a present, which she bought.

There was no response. Just those blank eyes, staring as if from a dark pit of infinite despair. A casual observer could not know that Lance DuFort was still alive beneath the dullness of his gaze. But he was, he was taking everything in. He watched the beautiful woman across the room read to him. He knew she could not possibly love him as a woman, not after what he had done. He saw the fragile Asian beauty read to him and pray for him and knew she was such a woman who would think him a fool and a scoundrel. Yet, these women continued to care for him.

Then, he noticed the caregivers. *What a burden it must be to care for me,* he thought. Despite the difficulty of handling his body's deadweight, cleaning his filth, and feeding him every bit of nutrition he ingested, he noticed that most of them treated him with tender care. This was tender care that he had never shown anyone. He wouldn't even have considered caring for someone in his helpless condition. I would have said, *What can they do for me?*

One evening, when Gwynn was gone and Lance was alone, a young nurse came into the room to check on him. She wore an inexpensive silver cross and was obviously tired. She checked his medication, looked at his vital signs, and touched his head. She bowed her head. She began to pray. Her prayer was for his miraculous healing.

Suddenly, there was a tingling sensation, beginning at the crown of his head, where her soft hand touched his hair, to the bottom of the toes, which he could no longer feel. He tried to move his toes and realized he was still paralyzed. Instantly, he realized what was being healed. It was not his body being healed, but Lance DuFort: mind, spirit, and soul. He sensed a kind of light entering his mind, emotions, and wounded spirit. He was bathing in an invisible pool of healing light.

There was no change the outside world could see. He didn't leap up and walk. His paralyzed arms and legs did not begin to move. He did not start to speak or ask questions. He just lay there bathing in the unselfish love of a nameless nurse.

Gwynn and Ahn noticed an eventual change. Lance still did not speak. There was no evidence of any change except a particular light in his deep, Gallic brown eyes. The women were unsure, but the light grew brighter as the weeks passed and fall arrived.

One evening, Gwynn and Ahn were there together. They silently prayed for him. He gazed up at them as they sat in silence. He finally spoke. The words were simple.

"Thank you."

The two women stared at him in amazement. Before the great silence, his speech contained anger, pain, resentment, and fear. "Thank you" was the last thing they expected him to say. He spoke again, words he had never spoken to Gwynn in their years together.

"I am sorry."

His eyes filled with tears. The two women could tell he was about to return to the silent light-in-darkness from which he had ever so briefly emerged. Then he spoke once more.

"Be careful. The snake is still in the garden."

With that, he closed his eyes and slept.

The two women sat for a long time in silent wonder. They had no idea what had changed Lance, but a change was evident. It seemed as if Lance DuFort was finally whole. His body was a wreck, but the human being was finally whole.

It was time for them to leave. They both touched his forehead and said a silent prayer.

Later that night, an orderly came into the room. He looked around to see if anyone was there and closed the door. Out of one of his pockets, he took a syringe and plunged it into the arm of the sleeping man, who briefly opened his eyes. The poison, taken from a blowfish, was meant to work quickly. It did.

Before he died, Lance looked at the man who was turning to leave; the last words the man heard were these:

"I forgive you."

NEW LIFE
SAN MIGUEL DE ALLENDE
SPRING 2003

MARIA MENDOZA BARDERO SAT ON the porch of the Hacienda de la Paz. Across the lawn, Bardero and Manny were playing soccer. The boy had talent. Beyond the lawn was a fence and wall. Beyond the wall was the vineyard. Beyond the vineyard was the pasture. To a casual observer, it was just another small ranch outside San Miguel de Allende. A closer observer would have noticed expensive security cameras.

Bardero was a careful man. The habits of a Watcher do not easily fade.

It was spring. Maria could feel the good earth coming alive as she felt the child growing in her womb. It would not be long before the three were four.

To the East, there were storm clouds.

"You two had better come in; a storm is coming."

Bardero looked up at her with a warm smile.

"It will pass as the seasons pass."

The two continued their game, but she noticed Bardero was watching the sky closely.

I am a lucky woman.

Bardero, who had long ago given up hope of a family, children, and domestic love, looked across the lawn at his wife. A gentle rain started to fall. He glanced at his stepson.

"It is raining. Your mother would like us to go in. Don't worry; it will not last long."

The rain softly fell as the father and son reached the long porch on which Maria was sitting. The boy ran into the house to get a soft drink. Bardero sat down beside Maria, gently taking her hand. For a short moment, each looked into the dark eyes of the other.

Bardero looked out beyond the lawn to the vineyard and pasture beyond.

Who would have imagined that one day I would have such a life?

"When I look into your eyes, I am lost in eternity."

"Yes. It is true for me as well."

Epilogue

THE DREAM OF ROGER ROMNY

HOUSTON, TEXAS

JANUARY 2005

ROGER ROMNY HAD LIVED AT the River Oaks condominium a floor below Ahn Winchester for a long time. It was convenient to his office, which was now the focus of his life. Arthur had accepted an appointment as attorney general when his predecessor left office and was now keying up for his election. Romny was already managing partner when Arthur resigned to seek public office and remained so. There was no new chairman of the firm.

After the murder of Stephen Winchester and his own severe injuries, Roger's then-wife had left him. He eventually remarried a woman whom he met at Houston's Second Baptist Church. Before the bombing, Romny was never religious in any way. His months in the hospital and the departure of his wife for a husband without his physical issues left him alone with plenty of time to ponder life, his future, and the swiftness with which youth, health, and vigor disappear. Most men delay the realization of their limitations and mortality until later in life. He was lucky enough to have been forced to ponder them earlier in his mid-40s.

Eleanor, his wife, contracted cancer in late 2003. It was not discovered until it was too late to stop its inevitable progression. Now, he was alone again. The firm had become his life. This time, however, it was different from when he was injured in the killing of Stephen Winchester. He had many friends, a church community, and many community activities. In his late 60s, he was content. Yet, there was an emptiness in his life. Eleanor had accepted his physical limitations without even the slightest hesitation. Their friendship and later love was not based on his physical prowess, intellectual ability, money, or position. Her love had changed his life as much as any single event.

I miss Arthur. In the beginning, I was not a friend to Arthur—far from it. If I had not suffered my injuries, I would never have enjoyed the most important collegial friendship of my life. His leadership and friendship allowed me to become a good managing partner.

In his reverie, he reflected on all the transactions and litigations they shared over the years. Their mutual support enabled the firm to grow and prosper as the legal practice was changing and consolidating. Winchester & Wells continued to be a force in the Houston legal community, the state of Texas, and even nationally. The growth of the firm had made Roger Romny a wealthy man.

I owe so much to Arthur. I have never repaid him for his friendship, and I have never let him know just how despicable and conniving I was before the "accident." Someday, I must tell him everything. He deserves to know.

It was getting late; the night was cold and rainy, and a mist was in the air. He could see the city's lights below and in the distance. He fell asleep, and in his sleep, he dreamed. He was old and near death. His career was over. The law firm was now in other hands. He was too elderly for any of his hobbies and avocations. He could barely leave his home. He could no longer even go out for a morning or a meal.

In this dream, he was sitting in the condominium in River Oaks, staring at the city below. The cold and icy hand of death was upon him. In the corner of the room, a light shone in the darkness. It was no ordinary light. It changed colors from green to yellow to blue until it became a deep and abiding red. The red blood of a sacrifice. In his dream, a figure clothed in a coat of many colors came out of that supernatural light and spoke.

"This is not your night. Your day will come, but this is not the day."

Then Roger saw in his dream a parade of lawsuits and transactions past, present, and future. He saw crowded and busy days in the office stretching from his first years as a lawyer out into the future. He saw a parade of transactions closing, suits being settled, partnership meetings, and annual distributions. He had no one with whom to share his lonely life. He had no one to spend his earnings on or love. He was at the top and found it a lonely place. In his dream, Roger wished it otherwise. But in his dream, his life could not be different. Nor could it be different in reality. This he knew. He had known love. Now, he must learn selfless service.

He thought back to the beginning of his friendship with Arthur. He remembered his attempts to be sure that Arthur never made partner. He saw in his mind the explosion that left him with permanent wounds and killed Stephen Winchester. He saw the failure of the Marshland Savings Association and the collapse of the financial system in Texas. He saw the collapse of E-Titan. He saw in his dream difficult times at the firm, as many of its oldest clients, including its largest banking client, failed. He remembered Arthur's calm, plodding leadership during those years.

He remembered his failures and infidelities. He saw all the people he had used and hurt before his injuries—and some since. He remembered his wife's desertion during his illness.

He remembered his inner healing through Eleanor's love. He remembered their love, and he missed her. He remembered his loneliness and saw the loneliness extending out into the future.

What is the purpose of it? What is the purpose of all this struggle? What is the purpose of all this failure and loss? What is the purpose of it all, even my success? In the end, does it mean nothing? What is the purpose of it all?

The figure in his dream began to speak.

"The purpose is not in history or events. For better or for worse, the meaning is in what humans make of it. Human history and human lives are stages upon which the play of life is set. I have set the stage. It is for you to create its meaning. The stage is not the meaning of the play. The meaning of the play is the life of the characters. Yet, life is not 'sound and fury, signifying nothing.' The deepest meaning is the love you share and the meaning it gives. That is the only meaning. The only thing that abides forever is love, for love is what I Am, and no love is ever lost in Me."

Then, in his dream, Roger saw his life as it was, played out in the second half of the 20th century. He saw all of the events of that history. He saw the wars. He saw the death of so many innocent young people in those wars, some for little or no reason at all. He saw the political intrigues and the victory of corruption and decay. In his vision, he saw all the economic booms and busts of his business life, past and future. He saw the end of Winchester & Wells, to which he had given his life. He saw the victory of fools and the defeat of the wise.

In his dream, he saw the innocent's corruption and the unexpected salvation of the corrupt. He saw all the marriages that begin with the fiery anticipation of youth and their end in disillusionment and divorce. He saw all the families starting in hope, ending with hope fulfilled or the end of hope. He saw the endless, impossible-to-understand foolishness and suffering of humanity. He saw in his dream all the seemingly meaningless chaos of history.

Above it all, he saw a figure, bloody from the lash, bruised by beatings, and pierced by nails. He saw that figure looking down upon him in sadness and pain. He felt the vulnerable, suffering love of that figure freely given, sharing itself with the world, and the figure drawing into himself all the pain, all the loss, all the destruction, all the decay, and death of the world from its foundation. He saw the vulnerability and suffering of the One who shared in all life's meaninglessness and drew it into himself. He saw himself sharing with the sufferer in his suffering.

Then, in a moment, he saw the figure of his dream transformed into light, a beam of light having the shape of a heart. He saw himself transformed into a version of that light.

Roger Romny awoke. It was morning, the sky was clear, and the day was warm. It was time to go to the office. His dream and its meaning could wait.

9798330391851